Democracy, Civil Society and the State

AFRICAN BOOKS COLLECTIVE LTD

End Street,

SOUTHERN AFRICA REGIONAL INSTITUTE
FOR POLICY STUDIES (SARIPS)

STATE AND DEMOCRACY SERIES
Series Editors: Lloyd Sachikonye and Ibbo Mandaza

Titles in this Series

Democracy, Civil Society and the State

Social Movements in Southern Africa

Lloyd Sachikonye (Editor)

SAPES BOOKS

HARARE

First published 1995
by SAPES Books
P.O. Box MP 111
Mount Pleasant
Harare
Zimbabwe

Typeset by Southern African Printing and Publishing House (SAPPHO) (Pvt) Ltd,
338 Herbert Chitepo Avenue, Harare, Zimbabwe

Cover Design by Paul Wade (Inkspots)

Printed by Natprint (Pvt.) Ltd., Harare, Zimbabwe

ISBN 1-77905-028-3 paperback
ISBN 1-77905-035-6 hardback

Contents

Acknowledgements

Many people and institutions assisted me in the course of the Research Project on Social Movements and in the editing of this collection of studies based on the project. Here, I can only single out a few. My profound thanks are due to Dr. Ibbo Mandaza, Executive Director of the SAPES Trust which facilitated the project, and to Dr. Mapopa Chipeta and Dr. Guy Mhone who co-ordinated the studies and workshops relating to the project. The assistance provided by the SAPES Trust staff, in particular by Joyce Kazembe, Maurice Mutowo and Jonathan Kadye was much appreciated.

I am most grateful to the discussants at the two workshops which assessed the initial drafts of the findings presented in this book. Amongst others, I must mention here, with thanks, Lloyd Ching'ambo, Norbert Tengende, Thomas Deve and Adebayo Olukoshi. In August 1993, I received an invitation from the Department of Sociology at the University of Lund in Sweden to participate in a workshop on *Social Movements in the Third World*. The workshop provided a useful forum for exchange of comparative perspectives on social movements and the democratic process in developing societies and so I am thankful to the organisers of inviting me.

The Library staff at the Institute of Development Studies were extremely helpful in facilitating access to material and I thank them. Miss Musakwa and Mrs. Kupamupindi typed various drafts of the chapters included in this book in their usual painstaking and cheerful manner; I must express to them my sincere gratitude. Finally, my wife, Taka and the "gang of three", Kamambo, Goki and Panashe provided invaluable support but also welcome distraction throughout the course of the project and the writing up. I am indebted to them. Of course, none of the above are responsible for any shortcomings of this book.

Lloyd M. Sachikonye
Harare
January 1995

Notes on the Contributors

Lloyd Mambo Sachikonye is currently chairman of the Department of Agrarian and Labour Studies at the Institute of Development Studies, University of Zimbabwe. He holds a BA and MSc in Politics from Ahmadu Bello University, Nigeria and a Ph.D in Politics from the University of Leeds. His main research interests are in labour and agrarian studies, and the role of social movements in the democratic process.

Donald Chanda was formerly Lecturer in the Department of African Development Studies, University of Zambia, Lusaka.

Eugenio Macamo is Lecturer in the Faculty of Economics, Eduardo Mondlane University, Maputo.

Louis Masuko is currently chairman of the Department of Economics and Technology Studies at the Institute of Development Studies, University of Zimbabwe. He holds an MSc degree in Economics.

Blade Bonginkosi E. Nzimande was formerly Director of the Education Policy Unit at the University of Natal (Durban). He holds a Ph.D in Sociology from the University of Natal. His major research interests are in education policy development, affirmative action, civil society and the state.

Ray Russon is Lecturer in the Department of Sociology at the University of Swaziland and currently a Research Fellow in the Sociology Department at the University of Witwatersrand. He gained his BA in Administration and Sociology from the University of Swaziland and MA in Sociology from the University of New South Wales Australia. His major research interest is in Social Policy and Social Welfare.

Mpumelelo J. Sikhosana is presently a Research Fellow in the Education Policy Unit at the University of Natal. He holds an MA in Industrial Psychology from the University of Natal (Pietermaritzburg). His main areas of research interest are democratic transitions, civil society and the state, human resources development and education policy development.

Introduction

Lloyd M. Sachikonye

The current political and economic reforms in most African countries have stimulated debate on the definition and content of democracy and civil society in the African context. These reforms were largely initiated by popular struggles in the late 1980s to force the unseating of authoritarian regimes. Strident demands for the dismemberment of the one-party state, military regimes and statist economic controls were articulated in much of Sub-Saharan Africa. These demands still persist where the incumbent regimes have not yet conceded to democratic change. The popular demands for political and economic change have been influenced by debates on the relationship between democracy and development, between state and civil society, and on the significance of the role of international forces in contributing to the reform process. (Anyang' Nyong'o, 1987; Mamdani, 1991; Mandaza and Sachikonye, 1991). In turn, the wave of popular struggles for democratisation has provided a stimulant and context of contemporary debates on the prospects, indeed the sustainability, of current political and economic reforms (Bangura and Gibbon and Ofstad 1992; Leftwich, 1993; Qadir *et al* 1993).

There is a direct relationship between contemporary political and economic changes, stalemates and reverses and the content of the intellectual discourse. It is a remarkably illuminating conjuncture in which there is constant feedback between political practice and theoretical reflection. But the outcome of the current political and economic changes is uncertain; the heady optimism of the late 1980s has begun to dissipate. Some autocratic regimes have made substantial concessions but others still resist and frustrate mass demands for democratic change by manipulating the political system often through the electoral process to block the ascendancy of popular opposition forces. In other instances, economic conditions, especially those associated with structural adjustment, have not provided the requisite stability for irreversible democratic transition.

This volume brings together studies which reflect on these debates on the concept and process of democracy, and on the relationship between state and civil society. The immediate context of the reflection on these concepts and processes is Southern Africa in the present conjuncture, a conjuncture fraught with both risk and promise. The democratic transitions in Angola and Mozambique may still degenerate into protracted feuds characterised by much violence and inconclusiveness. Angola is a particularly sad example. In South Africa, the April 1994 elections have so far proved a decisive stabilising factor, as the major political forces in that country accepted the verdict of the voters. In the remainder of the states — Lesotho, Namibia, Zambia and Zimbabwe — the democratic transitions may be sustained in spite of periodic lapses into heavy-handed authoritarianism and lack-lustre economic performance. In Swaziland, the pressure will continue for the democratic change which will inevitably restrict the autocratic propensities of the monarchy.

However, the studies in this volume do not attempt to assess the role of all the major forces engaged in the democratisation process. That would be very ambitious on our part. Instead, we place greater attention to the role of social movements in contributing to democratisation. Social movements have tended to be curiously neglected in the analysis of civil society and the democratisation process in the post-independence period. It has been more fashionable to carry out state-centred analyses revolving around state structures, political and economic processes to the neglect of the role of social movements in invigorating civil society and thereby impinging on the state itself. In this volume, we present the findings of studies on social movements which include labour, cooperatives, civil organisations, students, women and youth; and on the role of other key institutions in civil society such as churches. These studies constituted a project on *Democracy, Civil Society and the State: Social Movements in Southern Africa* supported by the Southern African Political Economy Series (SAPES) Trust. The studies were undertaken between 1991 and 1992 and the initial findings presented at two workshops organised in Harare in November 1992 and March 1993.

Conceptual Overviews

The first part of the book explores the key conceptual issues which form the substance of the empirical material presented in the national case studies in the second part. A critical survey of existing literature on democracy, civil society and social movements is conducted in the chapters by Sachikonye, Nzimande and Sikhosana. That democracy is a highly controversial concept because of its ideological connotations is acknowledged, and several contending perspectives are outlined. The first perspective provides a formalist and minimalist definition of democracy in terms of multi-partyism, periodic elections, governmental succession by constitutional and electoral procedures guaranteed under the rule of law. This minimalist definition is associated with the conservative variant of liberal democracy. It must be set against a more expansive and substantive definition of democracy which argues for the inclusion of such content as redistributive socio-economic reforms, broad popular participation and human rights. In the chapter by Sachikonye, the minimalist and formalist definition of democracy is questioned with specific reference to Francis Fukuyama's claim that there is no alternative to liberal democracy, and that capitalist democracy represented 'the end-point of mankind's ideological evolution and the final form of human government' (Fukuyama, 1992). This sweeping claim ignores the obvious limitations of liberal democracy, its inherent social inequalities and elitist forms of rule rather than broad popular participation in political and economic spheres. Yet Fukuyama is not an isolated exponent of this claim which also associates democracy with the "free market" system. Much of the Western discourse (including that of international financial institutions, which finance most of the adjustment programmes in developing countries) has centred on this assumed linkage between political and economic liberalisation. We dispute this thesis. Both explicitly and implicitly, the chapters in this volume veer towards the second position which argues for substantive forms of democracy in terms of broad popular participation in political and economic decision-making and control.

The definition of the concept of civil society is similarly heavily contested as Nzimande and Sikhosana show clearly in chapter 2 in their critique of some of the current conceptions. In a concise review of the conception of civil society in the writings by Marx, Engels and Gramsci, they argue that in the South African context, the concept has been abstracted from its theoretical and historical meaning. Like the concept of democracy, as we saw above, the concept of civil society has been used in a liberal sense, ignoring the history of the substantive critique of liberal democracy within radical scholarship. In the liberal conception there is a conflation of civil society as a sphere of struggle with mass organisations and the absence of an adequate analysis of the state. According to this liberal perspective, the state is inherently bureaucratic and undemocratic.

Nzimande and Sikhosana argue that the separation of civil society and the state is an embodiment of human alienation and reflective of sophisticated forms of the institutionalisation of capitalist exploitation throughout society. This separation masks the real nature and basis of exploitation in modern bourgeois societies. The 'freer' bourgeois society seemed to be, the more exploitative it became; this is what they understand to be Marx's perception of the essence of the separation between civil society and the state. But as they further argue, we cannot talk of an 'autonomous civil society' without addressing its class nature. Indeed, the deeper an analysis of civil society went, the clearer its inseparable relation to the state became. The counter-posing of civil society to the state, as in most liberal conceptions of the relationship between the two, is mistaken. The relationship between the state and civil society is a continuous and dialectical one. At different movements, or even at the same instance, in political struggles, in capital accumulation, state and civil society can operate in tandem. At other moments or instances they operate as opposites; and still in others as parallel processes. Finally, Nzimande and Sikhosana briefly outline their critique of the conception of civil society in the recent contributions by Swilling, Glaser and Slovo.

The section on conceptual overviews concludes with a discussion of another problematic concept, that of social movements. A minimalist working definition is that a social movement represents some collective action with some stability over time and some degree of organisation oriented towards change or conservation of society (Garre'ton, 1993). A more explicitly political definition is that social movements are organised social groups which are mobilised from below in pursuit of goals that challenge the established order of things, especially that of political forces with a stake in the state (Lindberg *et al* 1992). Thus social movements are by definition autonomous from the state and their goal is to change society or parts of it, or other relations crucial to them. This definition is somewhat narrow since social movements can be conservative or reformist rather than necessarily radical. The case-studies in the second part of the book illustrate their centrality as organs in civil society which have often played an active part in the democratic process. Their degree of autonomy from the state varies but most are not completely divorced from it, nor from such mass political movements as nationalism or national liberation movements. Their complex relationship with the state and the political process forms the substance of the national case-studies on South Africa, Swaziland, Mozambique, Zambia and Zimbabwe.

National Case-Studies and their Significance

It was widely expected (at the time of our writing) that the national liberation movement, principally the African National Congress (ANC) would constitute the majority element in the first post-apartheid government in South Africa. If this expectation was borne out in the elections in April 1994, this political success was, in no small measure, a vindication of the mass democratic movement whose pressure in the 1980s forced the apartheid regime to begin to crack. In this democratic movement, variously termed the United Democratic Front (UDF) and the Mass Democratic Movement (MDM), the role of such constituent social movements as labour, youth, students, women and civil organisations amongst others was critically important. In chapter 3, Nzimande and Sikhosana observe that the democratic anti-apartheid struggle was understood in its totality, and not merely as a preserve of the national liberation movement. Even more important was the awareness that although the ANC was viewed as the vanguard of the national liberation struggle, it in itself could not effect radical change without the participation of mass organisations (encompassing social movements) as part of the national democratic revolution. However, the optimistic expectations regarding a democratic transition can still be disappointed. This can occur, particularly if the experience of those other African countries which had experienced mass mobilisation before independence and went on to witness a demobilisation of those mass organisations after the attainment of majority rule, is replicated.

In their evaluation of the role of civil organisations in the democratic transition, they pose the question of how these organisations and social movements can continue as active elements within the national democratic revolution without simultaneously sacrificing their autonomy. Whether the labour movement (Congress of Trade Unions of South Africa), which has adopted a relatively sophisticated approach to this question will retain its independence together with its formal partnership in the triple alliance with the ANC and the South African Communist Party (SACP) will depend on the balance of class forces in the post-apartheid South African state.

In his chapter on Swaziland, Russon shows clearly the centrality of the role played by various social movements in the independence struggle, and currently by a mass democratic movement pushing for political change from an authoritarian monarchy. As in most African countries, the nationalist movement was a major social movement and an integrating force in Swaziland which pulled together conservative, moderate and radical tendencies. However, in Swaziland, nationalism experienced internal contradictions as the monarchy amassed all political power, and attempted to demobilise mass organisations and political groupings through such draconian measures as the State of Emergency and the repeal of the independence constitution. Throughout much of the 1970s and the 1980s, various social movements including workers and students sought to widen democratic space which the monarchy had constricted. The significance of the People's United Democratic Movement (PUDEMO), in which Russon himself has played a notable role is that it represents and unites various mass organisations with bases in social movements such as youth, labour, women human rights and consumer groups. To PUDEMO, the strength and strategy of mass democratic movement in neighbouring South Africa constitutes an inspiration. It was no accident therefore that after a historic congress in Soweto in February 1992, PUDEMO "unbanned" 'itself in Swaziland and stepped up its mobilisation campaign. However, as in South Africa, the outcome of the present democratic struggles is not obvious. But while Swaziland still has not gone as far as Malawi in conceding that a referendum on multi-partyism be held, the vibrancy of its civil society could become a decisive factor in the momentum for democratic change.

A much sombre picture is painted of the prospects of democratisation in Mozambique, which until the ceasefire in 1992, had been wrecked by a devastating civil war fuelled by South Africa amongst other bellicose sponsors. The current peace settlement is still fragile but elections were successfully organised for October 1994. In his chapter, Macamo argues that the war was the major political, social and economic constraint in the process of democratisation in Mozambique. Of course, the causes of the war itself were complex but the principal ones related to the failure to achieve political and ideological reconciliation at independence and externally instigated civil war. The serious rift between the Mozambican state, the church and rural chieftainships, for example, was one visible expression of an ideological conflict which also had repercussions on Frelimo's hold on power in centres of traditional authority in the countryside. The war also constrained the growth of an indigenous entrepreneurial class. Macamo nevertheless sees hopeful signs in the successful rapprochement between the state and the church, and an enhanced partnership between them in reconstruction, especially in the war-shattered rural areas. Frelimo's ideologically-driven strictures on civil society, particularly on the church itself but also labour, student and youth organisations have been removed as part of the democratic process. At the same time, however, economic liberalisation threatens to undermine whatever social gains had been attained in Mozambique's tumultuous post-independence era. Whoever forms the government after the October 1994 elections will face a Herculean task not only in the reconstitution of the economy but also the deepening of a democratic political culture and the post-war civil society.

If the prospects of the October 1994 multi-party elections in Mozambique were initially uncertain, those in Zambia in October 1991 were quite decisive in toppling the UNIP government under Kenneth Kaunda by the Movement for Multi-Party Democracy (MMD) under Frederick Chiluba. Donald Chanda in his chapter provides an account which centres on the formation and meteoric rise to power of the MMD, a loose congeries of various social forces and politicians disillusioned by two decades of one-party state rule. The MMD grouped together business interests, the intelligentsia, labour, informal sector producers, peasants and the lumpen-proletariat. It was an unwieldy but powerful movement with the dominant objective of ushering in a multi-party system. In spite of initial disadvantages such as constrained access to the mass media, the MMD won by a handsome margin in October 1991. Chanda's account of the MMD rise to power ends soon after its election victory and therefore does not reflect on the creeping authoritarianism signalled by the State of Emergency in early 1993 and the detention of opposition politicians. It also does not evaluate the significance of the spate of ministerial and parliamentary resignations in 1993 and January 1994. The MMD has certainly begun to unravel under the weight of austerity measures stemming from adjustment, but also from inter-ethnic squabbles and alleged pervasive corruption. In his conclusion, Chanda raises the question of whether the democratic change of government such as the Zambian one in 1991 signified the maturity of a diversified petty bourgeois class, alternating in state power under a new political culture. Or whether it represented a new context which the people's role was more representative and decisive therefore marking a new level of state organisation and political consciousness. It is now somewhat more difficult to answer these questions in the affirmative in the light of recent political developments. Indeed, some analysts have observed that the nature of the MMD seems to reproduce the structural conflicts and factional intrigues which transformed UNIP from one of Africa's most effective mass movements into a shell for transmitting presidential orders (Baylies and Szeftel, 1992).

The last two chapters on Zimbabwe by Sachikonye and Masuko evaluate the relations between the state and social movements, principally the labour, student and cooperative movements. Although Zimbabwe never formally renounced the multi-party system nor pursued an ideological vendetta with the church (as in Mozambique) nor attempted to systematically co-opt all social institutions (as in Swaziland), its conduct of relations with the labour and student movements has been characterised by authoritarian tendencies particularly from the mid-1980s onwards. This occurred in a context in which the social contract with these forces collapsed after a post-independence honeymoon. Selective repression of unions and students has been accomplished through the banning or draconian handling of strikes, demonstrations and boycotts. Legislation to undermine the power and cohesion of unions, and to whittle the autonomy of universities (representing as they do a major civil society institution) has been a source of tension in these relations. In sum, civil society institutions have sought to resist wholesale co-optation by the state. State control over the bulk of the mass media, district and local government institutions confer significant advantages to the ruling ZANU-PF party. However, this pervasive control should be set against the autonomy exercised by church-based organisations, organised business interests, the independently-owned press and various professional associations. In his chapter, Sachikonye observes that the strategic options of labour and student movements are somewhat limited in terms of political mobilisation against what they perceive as an authoritarian and unresponsive state. The prospects of a counter-hegemonic alliance are currently not very bright, given the current fragmentation of the opposition parties.

Nor does Masuko detect particularly rosy prospects for agricultural collective cooperatives in the context of structural adjustment, stalled agrarian reform and an ideologically inhospitable context. Similarly, there are very limited options, in economic and political terms, open to the cooperative movement. Although the movement could constitute a useful vehicle of rural democratisation, its further development will be conditioned by a dialectical relationship between voluntariness, a gradual learning process and state assistance. If any of these elements does not exist in sufficient measure, Masuko argues, the internal disarticulation of the cooperative movement becomes a distinct possibility. Once again, we can see that it is not illuminating nor useful to attempt a neat compartmentalisation between state and civil society institutions.

References

Anyang' Nyong'o, P., *Popular Struggles for Democracy in Africa*, London, ZED, 1987.

Bangura, Y., Gibbon, P. and Ofstad, A., (eds) *Authoritarianism, Democracy and Adjustment: The Politics of Economic Reform in Africa*, Uppsala: Scandinavian Institute of African Studies, 1992.

Baylies, C., and Szeftel, M., "The Fall and Rise of Multi-Party Politics in Zambia", *Review of African Political Economy* No. 54, 1992.

Fukuyama, F., *The End of History and the Last Man*, London and New York, Penguin, 1992.

Garreton, M., "Social Movements and the Politics of Democratisation". Paper presented to the Nordic Conference on *Social Movements in the Third World*, University of Lund, August, 1993.

Leftwich, A., "Governance, Democracy and Development in the Third World". *Third World Quarterly*, Vol. 14 No. 3, 1993.

Lindberg, S., Friedman, K. and Lundberg, S. *Social Movements and Strategies in the Third World*, Department of Sociology, University of Lund, 1992.

Mamdani, M., Mkandawire, T. and Wamba-dia-Wamba "Social Movements, Social Transformation and the Struggle for Democracy in Africa". Codesria Working Paper Series, 1988.

Mamdani, M. "State and Civil Society in Contemporary Africa: Reconceptualising the Birth of State Nationalism and the Defeat of Popular Movements". *Africa Development*, Vol. XV No. 3/4, 1991.

Mandaza, I. and Sachikonye, L. (eds) *The One-Party State and Democracy: The Zimbabwe Debate*. Harare: SAPES, 1991.

Neocosmos, M. "Political Liberalisation in Lesotho and Swaziland: Recent Developments". Paper presented to a Workshop on *Experiences of Political Liberalisation in Sub-Saharan Africa*, Centre for Development Research, Copenhagen, June 1993.

Qadir, S., Clapham, C. and Gills, B. "Sustainable Democracy: Formalism vs Substance". *Third World Quarterly*, vol. 14 No. 3, 1993.

Part 1: Conceptual Overviews

1

Democracy, Civil Society and Social Movements: An Analytical Framework

Lloyd M. Sachikonye

The Concept of Democracy

The concept of democracy is a heavily contested one. In spite of its significant capacity for mobilisation in the political transformations in Africa and Eastern Europe in the past seven years, there does not exist consensus on the definition of democracy. Arguably, democracy means different things or processes to different social interests. However, in the contemporary discourse on democracy, the concept has become associated with a political system in which multi-partyism exists, periodic free and fair elections based on universal suffrage are conducted, and press freedom, human rights and rule of the law guaranteed. Governments and politicians are required to uphold and abide by the constitution; checks and balances in the exercise of power exist, and the independence of the judiciary and the key role of parliament in the legislative process. In this discourse, the minimalist definition of democracy relates primarily to political pluralism based on constitutional arrangements.

These attributes of political pluralism have historically been associated with Western liberal democracy. They represent an outcome of long, drawn-out social and political struggles over several centuries between different social interests but primarily against structures of feudalism, aristocratic absolutism and privilege. In the liberal democracy discourse, 'contestation open to participation' is sufficient to identify a political system as *democratic*. As it has been asserted:

> Democracy is government *pro tempore*. Conflicts are regularly terminated under established rules. They are "terminated", temporarily suspended, rather than resolved definitively. Elections fill offices, legislatures establish rules, bureaucracies issue decisions, courts adjudicate conflicts, and these outcomes are binding until and unless they are altered according to rules. At

the same time, all such outcomes are temporary, since losers do not forfeit the right to compete in elections, negotiate again, influence legislations, pressure the bureaucracy, or seek recourse to courts. (Przeworski 1991:10).

These processes in liberal democracy are what guarantees its stability and legitimacy. For even constitutional rules themselves are not immutable because "rules too can be changed according to rules". This definition of democracy has infused the contemporary discussion on democracy outside the West; it has achieved the status of definitiveness in the West itself. Following the collapse of authoritarian socialism in Eastern Europe and of one-party state and military regime models in Africa, Asia and Latin America, Western liberal democracy has become a major reference point for debates on democratic transitions in these societies. These debates, are, however conducted against the background of triumphalism in the West, a triumphalism based on the ideological ascendancy of liberal democracy and capitalism in the post-Cold War era. One major representative of that triumphalist school is Francis Fukuyama who has argued that there is no satisfactory alternative to liberal democracy, and asserted that capitalist democracy represents 'the end-point of mankind's ideological evolution and the final form of human government' (Fukuyama, 1992). While earlier forms of government were characterised by grave defects and irrationalities that led to their eventual collapse, Fukuyama has argued, liberal democracy was arguably free from such fundamental internal contradictions. Whatever social problems still beset liberal democracies were problems of incomplete implementation of the twin principles of liberty and equality on which these democracies were founded, rather than of flaws in the principles themselves *(Ibid)*. According to this argument, liberal democracy is the only coherent political aspiration that spans different regions and cultures around the globe, while liberal principles in economics — "the free market" — have spread and succeeded in producing unprecedented levels of material superiority *(Ibid.* xiii).

The claims for liberal democracy and capitalism have a certain resonance in the post-Cold War context. Former socialist societies are eagerly embracing liberal democratic and capitalist structures. The authoritarian regimes in the Third World have few options except to genuflect to the same. But how useful is the minimalist and constitutionalist definition of *democracy*; and how valid are the claims for *liberal democracy* and the "free market" system?

As we have already observed, the concept of democracy has been loaded with Western historical and ideological baggage. Not unsurprisingly, the proponents of liberal democracy strive for it to achieve a hegemonic status globally. Yet there exist serious flaws in the concept and practice of liberal democracy. First, even ardent advocates such as Fukuyama concede that liberal democracies continue to be plagued by major social inequalities such as unemployment, pollution and crime (*Ibid.* 288). In addition to these inequalities, the question remains unanswered on whether there are no other deeper sources of discontent within liberal democracy. This frank admission from so determined an advocate of liberal democracy is very damaging to his thesis, not least given his insistence that liberal democracy uniquely satisfies the desire for 'recognition' that he locates at the heart of the historical process (Miliband, 1992:109). The deep flaws in liberal democracy should not be explained away. These flaws relate to the constitutionalist and material dimensions for liberal democracy. In liberal democratic regimes, 'democratic procedures' can be manipulated by elites and by the communications media which they control and do serve "to pour out a torrent of obfuscations, half-truths and lies" *(Ibid.)*. In this critique in which liberal democracy is equated with capitalist democracy, the latter is viewed as "oligarchic rule tempered by democratic forms". While this critique does not dismiss the importance of constitutionalism or democratic procedures, such structures and measures under capitalist democracy are also means of containing pressures from below.

A second strand of critique goes beyond Fukuyama's inadequate acknowledgement of the inequalities inherent in capitalist democracy. This critique argues that:

> democracy requires more than the maintenance of formal 'liberties' . . . Without substantial reforms and redistribution of economic assets, representative institutions − no matter how 'democratic' in form − will simply mirror undemocratic power relations of society. Democracy requires a change in the balance of forces in society (Gills and Rocamora, 1992).

This advocacy of progressive democracy is counter-poised to liberal or capitalist democracy. The case for extending the definition of democracy beyond its constitutionalist forms so as to include matters of social and economic content is a persuasive one in our view. The two dimensions, of form and content, should not be separated; they both constitute the substance of democracy. Those who are dissatisfied with the minimalist and formalist definition of democracy argue for the inclusion of such criteria as redistributive socio-economic reforms, broadened popular participation, social justice and human rights (Qadir *et al*, 1993).

A third strand of critique of liberal democracy relates specifically to the structures and ideology of capitalism. The capitalist system is defined as a system of economic organisation that demands the existence of a relatively small class of people who own and control the main means of industrial, commercial and financial activity as well as a major part of the means of communication. These people thereby exercise a totally disproportionate amount of influence on politics and society both in their own countries and beyond (Miliband, *op cit*). Yet democracy is based on the denial of such preponderance of control and influence which requires a rough equality of condition. Capitalist democracy is presented as the political system most supportive of economic growth but this prescription is basically an orthodoxy of hegemonic power holders who present it as a matter of natural law, whether economic or developmental, rather than as a specific product of historical conditions (Gills and Rocamora, *op cit*). The economic prescriptions advocated for developing countries have been explicitly connected to political liberalisation in the form of liberal democratic constitutionalism. This version of democracy is the political corollary of economic liberalisation. Democratisation is thus considered the necessary and natural product of submission to the rationality of the world-wide market.

Democracy in Developing Countries

The discourse on democracy at the present conjuncture has been shaped by the prevalent triumphalism of capitalist ideology in the context of the collapse of the orthodox socialist model, most dramatically in Eastern Europe. In developing countries, the transitions to democracy have largely assumed the embrace of formal structures of multi-party democracy but also the adoption of versions of the free market system. The options relating to development strategies have dwindled particularly where access to finance from the international financial institutions (IFIs) is crucial. Conditionalities which are attached to borrowing by developing countries have locked these countries into the international capitalist system much more firmly. Structural adjustment programmes often entail the liberalisation of investment and labour conditions, privatisation of public enterprises and significant cut-backs on social services such as education and health. Stabilisation measures supported by the IFIs have often resulted in steep devaluations and inflationary conditions while wholesale trade liberalisation has undermined domestic industry. Thus accompanying the transitions to multi-party democracy has been a generalised offensive for the liberation of 'market forces' aimed at the ideological rehabilitation of the superiority of private property, legitimation of social inequalities and anti-statism of all varieties (Gills and Rocamora *op cit*). It is, however, somewhat early to draw any definitive conclusions regarding the outcome of contemporary transitions to democracy, transitions being undertaken simultaneously with economic liberalisation. The austerity measures associated with economic liberalisation have often created bases of opposition to the newly installed democracies. The simultaneous pursuit of economic and political liberalisation has been fraught with dangers for the incumbent democracies. The pains of economic adjustment have been justified as 'temporary' hardships that are balanced by the benefits of a freer democratic political culture:

but unfortunately for them, the poor and dispossessed cannot eat votes! In such circumstances, low intensity democracy may 'work' in the short-term, primarily as a strategy to reduce political tension, but is fragile in the long-term, due to its inability to redress fundamental political and economic problems (Gills and Rocamora, *op cit*).

In Africa, especially, the sustainability of the democratic transitions is quite fragile as a consequence of the implementation of unpopular economic adjustment measures.

A major problem of the newly installed democracies concerns the legitimacy of these economic reforms which typically are not based on wide consultation and consensus between the social interests concerned: government, employers, unions and consumer groups. Governments face the choice of either involving a broad range of political forces in the shaping of reforms, thus compromising their economic soundness, or of trying to undermine all opposition to the reforms. Confronted with this dilemma and the resistance that the social costs of reforms inherently engender, "governments tend to vacillate between the technocratic political style inherent in market-oriented reforms and the participatory style required to maintain consensus" (Przeworski *op cit* 183). The vacillation characterises most African states which have installed democratic regimes but the clearer trend is towards authoritarian economic measures which require recourse to coercive methods to undermine those social forces (unions, the intelligentsia, consumer associations amongst others) which have opposed adjustment measures. If democratic conventions have been largely ignored in the design and implementation of adjustment measures, a repressive and undemocratic response has characterised state response to this opposition. The construction of democracy within the context of economic liberalisation has therefore proved to be problematic. Yet it is not a problematique only restricted to democratic transitions in Africa. Eastern Europe also confronts the twin challenge of democratisation and economic reform:

> Once democracy is weakened, pursuit of reforms may become politically destabilising. At some point, the alternative may become either to abandon reforms or to discard representative institutions altogether. Authoritarian temptations are inevitable. The clamour of discordant voices, the delay caused by having to follow procedures, and the seeming irrationality of conflicts inescapably cause impatience among the proponents of reforms. For them, reforms are obviously needed and transparently rational: doubts, oppositions, insistence on procedures appear to be symptoms of irrationality. Technocracy hurls itself against democracy and breeds the inclination to proceed against popular resistance: to suppress *glasnost* in order to continue with *perestroika* (Przeworski, *op cit.* 187).

This insight into the tension between democratisation and economic liberalisation demonstrates the need for a broader definition of democracy because the narrow constitutionalist definition of democracy shows itself to be inadequate, as we observed above. Levels of accumulation impinge on the prospects of democracy in developing countries. For instance, the low levels of national integration restrict democratisation to an urban phenomenon, relegates peasants to the fringes of civil society, and undermines their capacity to develop national strategies and enter into broad democratic coalitions (Bangura, 1992). We have seen how far from settled the definition of democracy is: it is a contested concept. The constitutionalist and minimalist definition is incomplete; the material content of democracy is a major feature and therefore should be incorporated into the definition. We now turn in the next section to a discussion of the sources of pressure for democratisation.

Civil Society and the State

The discourse on democracy devotes considerable attention to the concept of civil society but particularly to its relationship to the state. Just as the neo-liberal variant of the concept of democracy stresses economic liberalisation as its condition and guarantee, so it is argued that civil society thrives better if separated from the state. The liberation of civil society from the clutches of the state is the major condition for democratisation, according to this perspective. But how valid is this perspective? In this section, we attempt a definition of civil society and argue against its analytical divorce from the state. We show that there is some ideological basis for the postulation of the argument that: democracy is best upheld under a capitalist 'free market' system in which civil society has been weaned away from the state.

One working definition is that in the most abstract sense, civil society can be conceived as an aggregate of institutions whose members are engaged primarily in a complex of non-state activities — economic and cultural production, voluntary associations and household life — and who in this way preserve and transform their identity by exercising all sorts of pressures or controls upon state institutions (Keane, 1987:14). Civil society would include such organisations as professional associations of one sort or another, student bodies, independent communications media, chambers of commerce, trade unions, cooperatives and non-governmental organisations (NGOs) of one variety or another. The church and its affiliated organisations constitute another important rump of civil society. However, as Nzimande and Sikhokosana argue in the next chapter, the origins and use of the concept of civil society spans several centuries with the concept featuring significantly in the writings of Hegel, Marx and Gramsci. Whereas the concept was anonymous with the 'commonwealth' or 'political society' in English political thought in the 16th and 17th centuries, it underwent some modification in Hegel's distinction between the state and civil society. Marx transformed Hegel's distinction between the state and civil society by denying the universality of the state and insisting that the state expressed the peculiarities of civil society and its class relations (Wood, 1990:61). Gramsci appropriated the concept of civil society to define the terrain of a new kind of struggle which extend the contest against capitalism not only to its economic foundations but to its cultural and ideological roots in everyday life.

In the neo-liberal version of the discourse on democracy, civil society is viewed as playing a critical role against statism of various shades, but primarily the statism associated with a prominent role of the state in economic activity. Indeed civil society has been likened to conceptual portmanteau

which indiscriminately lumps together everything from households to voluntary associations to the economic system of capitalism *(Ibid)*.

It has been argued that in Eastern Europe, the concept has been simultaneously utilised in the defence of political rights and the restoration of capitalism. While the separation of the state and civil society in the West gave rise to new forms of freedom and equality, it also created new modes of domination and coercion. As Wood has further argued, one way of characterising the specificity of civil society as a particular form to the modern world — the particular historical conditions which made possible the distinction between state and civil society — was that it constituted a new form of social power in which many coercive functions that once belonged to the state were relocated in the 'private' sphere, in private property, class exploitation and market imperatives *(Ibid)*. It was this 'privatisation' of public power which created the historically novel realm of 'civil society'. Other theorists concur when they observe that civil society has no "natural innocence" because repressive power relations also exist in civil society (Keane, *op cit*; Bangura and Gibbon, 1992:20-21). These observations tend to undermine the almost uncritical adulation that has accompanied most discussions on civil society, discussions in which it has been presented as a necessary counter-poise to the state.

If civil society institutions are not inherently democratic, is it valid to insist on their analytical separation from the state as the neo-liberal discourse does? It is not a valid exercise to do so. Without the protective, redistributive and conflict — mediating functions of the state, struggles to transform civil society become "ghettoised, divided and stagnant, or will spawn their own new forms of inequality and unfreedom" (Keane, *op cit*15). Further, civil society does not exist independently from the state; there is an inter-penetration between the two. As it been cogently argued:

for the notion of civil society to make sense it must involve some structuring of relations that distinguishes it from just being a society. It is the relationship to the state that is this structuring principle. Civil society is situated in rules and transactions which connect state and society (Beckman, 1992).

For example, chambers of commerce organise and represent business interests in a public arena as defined primarily by relations to the state via legislation, tax and license provisions. Thus the construction of civil society is centred on rules that regulate relations between competing interests in society; the protection of the state is sought in the pursuit of productive and reproductive life. The enforced separation between the state and civil society in the neo-liberal mould is therefore conceptually untenable.

However, the weaning away of civil society from the state represents more than an intellectual fashion. It has been defined as a "hegemonic ideological project of our time" which extols economic liberalisation and anti-statism *(Ibid.)*. In an effort to de-legitimise the principal ideological rival — economic nationalism — neo-liberals seek to delegitimise the state, the main locus of nationalist aspirations and resistance to the neo-liberal project. In order to undercut the claims by the state to represent the nation, its alien nature is emphasised; its retrogressiveness is explained in terms of separation from civil society.

The tension between stressing a measure of independence to civil society and according primacy to the state in the liberation and reconstruction processes also exists in the South African debate on civil society. The main elements of that debate are outlined in the following chapter by Nzimande and Sikhosana. Here we only briefly allude to the implications of two positions as they have been expressed by proponents of the liberation movement. That civil society must be built up and strengthened in its own right is strongly argued for; the unions in the workplace, civic associations in the townships, village communities in rural areas must be guaranteed autonomy from the political parties and the state (Mayekiso, 1990). Observing that "the masses are not interested in political parties as such" but more concerned with access to houses, schools and health care, it was argued that civil society must project its own interests as distinct from those of the liberation movement in South Africa. Civil society institutions, if bestowed with some measure of independence, would have the capacity to push for changes beneficial to society. There is expressed pessimism about the capacity of the liberation movement to articulate the interests of civil society: "because of the nature of the broad alliance of social forces that the ANC has come to represent, there may well be limits beyond which that party cannot go in terms of radical policy, until it is driven forward by the insistent voices of a well-organised civil society" *(Ibid.)*. The argument for a democratically constituted and strong civil society which exerts strength on state institutions can hardly be faulted. Conceptual ambiguity, however, emerges when the dichotomisation of state and civil society is attempted. In his critique of this counterpoising of civil society to the state, Singh has argued that:

> in addition to asserting the importance of civil freedoms long suppressed by the apartheid state, the struggle for transformation will also require strong state interventionism in order to correct massive structural imbalances in the political and economic spheres. At that point, an antagonistic model of civil society — state relationship, thereby privileging one at the expense of the other, will be less illuminating (Singh, 1990).

Rather it is necessary to mediate in a much more subtle way the contradiction between necessary state intervention and control on the one hand and the need to build up a strong, vigorous and empowering civil society on the other. The major question which arises when the liberation movement developes over-arching and integrative programmes of reconstruction with their own kind of logic and legitimacy relate to the ground rules for sustaining the distinction between mobilising on behalf of civil society, and mobilising on behalf of party-specific programmes in order to check the tendency to subsume the organs and structures of civil society to party purposes and agendas *(Ibid.)*. The conceptualisation of the civil society — state relationship will remain a subject of debate and source of contention on the question of political strategy. However, the forceful separation of the two sets of forces is analytically not very useful, as we observed above.

Let us now turn to the more general question of the density of civil society in Africa given the recognition of its role in the democratisation process. If civil society is quite visible in urban Africa, it is very sparse within the rural sector. Indeed, it has been questioned whether civil society, in the conventional sense, exists in rural Africa. Arguing that there was much obsession in the search for a civil society in Africa "through European eyes", Mamdani has urged the need for a historical perspective on the issue (Mamdani, 1993). The two distinct legal structures, the modern and customary legal structures, had an impact on the development of civil society in the colonial context. If it is accepted that civil society existed where there was differentiation of power, then the rural power structures centred on chiefs, spawned struggles which found expression in ethnic movements ranged against colonialism. The struggles within the ethnic structures were between the beneficiaries and victims of the colonial system. The forces ranged against each of her constituted the basis of a rural civil society. Vestiges of colonial state structures remain in rural areas with inhibitive consequences on the fuller development of a rural civil society. Urban-based movements have encountered constraints in penetrating through these structures. Most rural reforms have tended to be based on state initiatives whether in Burkina Faso, Libya, Ghana or Uganda. Otherwise, the earliest formation of civil society consisted of white settlers in the African context; it was later augmented by immigrants, the emergent domestic middle class and the working class. At independence, the de-racialisation of civil society occurred but decolonisation was incomplete.

The density and outlook of civil society institutions have a bearing on the democratisation process. Civil society and the state must become the condition of each other's democratisation (Keane, *op cit.*). That democratisation process depends on the extent to which the totality of civil society would temper the political instinct characteristic of a dependent and compradorian post-colonial state, at times variously constituting a key element within the state, and at other times variously posing as opposition when the state has become so weak as to self-propel itself towards the one-party state (Mandaza, 1991:39). Admittedly, the growth of this civil society has been uneven within and between countries but associations representing workers, professional, occupational groups, students, women and business interests have lately more active, robust and better organised in the pursuit of their interests. (Beckman, 1992; Sachikonye, 1992). They have made it more difficult for states to engage in coercive authoritarianism at their will with impunity, and their resistance has been instrumental in broadening the democratic space. In post-white settler civil societies, the bourgeois associations which represent specific economic interests in manufacturing, mining and agriculture have played a key role in limiting the state's control over economic and social life.

One argument is that the density or otherwise of civil society determines the trajectory of democratic struggles. Authoritarian regimes with a dense civil society tend to be more precarious than those with a "thin" one (Gibbon, 1992:166). However, where a dense civil society was composed largely of "traditional" or "neo-traditional" elites, these might prove amenable to certain forms of state subordination:

without disturbing the dictatorial form of rule. While secular and modern civil societies are less easily subordinated, except through "corporatist" types of relationships, which adjustment renders impossible *(Ibid.)*.

Indeed, a cursory glance at the elements of civil society which have been central in the drive for the restoration and consolidation of multi-party politics and structures in such diverse countries as Kenya, Zambia and Zimbabwe confirms that labour and student movements, domestic business interests, consumer associations, and professional associations representing the intelligentsia, have been especially active. While these forces represent sources of pressure for democratisation, they also achieve their development through access to state patronage, resources or legal structures, as we observed above. The overall impact of structural adjustment has been the reduction of the size of state institutions and by the same token, the contraction of resources from which some civil society organs have depended for their growth (Gibbon, 1993, *op cit*). This brings us back to our original argument that the compartmentalisation of the state from civil society is more confusing than illuminating. In the next section, we examine more closely an active constituent of civil society: the social movement, which is the subject of focus in this volume.

Social Movements and the State

The concept of social movement like those of *democracy* and *civil society* is not a simple and an unambiguous one. Only a working definition can be outlined here. Social movements are defined as organised social groups which are mobilised from below in pursuit of goals that challenge the established order of things, especially that of states and political parties with a stake in the state (Lindberg, Friedman and Lundberg, 1992:5). According to this perspective, social movements are by definition autonomous from the state and their goal is to change society or parts of it or other relations crucial to them. They differ from local protest groups by being more permanent, and also by their potential to appeal to groups of people beyond a particular boundary *(Ibid.)*. A more nuanced definition is that social movements represent some collective action with some stability over time and some degree of organisation oriented towards change or conservation of society (Garreton, 1993). Some analysts distinguish between (a) traditional social movements (such as labour and peasant movements and populist mobilisations) which draw upon a nation-wide constituency and aimed at influencing government policy, or engage in broad-based conflicts along the lines of social class; and (b) 'new' social movements which encompass protest and conflict, lobby and pressure government agencies over development and social issues (Lehman, 1990:148). Such new movements include cooperatives engaged in housing, consumer and other social services. They tend to be organised on an *ad hoc* basis and some of their issues for mobilising around have included urban land invasions, rural land rights, women's and human rights and self-help development projects. However, social movements have also been defined as an alternative or response to de-participation and ideological vacuity, but also as movements of self-reflectivity (Ake, 1993). Central in their core character and identity is their representation or projection of social interests, which the existing state and institutions cannot project for one reason or another. But this does not necessarily imply that a social movement cannot be subsequently incorporated into the state itself.

Furthermore, the concept of social movement has been considerably broadened to encapsulate a wider historical context. This is the position developed by those analysts who have defined social movements as anti-systemic movements (Arrighi, Hopkins and Wallerstein, 1989). They have postulated that the social movement and national movement were the two principal varieties of movements which emerged in the 19th century. The social movement defined oppression as that imposed by employers over wage-earners, by the bourgeoisie over the proletariat while the national movement defined oppression as that by one ethno-national group over another *(Ibid.)*. However, the two movements, sometimes found sufficient tactical congruence to enable them to collaborate politically. By the 1970s "a break with the past" was discernible with the emergence of a new kind of anti-systemic movement (or movements within movements) in different parts of the world (the student, black and anti-war movements in the United States), the student movements in Japan and Mexico; the labour and student movements in Europe; the Cultural Revolution in China and the rise of women's movements. The anti-bureaucratic thrust of this latter wave of social movements was partly explained by the decreasing capacity of bureaucratic structures to fulfil the expectations on which the emergence and expansion of old-style movements had been based, and partly by the increasing efficacy of direct forms of action.

Finally, another perspective distinguishes between social movements as a collective response reacting to specific tensions or contradictions in society and oriented towards resolving them; and the Social Movement (in capital letters) as the "bearer of the sense of history and major agent of global social change" (Garreton, *op cit.*). Such Social Movements with a national or global perspective would include nationalist and national liberation movements, the peace and non-aligned movements amongst others. These broader social movements contain within them different types of social movements representing specific sectors of society. Of course, the co-optive potential of the broad Social Movement such as the nationalist movement in relation to its constituent movements such as labour, women, youth and co-operative movements should not be under-estimated. One observation that has been made is that the historic compromise — between the nationalist movement and colonial authorities — which ushered independence was premised on the pre-emption of movements of peasants, labour, women, youth and oppressed nationalists which had gathered momentum at the end of World War 2 (Mamdani, 1991). In the process, from a popularly-rooted conception, nationalism was reduced to a state ideology at independence. The various social movements which had lent that nationalism some vibrancy were demobilised in most cases.

However, just like in the debate on civil society's relations with the state, there has been generated a great deal of interest in those between social movements and the political process. We have already observed that most contemporary social movements in Africa were also constituent elements of the nationalist or national liberation movement which inherited the colonial state. As key elements within civil society, social movements are not totally divorced from the state. The growth of some of the movements is linked to the disbursement of state resources as in public sector investment to increase employment, the size of unions, development projects from which cooperatives benefit, provision for tertiary education which swells the numbers of the intelligentsia. There arises therefore a recurring dilemma as in the case of civil society — state relations, a dilemma concerning the measurement and efficacy of the autonomy of social movements from the state. Opinions differ on whether it is realistic for social movements to detach themselves from the political process and the state. One strand of opinion sees the potential of social movements in shaping social relations at the level of the state and elsewhere, at politicising previously uncontested relations and re-politicising previously settled relations. However, if these social movements are to realise that potential to effect social change, they needed to exert control over the state apparatus (Arrighi *et al. op cit*). Consequently, the primary objective of the old-style social and national movements had been the capture of state power.

Another strand observes that he same generalisation about their quest for state power cannot hold for most contemporary social movements. Some have parochial objectives, theya do not necessarily aim to fundamentally transform society, but can be reformist, if not conservative. Some analysts go further to argue that most social movements:

do not regard the state or its institutions and particular membership or militancy in political parties as adequate or appropriate institutions for the pursuit of their aims. Indeed, much of the membership and force of contemporary social movements is the reflection of people's disappointment with, and their search for alternative to, with the political process, political parties and the state . . . (Frank and Fuentes, 1989).

These analysts nonetheless concede that this disengagement strategy has limitations. The capacity of social movements to effect transformation outside the political process is very modest. The more powerful and uncontrollable the forces of the global economy, especially in the present period of world economic crisis, the more they generate social movements which claim both immunity from these forces and which promise to overcome them for their membership. Therefore, objectively irrational hopes of salvation "appear as subjectively rational appeals to confront reality — and to serve oneself and one's soul through active participation in social movements; the message becomes the medium (*Ibid.*).

The marginalisation of social movements in the political process was amply demonstrated in the transformations which have occurred in Eastern Europe in recent years. The question of access to state power became a central issue. In the context of political power vacuums, Eastern European social movements found themselves 'obliged' to reorganise in order to capture and exercise state power (Frank, 1990). The examples of Solidarnosc in Poland, Civic Forum in Czechoslovakia and *Neues Forum* in the former East Germany spring to mind. These did not fully succeed in forging that transition to executive power. However, the broad question of the institutionalisation of movements into parties and state power emerged again much more clearly.

In Southern Africa, the broad national liberation movement has been confronted precisely with a similar problematique of transforming into political parties and state structures. It is a much more pressing question in South Africa as the national liberation movement constitutes a majority-rule government in the first post-apartheid government elected in April 1994. The different social movements — the labour and community-based movements, rural and urban squatter movements amongst others — which constitute the national liberation movement will be confronted with the challenge and dilemma of exerting adequate pressure on the political structures and the post-apartheid state. This is one of the central issues examined by Nzimande and Sikhosana on the relations between civil organisations and the national liberation movement in chapter 3 in this volume. The dilemma for those social movements which have been active in the liberation process is whether to partake in an institutionalisation process and remain key agents in political transformation or to assert some autonomy from the new political and post-apartheid state structures. The prospects of the assertion of their power and autonomy in the new power structure are mixed if the experiences in Angola, Mozambique and Zimbabwe are pointers at all — where the national liberation movement subordinated and demobilised those social movements that had been active agents in the liberation process.

We observed briefly above that global economic developments exert some impact on developing countries, as do conditionalities inserted into structural adjustment programmes. Social movements particularly those organised around labour and consumer interests have been especially vocal against unilaterally imposed adjustment measures. Economic grievances have therefore sometime provided the basis of broad-based coalitions against incumbent regimes. Economic grievances combined with opposition to the monolithic one-party structure provided the basis for an enormous groundswell against the Kaunda regime in 1991. At the same time, however, states can pursue corporatist strategies which result in the institutionalisation of the movements. The problematique of the state-social movement relationship is again replicated in those instances.

Social Movements as a Focus of Enquiry

In the preceding sections we have observed the serious limits of multi-party democracy, essentially a derivative of liberal democracy with its inherent weaknesses. It was argued that the formal, constitutionalist forms of democracy were insufficient in themselves in guaranteeing minimal material content to democracy. Hence the need to broaden the concept of democracy to include socio-economic arrangements based on a mixed economy in which relative shares of the private and public sectors were reversed; the main means of economic activity were under one or another of public, social and cooperative ownership, with the greatest possible degree of democratic participation and control (Miliband, *op cit.*). Such a democracy would certainly embody some features of liberal democracy including the rule of law, the separation of powers, civil liberties, political pluralism and a vibrant civil society. In addition, in this more progressive form of democracy, the objective would be the democratisation of the state and society at all levels, giving the notion of citizenship a far truer and larger meaning than it could ever have in a class-divided society (*Ibid.*).

In this democratisation process, political parties and state institutions are not the sole actors nor guarantors that all sections of society are adequately represented in the political process and have reasonable opportunities to improve their material well-being. This is the context in which civil society institutions can play a key role in articulating the interests of the under-represented sections of society. They also guard their autonomy *vis-a-vis* the corporatist strategies of the state. Some of the more dynamic institutions or forces within civil society are social movements, as we have already pointed out. We saw that these movements embody specific political, economic and cultural demands and these are expressed in the exertion of pressure on the political system, on the state and on the economy. Yet there have not been many systematic studies on the formation and objectives of social movements, and on their relations with orthodox political parties and the state. There has been a tendency to take a state-centred perspective on these movements, a perspective which uncritically accepts their subordination (or the case for such subordination) to the state. In the series of studies presented in this volume, we are critical of this complacent perspective.

This change of perspective — to an analysis of social struggles from the point of view of democratic struggle — can be grasped in terms of a shift from a geographical to a social perspective (Mamdani, 1991, *op cit*). The view from the valley (where social movements are located) in equally important as the view from the mountain-top (where state institutions pursue their hegemonic objective). However, as we also acknowledged, there is no clear-cut separation between the state and civil society, and therefore between the state and social movements in reality. This tension between an umbilical relationship and the struggles for autonomy constitute the dialectic in the state-social movement relationship. This is also reflected in the case-studies presented in the volume. What makes the studies illuminating is their capacity to bring out this relationship of accommodation and conflict in a context in which struggles for further democratisation deepen. This is a sufficient justification for an extended focus on social movements as a subject of enquiry in social science and political theory.

References

Ake, A., Oral Presentation on "Globalisation and Social Movements" Nordic Conference on *Social Movements in the Third World,* University of Lund, August 1993.

Arrighi, G., Hopkins, A. and Wallerstein I. *Anti-Systemic Movements*, London, 1987.

Bangura, Y., "Authoritarian Rule and Democracy in Africa: A Theoretical Discourse" in P. Gibbon, Y. Bangura and A. Ofstad (eds.) *Authoritarianism, Democracy and Adjustment,.* Uppsala, Scandinavia Institute of African Studies (SIAS), 1992

Beckman, B., "Empowerment or Repression: The World Bank and the Politics of African Adjustment" in P. Gibbon *et al* (eds.) *Authoritarianism, Democracy and Adjustment*, Uppsala: SIAS, 1992.

----- "The Liberation of Civil Society: Neo-Liberal Ideology and Political Theory in an African Context" Paper to a Workshop on *Social Movements, State and Democracy,* Dehli University and the Indian Statistical Institute, New Dehli, October 1992.

Frank, A. G., "Revolution in Eastern Europe: Lessons for Democratic Social Movements (and Socialism)" *Third World Quarterly*, Vol. 12 No. 2.

----- and Fuentes, M., "Nine Theses on Social Movements" *Economic and Political Weekly*, 27 August 1989.

Fukuyama, F., *The End of History and the Last Man*, London and New York, Penguin.

Garretin, M., 'Social Movements and the Politics of Democratisation' Paper presented to the Nordic Conference on *Social Movements in the Third World,* University of Lund, August 1993.

Gibbon, P., "Structural Adjustment and Pressures Towards Multi-Partyism in Sub-Saharan Africa" in Gibbon, P. *et al* (eds.) *Authoritarianism, Democracy and Adjustment*. Uppsala: SIAS, 1992.

Gills, B., and Roccamora, J., "Low-Intensity Democracy" *Third World Quarterly*, Vol. 13 No. 3, 1992

Keane, J., *Democracy and Civil Society* London and New Your: Verso, 1988.

Lindberg, S., Friedman, K., and Landberg, S., "Social Movements and Strategies in Third World Development", Report No. 28: Department of Sociology, University of London, 1992.

Mamdani, M., "State and Civil Society in Contemporary Africa: Reconceptualising the Birth of State Nationalism and the Defect of Popular Movements" *Africa Development* Vol. XV No. 3/4, 1991.

Mandaza, I., "Democracy in the African Reality" *Southern Africa Political and Economic Monthly (SAPEM)* Vol. 3 No. 4, 1990.

----- "The One-Party State and Democracy in Southern Africa: Towards a Conceptual Framework" in I. Mandaza and L.M. Sachikonye (eds) *The One-Party State and Democracy: The Zimbabwe Debate*, Harare: SAPES.

Miliband, R., "Fukuyama and the Socialist Alternative" *New Left Review*, 1993.

Oomen, T.K., "Social Movements and Collective Actions in the Third World: A Perspective". Paper to the Nordic Conference on Social Movements in *the Third World*, University of Lund, August 1993.

Plotke, D., "What's So New About New Social Movements?" *Socialist Review*, Vol. 90 No. 1, 1990.

Przeworski, A., *Democracy and the Market*, Cambridge: CUP, 1991.

Sachikonye, L.M., "Labour and Student Movements and the State in Zimbabwe" *Mimeo*, 1992.

Singh, M., "Deconstructing 'Civil Society'" *Southern Africa Report*, December 1990.

2

'Civil Society': A Theoretical Survey and Critique of Some South African Conceptions

Blade Nzimande

Mpume Sikhosana

Introduction and Background

The crisis in Eastern Europe, the failure of democracy in Africa and the apparent 'success' and 'stability' of western bourgeois democracies have all led to extensive soul-searching amongst socialists and Marxists on how national and socialist democracy can be brought about in the contemporary period. This failure of democracy has been attributed to, the following factors, amongst others.

First, in the case of Eastern Europe, the development of bureaucratic socialism has been cited as the reasons for the crisis.[1] Perhaps even more significant for our purposes here is the assertion in Slovo's bold article that the crisis in Eastern Europe is, amongst other things, an outcome of the "steady erosion of people's power both at the level of government and mass social organisations."[2] Slovo further develops his argument by pointing out that in fact the crisis can be traced to some of the Marxist classics whereby the question of the nature of established *socialist 'civil society* was never addressed. These comments by Slovo are fundamental and raise questions relating to civil society and socialist democracy which perhaps have not been taken by some of the respondents to this paper, which perhaps have not been taken up by some of the respondents to his paper: of 'civil society' and socialist democracy. It is some of these issues that this paper intends to address.

Second, the crisis in Africa has manifested itself most sharply in the persistent economic underdevelopment of many countries.[3] Some scholars have argued that the crisis in Africa is attributable to the lack of democracy in most African countries, in particular, one-party states.[4] To counteract the problems relating to democracy in Africa in recent times, there has been a movement demanding multi-party democracy in many African countries, even in the most protected enclaves of one-party states like Kenya, Zaire and most recently Malawi. Although

Mandaza is critical of explanations largely attributing the lack of democracy to the model of a one-party state, he argues that, for instance, the "Zimbabwe debate on the one-party state and democracy herein should give us deeper insight into the problematic of the state and democracy in the post-colonial situation".[5]

Third, some of the political successes and failures in Latin America in particular have been attributed to either the growth or suppression of 'civil society'.[6] In these and other 'third-world' countries, the growth of military dictatorships and the failure of some of the most bold experiments in democracy has also raised high on the agenda the question of democracy. In most instances, these debates have centred around the role of the 'social movements' and 'civil society' in building democracy in general. As a matter of fact, there is a growing usage of the concept of 'civil society' in both western Marxism and in Eastern Europe.[7]

In South Africa in particular, these debates have underlying common assumptions, some of which are:

i.   An uncritical revival of, and trust in, the concept of 'civil society' as the solution to establishing democratic regimes;

ii.   Related to the above, the notion that the development of strong independent, non-sectarian 'social movements' is a guarantee for democracy;

iii.   A tendency to simply abandon some of the fundamental concepts of Marxism-Leninism (for example, 'dictatorship of the proletariat' and 'vanguardism'), without adequate theorisation of why they are no longer applicable. This is sometimes accompanied by a very uncritical acceptance of some of the long-discredited liberal notions of democracy;

iv.   An evolutionary, rather than a revolutionary, conception of the transition to socialism, which is a very fundamental departure from the Marxist paradigm. The development of this conception is not unrelated to the growing pessimism found amongst many socialists after the collapse of East European socialism. Underpinning this evolutionary transition to socialism is the notion that the vehicle for achieving this is democracy, largely conceived in terms of liberal democracy;

v.   The stripping of the struggle for democracy of its class content, and the tendency to talk about 'democracy in general'. This underlies most of these responses to the crisis of socialism;

vi.   An implicit, sometimes explicit, assumption that a vibrant 'civil society' will act as a watchdog over the state to ensure that it behaves democratically. In virtually all of the interventions looking into the question of socialism and the democratisation of society is the absence of an analysis of the state and, more particularly, the role of the state in bringing about democracy; and

vii. The notion that 'organs of civil society' will create democracy only if they distance themselves from political organisations; consequently, democracy implies 'civil society' disengaging or distancing itself from the state.

As a theoretical contribution to the issue of building democracy, both in the national democratic phase of the South African revolution and under socialism, this chapter will engage some of the above issues.

The overall aim of the chapter is a critical review of some of the literature of the post-February, 1990, debates in South Africa on the question of 'civil society'. The specific objectives of the chapter are: firstly, an examination of the concept of 'civil society' as used by Marx and Engels, as well as by Gramsci, who has come to be known as the main classical theoretician of 'civil society'. A critical survey of the 'classics' is based on the assumption that no adequate conception of 'civil society' can be undertaken without a full assessment of the theoretical and historical meanings of the concept in the works of Marx, Engels and Gramsci.

Secondly, the chapter aims to critically evaluate some of the current usages of the concept 'civil society', basically showing that this concept is presently being used in South Africa in a liberal sense. The aim of the argument here is to show that the concept has been deployed in a pragmatic sense without adequate examination of its theoretical meaning and historical origins. Thirdly, the chapter attempts to lay the basis for a different understanding of 'civil society' by sharply posing the question of the relationship between 'civil society' and the state. This is done in order to show that 'civil society' cannot be understood outside of its relationship to, and articulation with, the state.

The Concept of 'Civil Society' in Marx and Engels

Narsoo makes a very important observation about the debates around the contemporary usage of the concept 'civil society' in South Africa, post February 2, 1990. He correctly observes that:

> it has become . . . fashionable to invoke the magic term 'civil society' as panacea for the ills of the failed East European regimes, the decline of the welfare state, the ailing economies of the African continent, and for the reconstruction in South Africa.[8]

More important is Narsoo's further observation that the term 'civil society' has become all things to all people. The use of the concept 'civil society' has permeated the national liberation and mass democratic movements, and has become a watch-word of the post February 2, 1990, phase of the South African struggle. It is for this reason that it is important to interrogate this concept more closely, with the starting point, as the examination of the meaning of the term in Marx and Engels' works.

The concept 'civil society' in the works of Marx and Engels goes to the very heart of the nature of bourgeois society and democracy. What is disturbing about the use of the term by analysts who claim to be Marxists is a lack of reflection on the *theoretical* status of the term in Marx's works and in Marxism as a whole. The term is used as if it appeared only in the contemporary period, with no history in Marx's works. It is argued here, as will be demonstrated below, that the concept 'civil society' has a specific *theoretical* and *historical* meaning in Marx's works in particular. Marx's usage of the term in his early works and non-usage in the later works is based on a particular theoretical understanding and meaning of the concept.

Examining Marx's works is by no means meant to give them the status of a catechism. Yet, it is our strong belief that the way in which Marx and Engels used the concept cannot be glibly passed over nor ignored; it impacts directly on the current debates. Over and above this, the understanding that Marx and Engels had of the concept affected the entire course of their work. Their work on this question is too significant to be ignored, particularly by people who claim to be part of the 'left'.

Therefore, tracing the meaning of 'civil society' in the Marxist classics should provide the theoretical backdrop against which to assess both the theoretical and political validity of the usage of this concept in contemporary South Africa.

The modern political usage of the term 'civil society' can be traced to Hegel. He used the term to distinguish between what he called 'political society', whose consummation was the state, and 'civil society', the sphere of private individuals pursuing their own interests. In Hegel's writings on this subject, the state is the rule of reason in society and the incarnation of freedom and, by implication, is the rationalisation of an otherwise 'irrational', egotistical 'civil society'.[9]

Marx's entry point in his *Early works* is the reverse of Hegel's views. Marx points out that the real theatre of history is not the state but 'civil society' itself. He begins by historicising this separation between political society and 'civil society' by firmly tracing it to the advent of bourgeois society. In his *Early works* he explains the separation in the following manner:

> the abstraction of the state as such belongs only to the modern time, because the abstraction of private life also belongs only to modern times. The abstraction of the political state is a modern product . . . In the Middle Ages there were serfs, feudal property, corporations of trade and of learned men, etc. This means that in the Middle Ages, property, trade, society and men were political; the material content of the state was delimited by its form; each private sphere had a political character or was a political sphere or politics formed the character of the private sphere. In the Middle Ages the political constitution was the constitution of private property, but only because the constitution of private property was the political constitution. In the Middle Ages the people's life and the state's life were identical. Man was the real principle of the state, but it was unfree man. So it is the democracy of unfreedom, perfected alienation. The abstract, reflected opposition only begins with the modern world. The Middle Ages embodied the real dualism, and the modern time the abstract dualism . . . [10]

This extract begins to clarify what Marx at this stage understood to be 'civil society'. Firstly, 'civil society' was born out of bourgeois revolution(s) as part of the freeing of the capitalist productive forces. The bourgeois revolution(s) that smashed the feudal order gave birth to civil liberties, and transformed the oppressed classes into 'equal' citizens alongside their old masters.

Secondly, the birth of civil liberties comes with bourgeois society, but, according to early Marx, these liberties do not constitute human emancipation and full freedom. At this stage, Marx was already fully aware of the abstract nature of this dualism in modern bourgeois society, perceiving it to be abstract in the sense that the state poses as an entity separated from 'civil society' which in turn poses as an autonomous sphere where people can pursue their own interests without hindrance. This means simply that whilst the separation between civil society and the state 'freed' the oppressed and exploited classes under feudalism, this was not real freedom, because the creation of a 'civil society' — the precondition for the creation of the modern proletariat — simply liberated the oppressed classes from one form of exploitation and led them to another. They were released from the oppression of the land-owning classes, but were then delivered to the bourgeoisie as the working class, resulting in a new form of exploitation and the oppression of the working masses.

The separation of 'civil society' and the state is an embodiment of human alienation and reflective of sophisticated forms of institutionalisation of capitalist exploitation throughout society. This separation serves to mask the true nature and basis of exploitation in modern bourgeois societies. What Marx is pointing out here is that the 'freer' bourgeois society seems to be, the more exploitative it becomes. This is what we understand to be Marx's perception of the essence of the separation between 'civil society' and the state.

Although Marx in his early works refers to this distinction, he uses 'civil society' in a descriptive rather than an analytical sense, taking its separation from political society as a given, as an outcome of bourgeois society. It is very clear that Marx was at this stage already indicating how property relations, even in modern bourgeois society, are the foundations of 'civil society'.

What remains unclear at this point is whether this separation, which Marx acknowledges, is real or apparent. According to Marx's concept of abstract dualism, we would argue that the separation is both real *and* apparent. It is real in so far as it is an expression of the actual liberation of serfs into modern citizens with voting rights; at the same time, it is apparent in that the separation between 'civil society' and political society does not abolish inequalities based on property. It is important to quote Marx in full in his essay *On the Jewish question* to illustrate this point:

> and yet the political annulment of private property has not only not abolished private property, it actually presupposes it. The state does away with difference in birth, class, education, and profession in its own manner when it declares birth, class, education, and profession to be unpolitical differences, when it summons every member of the people to an equal participation in popular sovereignty without taking the difference into consideration, when it treats all elements of the people's real life from the point of view of the state. Nevertheless the state still allows private property, education, and profession to have an effect in their own manner, that is, as private property, as education, as profession, and make their particular natures felt.[11]

Whilst the state, especially as embodied in bourgeois constitutions, claims to have abolished class, property and other social distinctions by giving 'equal' status to *all* its citizens, in actual fact, these distinctions are embodied in 'civil society'. From the above quotation, it can also be concluded that Marx was becoming acutely aware of how bourgeois political institutions reify 'civil society' into a 'private sphere'. Such reification is projected ideologically in the separation of the political state from 'civil society'. We would argue that already in these early works, Marx begins to anticipate the dissolution of this separation with the dissolution of bourgeois society. In fact, he makes the following conclusion in *On the Jewish question*:

> the actual individual man must take the abstract citizen back into himself and, as an individual man in his empirical life, in his individual work and individual relationships become a species-being; man must recognise his own forces as social forces, organise them, and thus no longer separate social forces from himself in the form of political forces. Only when this has been achieved will human emancipation be completed.[12]

In *The German Ideology*, Marx and Engels move closer to the actual material basis of 'civil society' as they begin to examine the material foundations of society. What is distinct, though, about *The German Ideology*, where the foundations of historical materialism are explicitly articulated, is that 'civil society' constitutes the entire social intercourse of individuals based on their economic relations. We would like to differ with Hunt when he argues that Marx's usage of the term can be divided into three watertight stages.[13] In fact, there is a common thread that runs throughout. As shown above, Marx was anticipating the ideological nature of the separation between the state and 'civil society', which he clearly articulated in *The German Ideology*.

Marx's use of the concept in his early works indicates that a full understanding of 'civil society' will lead to an analysis of property relations. In other words, it is not by chance that Marx moves to economic studies; rather, it is a further development in his analysis of the basis of 'civil society'. It is not his study of the capitalist economy that leads him to discover the real nature of 'civil society', but it is his study of 'civil society' that leads him to unpack the 'hidden abode' of 'civil society' as the real motor of history. It is this particular understanding that leads Marx to a materialist analysis and grasp of the state as simultaneously acting above society and as an institutional expression of relations in ('civil') society.

One very important piece of evidence in this regard is the way Marx defines 'civil society' in *The German Ideology*:

the form of intercourse determined by the existing productive forces at all previous historical stages, and in its turn determining these, is civil society . . . Already here we see how this civil society is the true source and theatre of all history, and how absurd is the conception of history held hitherto, which neglects the real relationships and confines itself to high sounding drama of princes and states.[14]

This is a continuation of Marx's earlier point that the separation between state and 'civil society' does not abolish private property and social relationships based on such property. By implication, such a conceptualisation would have led Marx to examine how private property constitutes the foundation of society.

From the above assertion, we would then like to assess why Marx hardly uses the term 'civil society' in his later works. There are two possibilities here: either he abandons the term because it is ideological and no longer a useful concept with which to understand the development of society, or his intention was to come back to the concept after his study of the 'economy'. In fact, the reason why Marx, particularly in *The German Ideology*, begins to expand the term to mean 'social relations' is because 'civil society' cannot be disconnected from the state. In other words, at this stage, the term 'civil society' is only used to show that separating the two shows a fragmented view of society. Already in this text he lays the foundations for his later works and a more proper conceptualisation of what has been referred to as 'civil society'. The following quotation is evidence of this:

Civil society embraces the whole material intercourse of individuals within a definite stage of the development of productive forces. It embraces the whole commercial and industrial life of a given stage and, in so far as it transcends the state and the nation, though, *on the other hand again, it must assert itself in its foreign relations as nationality, and inwardly must organise itself as state.*[15]

What this means is that the counter-poising of the state with 'civil society' represents a distorted understanding of the nature of bourgeois society. It also means that the question of the nature of the state is inextricably linked to 'civil society', thus rendering it impossible to conceptualise 'civil society' independently of the state. Similarly, though, this assertion should not be read to mean that the state can simply be reduced to 'civil society', in that under bourgeois society, it tries to act above, and mediate relations in, 'civil society'. It is because of this nature of bourgeois society that Marx abandons the term, and prefers to talk of social relations in general, with the mode of production as its underlying force.

It is in the above sense, therefore, that the state and 'civil society' cannot simply be seen as opposites but a complex articulation of the rule of the bourgeoisie under modern conditions. 'Civil society' is thus a liberal concept, which expresses, strangely enough, the relative success of bourgeoisie ideology in separating these spheres. The presentation of the state and 'civil society' as separate is ideological in the Marxian sense. According to Marx and Engels, ideology is not a fictitious presentation of reality but is rooted in the material conditions prevailing in society; yet, it is the inversion of those relations in society. Perceiving 'civil society' as distinct from the state is an inversion in the sense that it fails to see the interconnection between the two spheres and how the state is the expression of relations in 'civil society', whose foundations are the rule of the bourgeoisie.

On the other hand, we cannot rule out the possibility that Marx would have returned to the concept, particularly given the fact that he left *Capital Volume 3* at the point when he was about to discuss social classes. However, our reading of the development of Marx's conceptualisation of 'civil society' leaves us with no other conclusion than that at this mature stage, he would have abandoned the concept as a basis for understanding democracy and society as a whole.

In reaching the above conclusion, we differ in particular with Althusser's very strong argument that:

> The concept of 'civil society', as found in Marx's mature writings, and constantly repeated by Gramsci, to designate the sphere of *economic* existence, is ambiguous and should be struck from Marxist theoretical vocabulary — unless it is made to designate not the economic as opposed to the political, but the 'private' as opposed to the public, i.e. a combined effect of law and legal-political ideology on the economic.[16]

For us, abandoning the use of the term does not derive from an ambiguity of the term as such in Marx's writings. In fact, we feel that the way in which Marx uses the term represents a progressively mature view of 'civil society', leading him to see its limits in understanding capitalist society.

In the light of the above, we have no reason to believe that Marx's Engels' conceptualisation of 'civil society' can be discarded without a convincing argument of why its theoretical validity is doubtful under present conditions.

Gramsci's Conception of 'Civil Society'

Usage of the term 'civil society' in contemporary Marxist discourse is normally associated with Gramsci. It is therefore important to try and understand what Gramsci means by this concept. Althusser is, in fact, mistaken in attributing to Gramsci the notion of 'civil society' as meaning the economic sphere. Gramsci uses the concept in a manner not inconsistent with that of Marx and Engels, although he definitely enriches it.

It is argued here that in order to fully comprehend Gramsci's usage of the term, one needs to understand the context within which he was using it. Gramsci's primary concern, particularly in his *Prison Notebooks*, is the understanding of the question of contestation over state power. It is in this context, for instance, that he comes up with his concept of *hegemony*, and his understanding of the role of the state, intellectuals and the Communist Party is firmly grounded in this concept.

With regard to the role of intellectuals, it is important to quote Gramsci in full, insofar as this quotation clarifies his understanding of 'civil society' in relation to hegemony:

> what we can do, for the moment, is to fix two major superstructural 'levels': the one that can be called 'civil society', that is the ensemble of organisms commonly called 'private', and that of 'political society' or 'the State'. These two levels correspond on the one hand to the function of 'hegemony' which the dominant group exercises throughout society, and on the other hand to that of 'direct domination' or command exercised through the state and 'juridical' government.[17]

Here Gramsci is using the concept in a classical Hegelian way to distinguish between 'civil' and 'political' society. However, Gramsci's most important point is that the dominant class exercises power throughout both 'civil' and 'political' society. Hegemonic domination is primarily exercised via 'civil society', and direct domination through direct state repression.

Like Marx, Gramsci sees 'civil society' as the theatre of struggle and a terrain where real power is contested. He compares 'civil society' to the trenches in modern warfare:

. . . in the case of the most advanced States . . . 'civil society' has become a very complex structure and one which is resistant to the catastrophic 'incursions' of the immediate economic element (crises, depressions, etc). The superstructures of civil society are like the trenches of modern warfare. In war it would sometimes happen that a fierce artillery attack, seemed to have destroyed the enemy's entire defensive system, whereas in fact it had only destroyed the outer perimeter; and at the moment of their advance and attack the assailants would find themselves confronted by a line of defence which was still effective.[18]

However, there is a new element introduced by Gramsci with regard to the concept of 'civil society' and that is its resistance to change even in the face of serious political and economic changes or crises. It is not only the resilience of 'civil society' *per se* to which he refers here, but also to a more fundamental phenomenon: the dominant group's hold over institutions of society, even if only ideologically, in spite of crises and changes.

Given the above, one would assume that Gramsci had a dualistic understanding of bourgeois society, as consisting of both a 'resilient', sometimes 'autonomous' 'civil society', and a repressive political society, when, in fact, he is merely illustrating the different ways in which a ruling class exercises power. Gramsci himself criticises the separation of 'civil' and 'political' society, and uses this as a methodological, rather than a structural or organic, distinction to demonstrate how hegemony operates. Gramsci himself makes this point clear in his critique of ideologies of the free market system:

the ideas of the Free Trade movement are based on a theoretical error, whose practical origin is not hard to identify; they are based on a distinction between political society and 'civil society' which is made into and presented as an organic one, whereas in fact it is merely methodological. Thus it is asserted that economic activity belongs to civil society, and that the state must not intervene to regulate it. But since in actual reality civil society and the State are one and the same, it must be made clear that *laissez faire* too is a form of state 'regulation', introduced and maintained by legislative and coercive means. It is a deliberate policy, conscious of its own ends, and not the spontaneous, automatic expression of economic facts.[19]

The similarities between Marx and Gramsci's understanding of 'civil society' are striking, although these have usually been under-emphasised in Marxist discussions on this concept. Gramsci uses the concept to highlight aspects of political and ideological domination in much more precise terms than those developed by Marx himself.

'Civil Society' as a Liberal and One-Sided Concept

For our purposes, surveying the meaning of the term 'civil society' in Marx and Gramsci's works leads to these conclusions.

First, the distinction between 'political' and 'civil society' in Marx and Gramsci's works is methodological (descriptive) and not a theoretical one. In other words, one cannot treat 'civil society' without simultaneously addressing the question of the state, and the entire set of social relations underpinning society.

Secondly, the current conceptualisation in most of the contemporary debates in South Africa involves separating the state and 'civil society'. This is a Hegelian conceptualisation, rooted neither in Marx's nor in Gramsci's use of the concept. However, this conceptualisation is also a mechanical inversion of Hegel. If for Hegel the state was the incarnation of reason that had to mediate over the 'selfish civil society', for the protagonists of a 'vibrant civil society', 'civil society' is the incarnation of reason that has to act as a watchdog over the state. In fact, the current usage, as will be illustrated below, is a liberal one, and a misreading of Marx and Gramsci.

Thirdly, an argument for a 'civil society' independent of the state cannot be theoretically sustained because it obscures the fundamental role of the state in bringing about democracy.

Based on the above assessment it is important to concretely illustrate how contemporary usage of this concept in South Africa indicates a very one-sided approach to the question of building democracy.

Democracy and 'Civil Society': An Overview of Contemporary South African Debates

The discourse of 'civil society' has been used in a variety of ways, both in the everyday language of the national liberation and mass democratic movements, as well as in some of the theoretical reflections on the crisis of Eastern European socialism. However, some of the more significant published debates have raised this question within the context of the broad umbrella of 'democratic socialism'. From our survey of this literature, there are a number of variants of democratic socialism; these include Swilling's notion of 'associational socialism', Glaser's 'logic of democratic participation', and the variant found within the ranks of the South African Communist Party (SACP).

The intention of critically evaluating these positions is not aimed at an overall assessment of the totality of their arguments on various aspects of the crisis of Eastern European socialism, nor is the aim to evaluate the concept of 'democratic socialism' as such.[20] Rather, our primary concern is to evaluate the usage of the concept of 'civil society' and its relation to democracy. A brief evaluation of Swilling, Glaser and Slovo's ideas will be undertaken, as examples of the way the concept 'civil society' has been defined and utilised.

In order to illustrate some of the core ideas informing Swilling and Glaser's variant of 'democratic socialism', a few quotations will suffice. After criticising what he calls naive visions of 'civil society' as expounded by proponents of a free-market economy, Glaser presents his vision of the relationship between 'civil society' and democracy:

> this positive vision of civil society, goes beyond the call for individual freedoms, since it urges active use of otherwise formal 'rights' to establish the richest possible array of voluntary activity, perhaps supported by the state . . . It is also distinct from the (also important) demand for 'direct democracy', since it does not render individuals and voluntary organisations accountable to local majorities or spontaneous crowds . . . Freed of its naive free market connotations, the idea of an autonomous civil society is a crucial counter-weight to the ambitions of any state.[21]

Swilling advances arguments that are similar to those of Glaser. It is important to quote him in full in order to completely grasp the essence of his arguments about the role of 'civil society' in building democracy and socialism:

> Civil society has emerged as the codeword for the associational life of a society that exists somewhere between the individual actions of each person (what some might call the 'private realm') and the organisations and institutions constituted by the state (or 'public realm'). It is where everyday life is experienced, discussed, comprehended, contested and reproduced. This is where hegemony is built and contested . . . The New Right, liberal intellectuals and even sections of the liberation movement are of the view that civil society should include the profit-driven shareholder-owned, industrial-commercial sector. This author is of the view that a true 'civil society' is one where ordinary everyday citizens, who do not control the levers of political and

economic power, have access to locally-constituted voluntary associations that have the capacity, know-how and resources to influence and even determine the structure of power and the allocation of material resources.[22]

Slovo's paper by its very nature, does not encompass everything and it might perhaps be regarded as unfair to criticise him for what he does not say. However, it is important to question his usage of the concept of a 'socialist civil society'. Slovo argues that:

> Lenin envisaged that working class power would be based on the kind of democracy of the Commune, but he did not address, in any detail, the nature of *established socialist civil society*, including fundamental questions such as the relationship between the party, state, people's elected representatives, social organisations, etc.[23]

We believe that Slovo's use of the term 'socialist civil society' without any theoretical clarification is a serious omission on his part. In fact, by so doing, Slovo is committing a mistake similar to that of the other 'democratic socialists' as highlighted above: viewing the development of 'civil society' as one of the key elements in democracy, without demonstrating how this is so. The fact that Slovo specifically uses the concept of 'socialist civil society' is important, in the light of what Marx, Engels and Gramsci said, to assess the theoretical validity of this concept.

The *first* weakness in the above conceptions of 'civil society' is the separation of 'civil society' from the state. Furthermore, particularly in the case of Glaser, another weakness is the counterpoising of 'civil society' with the state, arguing that an independent 'vibrant civil society' can act as a check against the state. This is a distortion of Marxism and its conception of the state, whereby the state is seen as the institutional, political expression of relations in ('civil') society. In fact, we would argue that the theoretical strength and perhaps the scientificity of Marxism lies precisely in having exposed the fact that the state in capitalist social formations is the political expression of relations in 'civil society'. Marxism also exposes the fact that the separation between 'civil society' and the state is largely an ideological one, hiding the true character and source of exploitation and oppression in capitalist social formations.

The *second* weakness related to the above is that of narrowly presenting the task of building democracy only in terms of 'civil society'. This is extremely one-sided, and the question of democratisation cannot be separated from the question of the contestation and seizure of state power. It is our argument here that unless the national liberation movement holds state power, the process of democratisation in South Africa cannot even begin to be set in motion. These variants of 'democratic socialism' end up limiting the issue of building democracy to the task of developing an 'autonomous civil society', as if this on its own is adequate for the purposes of building either a national or a socialist democracy.

The weakness of these arguments is even more sharply revealed when Swilling suggests what should and should not be included in 'civil society'. It is as if institutions of capital and its reproductive organs could easily be removed from 'civil society'. The end results of these arguments are no different to those of liberals. In the same way as liberals want a private sphere free of state intervention, these 'democratic socialists' also want a 'civil society' free of state interference.

The *third* area of weakness in these arguments is that there is an underlying assumption that the state has no role at all to play in the process of democratisation. The state, by its very nature, is presented as being incapable of playing a role in the democratisation process. This is simply incorrect. However, even more serious is that this assumption blocks the exploring of the question of the nature of the national democratic and socialist states that should be constructed in order to deepen democracy.

A related argument is that 'civil society' will act as a watchdog over the state, although the net outcome of such an approach is the opposite of what it claims to be fighting for — that is, abandoning the terrain of the state to the whims of state bureaucrats and capitalist institutions. Thus an important issue is obscured: how can what these 'democratic socialists' term 'organs of civil society' play a role both inside and outside the sphere of the state? In other words, for them, the state ceases to be an arena of contestation; pressure groups from outside are sufficient to act as a check against its inherently undemocratic and bureaucratic character. If the state is unable to contribute to a process of democracy (whether it be a national democratic or a socialist one) one might as well forget about struggling for the capture or seizure of state power. The fact that the socialist states of Eastern Europe became bureaucratic and oppressed the very classes they claimed to be representing does not mean that a socialist state is inherently undemocratic.

The *fourth* and more serious omission in these arguments is their disturbing silence on the role of political parties and organisations in the process of building democracy. No matter how much one can engage in wishful thinking that the building of democracy is the task of an 'independent and vibrant civil society', political parties, whether they be bourgeois, petty bourgeois or socialist, *do* and *should* play a very significant role in this democratisation process. Bourgeois and petty bourgeois political parties always intervene to shape 'civil society' in a manner that will reproduce the type of society these parties stand for. It is incumbent upon, and perhaps the most important function of, a political party of the working class such as (SACP) to *unashamedly* struggle for the hegemony of the working class and a socialist agenda throughout all levels of society. To suggest that the building of democracy is a task for 'civil society' and its organs indicates plain naivete of the nature of political struggle. In fact, it is such a conceptualisation that has led to the problematic practice that is beginning to emerge in South Africa within the national liberation and mass democratic movements: for instance, issues around services and development in townships are for civics, and 'political issues' are for political organisations and parties.[24]

To develop the above point further, it is important to note that political parties are *class* parties, that is, they represent the interests of particular classes in society, whether they be the bourgeoisie, the petty bourgeoisie or the proletariat.[25] This is the essence of the *class struggle*, in that this struggle throws up political parties which stand for the interests of this or that class, or coalitions or fractions of classes. Even in colonial societies, national liberation movements contain within them a number of classes who constantly vie for political hegemony and supremacy. Political parties and national liberation movements strive to shape society in a manner consistent with their own interests. It is therefore inadequate to tackle the question of democracy without relating this to the question of class struggle and the role of political parties or movements thrown up by that class struggle. The notion of the development of democracy primarily through the building of a 'vibrant civil society', without taking into account the type of movement or political party is idealistic. This argument can be dangerous since it disarms the liberation movement or working class parties by encouraging them to desist from building mass organisations or intervening in so-called 'civil society'.

The *fifth* and perhaps most obvious weakness of the argument that the development of 'organs of civil society' within an independent sphere of 'civil society' is a guarantee for democracy, is that oppressive and capitalist institutions are also independent organs of 'civil society'. The coincidence between this argument and that of the ideologists of the free market is particularly striking. Furthermore, even the apartheid regime's programme of privatisation can be regarded as an attempt to relegate political and economic power to the sphere of a 'civil society' without state interference. Yet so doing, the regime is hoping to reproduce apartheid through an 'independent and vibrant civil society'.

The *sixth* weakness, particularly in relation to Slovo's usage of the concept of 'socialist civil society', begs one very fundamental question: if the 'separation' between 'civil society' and the state is, as Marx pointed out, an abstract dualism and a product of the transition from feudalism to capitalism, can we then theoretically sustain the notion of a socialist 'civil society'? From our understanding of the use of the concept by Marx, the separation is a product of the evolution of bourgeois society and one of the key tasks of socialism is to bridge this separation. In fact, we would argue that this separation is an institutional expression of the alienation of 'man' in capitalist societies: the separation of the 'social' from the 'political'. The separation is a reflection of the relegation of human social needs to the private sphere of 'civil society'. As indicated above, Marx specifically points out that one of the tasks of socialist transformation is that "man must recognise his own forces as social, organise them, and thus no longer separate social forces from himself in the form of political forces".

It is our belief here that if a correct approach to the question of building democracy is to be developed both in the immediate phase of national democracy and in the period of socialist reconstruction, we should spare no effort in exposing the weaknesses and distortions embodied in such views.

What the above critical review of the usage of the concept of 'civil society' shows is that an assessment of the crisis of Eastern European socialism which is based purely on the notion that the source of the crisis was largely the suppression of the development of a vibrant 'civil society' is not useful at all. An assessment should be based on an historical analysis of the development of those societies in their totality viz. the nature of social formations, the nature and role of the state and the communist parties that were in power, and the imperialist onslaught on socialist countries. It is only then that we can learn lessons from those countries for the future of national democracy and socialism in South Africa.

One of the latest inventions around the issue of 'civil society' is Mayekiso's notion of a 'working class civil society'.[26] This notion appears to be a theoretical advance in understanding the concept of 'civil society'; unfortunately, Mayekiso does not define it and instead contributes further to the confusion surrounding the deployment of this concept in South Africa.

There are two main weaknesses in Mayekiso's notion of 'working class civil society'. Firstly, he understands 'civil society' as being divided into two 'civil societies', one for the ruling class, and another for the working class, as demonstrated in the following line of argument:

> on the one hand, it is clear in South Africa that the most developed organs of civil society serve the bourgeoisie . . . For working class people, on the other hand, the organs of civil society include civic associations, trade unions, the women's groups . . . and other organisations, formal and informal, that represent the interests of poor and working people.[27]

Given this line of argument, the theoretical assumption underlying the concept of 'working class civil society' is that the struggle is between two 'civil societies', and the transformation of society is the victory of 'working class civil society' over that of the bourgeoisie. To present civil society as divided into two is an erroneous understanding of the nature of bourgeois societies.

The second weakness in Mayekiso's argument is that his concept conflates working class mass organisations with 'working class civil society', a persistent mistake of protagonists of 'civil society'. The two are not the same. The existence of 'civil society' presupposes the existence of repressive and exploitative relations in society. The separation between state and 'civil society' — the birth of liberalism actually — has been the mode of subjugation of the working class under the era of bourgeoisie dominance. Therefore, the concept of a 'working class civil society' is contradictory.

Arguments for an autonomous 'civil society' are the greatest disservice to Marxism itself. With a stroke of the pen, they wipe out the entire Marxist critique of liberal and bourgeois democracy. It is as if Marxist theory has not undertaken more than a century of critique of capitalism and its political institutions. All of a sudden, without much reference to these debates, we are told that the Marxist mistake was to throw away the baby with the bathwater (i.e. throwing away capitalism with its liberal freedoms), as if socialism is simply an incremental building upon liberal bourgeois freedoms!

Finally, it is important to highlight a few more theoretical issues in order to further illustrate the weaknesses of the concept 'civil society'. In the usage of this concept it has been conveniently forgotten that the nature and structure of 'civil society' is founded upon class relations in society. In bourgeois societies it is 'civil society' that is the real theatre of history, viz. class exploitation and class struggles. By implication, therefore, we cannot talk of an 'autonomous civil society' without addressing the class nature of that 'civil society'. The more we analyse 'civil society', the clearer its inseparable relation to the state becomes, and the clearer becomes the realisation that an 'autonomous civil society' is the material foundation and ideological projection of capitalist exploitation in its most sophisticated forms. The task of a socialist revolution, therefore, in so far as the issue under discussion is concerned, is to strive for the abolition of the state and 'civil society' in both their separation or interconnectedness. This task is presented by Marx and Engels thus:

> the working class, in the course of its development, will substitute for the old civil society an association which will exclude classes and their antagonism, and there will be no more political power properly so called, since political power is precisely the official expression of antagonism in civil society.[28]

In theoretical terms, the relationship between the state and the rest of society is a continuous and dialectical one. At different moments or even at the same instance in the 'daily operation' of society, in political struggles, in capital accumulation, state and ('civil') society can operate as the same thing; at other moments or instances as opposites; and still in others, as parallel processes. All these are complex articulations which actually defy a simplistic and basically un-Marxist notion of a separate state and 'civil society'.

The bourgeoisie and its ideologues, free marketeers in particular, want to present state and 'civil society' as separate and independent spheres, in order to hide the true material foundations of capitalist exploitation and the role played by the state in sustaining such an order. 'Civil society' in particular is presented as a 'heaven' within which individuals or groups of people can enjoy personal freedom and free competition.

It is therefore unacceptable for people who regard themselves as Marxists to deploy the concept 'civil society' in such an unproblematic manner. If the so-called 'left' intended something else by its usage of an 'autonomous civil society', it has a lot of theoretical explaining to do.

The implications of the (un)problematic usage of the concept of 'civil society' by the 'left', both in Europe and in South Africa, are best summed up by Wood thus: ". . . the new concept of civil society signals that the left has learned the lessons of liberalism about the dangers of state oppression, but we seem to be forgetting the lessons we once learned from the socialist tradition about oppressions of civil society"[29]

Mass Struggles, Political Power and Democracy

No doubt 'democratic socialists' and other protagonists of 'civil society' will throw their hands up in horror at what might seem to be a collapse of political and social life into one and, therefore, the subjection of 'civil society' to political life. Actually, this issue is the crux of the matter on the question of socialist democracy. It is in this area that 'democratic socialists', in the way they pose the question of democracy, obscure the very real socialist imperative of overcoming the contradiction between 'civil society' and the state. By arguing for the development of an autonomous 'civil society', they do not address this issue at all; instead, they fall into the very same mould of the separation of 'civil society' and the state under capitalism. This obscures the need for the creation of organs of (proletarian) state power that are simultaneously autonomous mass social formations able to act independently of the state. This is what the Soviets were originally, and it was intended to incorporate within them both these qualities as the only concrete political path for bridging social and political life as the highest form of human emancipation. It was not because they were organs of state power that the Soviets failed, but rather their autonomous character as mass social formations were progressively stifled by the Communist Party through the mechanism of a bureaucratic state. That this happened in Eastern Europe does not mean that there can be no organs of state power that are simultaneously mass-based and autonomous.

It was not, we would argue, due to the inherently bureaucratic character of the state that the Soviets became conduits of the party and the state bureaucracy. Rather it was due to the particularly stifling state form that developed in the Soviet Union (for example, tight control by the Party, merging of party with state apparatuses, important contextual problems of imperialism and its assault on the Soviet Union, outlawing of the opposition and undermining the heterogenous character of, and debates amongst, the Soviets).

Let us explore a bit further how organs of state power can simultaneously be part of the state and be autonomous mass social formations. One of the issues around this question is the debate between Kautsky and Lenin on whether or not Soviets should be transformed into state organisations. This is one of the most crucial areas of socialist theory and revolutionary practice; yet, it has hardly been given the attention it requires. It is, therefore, important to quote liberally in order to engage this issue.

In his pamphlet *The Dictatorship of the Proletariat*, Kautsky vehemently criticises the Bolsheviks in power for, amongst other things, converting the Soviets into organs of proletarian state power. He argues that:

> . . . the Soviet form of organisation is one of the most important phenomena of our time. It promises to acquire decisive importance in the great decisive battles between capital and labour towards which we are marching . . . But are we entitled to demand more of the Soviets? The Bolsheviks, after the November Revolution, 1917, secured in conjunction with the Left Socialist-Revolutionaries a majority in the Russian Soviets of Workers' Deputies, and after the dispersion of the Constituent Assembly, they set out to transform the Soviets from a *combat organisation of one class*, as they had been up to then, into a *state organisation*. They destroyed the democracy which the Russian people had won in the March Revolution.[30]

Kautsky's argument here is basically that, for democracy to have flourished in socialist Russia at the time, the Soviets should not have been transformed into state organisations. Obviously, this argument would today find favour amongst many of the 'democratic socialists', who say that they should have been left to be 'organs of civil society', independent from the state. We could further state that perhaps in this argument, taken to its logical conclusion in the present debates in South Africa, the Soviets would have constituted part of the 'socialist civil society' separate from the organs of the proletarian state. Indeed, it is largely because of hindsight that there is now talk of a 'socialist civil society'.

How did Lenin respond to Kautsky in this regard?

> Thus, the oppressed class (according to Kautsky — authors), the vanguard of all the working and exploited people in modern society, must strive towards the 'decisive battles between capital and labour', *but must not touch* the machine by means of which capital suppresses labour! — *It must not break up* that machine! — *It must not make use* of its all-embracing organisation *for suppressing the exploiters*! Excellent, Mr Kautsky, magnificent!

'We' recognise the class struggle — in the same way as all liberals recognise it, i.e. without the overthrow of the bourgeoisie.[31]

Lenin argues further that:

whoever sincerely shared the Marxist view that the state is nothing but a machine for the suppression of one class by another, and who has at all reflected upon this truth, could never have reached the absurd conclusion that the proletarian organisations capable of defeating finance capital must not transform themselves into state organisations . . . .[32] To say to the Soviets: fight, but don't take all the state power into your hands, don't become state organisations — is tantamount to preaching class collaboration and 'social peace' between the proletariat and the bourgeoisie.[33]

According to Glaser, this reply by Lenin is an example of statist thinking. However, the question that is essentially posed by Lenin in this reply to Kautsky, and which should be a key question pre-occupying all socialists at this point in time is this: After the overthrow of the bourgeoisie and its institutions, what type of proletarian organs of state power should be put into place? Marx had earlier answered in the *Communist Manifesto* that the bourgeois state machine should be replaced by the proletariat organised as the ruling class. In all the criticisms and reflections on the failure of Eastern European socialism, this question has hardly been engaged. We would argue that it is the very same organs of the working class which overthrew the bourgeoisie that should become the new organs of proletarian state power. In the case of Russia in 1917, it was the Soviets.

Otherwise, what institutions and organs should have become the organs of the new proletarian state power? With the Soviets having become the new organs of the proletarian state, there was no necessary connection between this transformation and the bureaucratisation that took place later. In fact, the Soviets as organs of state power in the proletarian state should have subjected the state to the popular will of the working people instead of the other way around. By so doing, the Soviets would have been autonomous mass social formations, wielding state power at the same time. The strengthening of this character of the Soviets would have deepened socialist democracy in the Soviet Union. This would have laid the basis for organs of people's power to subject the proletarian state to their will, whilst essentially remaining autonomous organisations of the working class and the Russian people as a whole. This is how Soviets operated initially. The reasons for the later reversal of Soviet democracy should not merely be sought in the assumed (inherent) bureaucratic character of the state, but also in the manner in which the Party conducted itself in its wielding of state power.

Conclusion

Although this debate cannot, and will not, be concluded now, it is important to end by summarising some of the main points raised.

The collapse of Eastern Europe has definitely raised a lot of debate about the question of democracy and the building of socialism. Despite major disappointments with the fall of the Eastern Europe project, one positive aspect that has emerged is the questioning of the very basis of socialism and Marxism. This is indeed healthy and in the finest tradition of Marxism and radical left scholarship.

In the case of South Africa, the emergence of the concept of 'civil society' has helped to sharpen our focus on the issue of the relationship between mass and political organisations; state and non-state formations; as well as the complexities of building true democracy. In that sense, the debate has enhanced our understanding of some of the issues taken for granted in the building of national and socialist democracy.

Nevertheless it is in such situations of profound crises and political change that intellectual productivity increases. During such periods, severe theoretical distortions and opportunistic analyses also emerge. It is also within this context that the emergence and abuse of the concept of 'civil society' should be understood.

In summary, therefore, the following points can be made about the usage of the concept 'civil society'[34] in South Africa. Firstly, the concept is being used uncritically and has been completely abstracted from its theoretical and historical meaning. In this sense, it is not at all useful in understanding the contemporary crisis of socialism and the question of democracy. Secondly, the concept is being used in a liberal sense, and ignores the whole history of the critique of liberal democracy within left scholarship. Thirdly, the concept is used in a manner that conflates or equates 'civil society' as a sphere of struggle with mass organisations.

Lastly, and perhaps most important is the absence of an analysis of the state by protagonists of 'civil society'. The state is assumed to be inherently bureaucratic and undemocratic. This assertion substitutes for a much-needed analysis of the way in which bureaucratic and authoritarian states have formed in the contemporary period. It is theoretically problematic to simply account for the emergence of such states through asserting that a vibrant and autonomous 'civil society' was either absent or suppressed.

The usage of the concept in South Africa in particular avoids the very key task of analysing the prospects for the transformation of the apartheid state into a democratic state. Despite the increasing focus on the nature and role of 'civil society', there are a lot of expectations about and demands on a future democratic state in South Africa. For instance, declarations, programmes and resolutions of the national liberation and democratic movements are littered with expectations about the role of a democratic state in economic development, housing, education, health, affirmative action, and in virtually every sphere of activity. In other words, the signs are pointing towards the emergence of an *overdeveloped post-apartheid state*. Yet, protagonists of a vibrant and autonomous 'civil society' hardly engage this very real possibility. They do not address the question of how 'civil society' will interact with or relate to such a post-apartheid state, and the implications of such a state for the thorough democratisation of the South African society.

Notes

1. Slovo, J. "Has socialism failed?" in *African Communist*, No. 121, 2nd Quarter, 1990.
2. *Ibid.*, p.35 — emphases added.
3. Turok, B. (1988) *Africa: what can be done?* London: Zed Press; Onimode, B. (1989) A political economy of the African crisis London: Zed press; amongst others.
5. Cited from Mandaza, I. (1991) "Introduction: the problem of methodology" (An introduction to the project "Democracy, civil society and the state: social movements in Southern Africa"), An unpublished SAPES mimeo, Harare.
6. *Ibid.*, p.3.
7. See, amongst others, Foweraker, J. and Craig, A. (1990) *Popular movements and political change*, London: Lynne Rienner Publishers; and Wood, EM (1990) "The uses and abuses of 'civil society' Socialist Register, 1990.
8. Havel, V. (1988) "Anti-political politics'" in Keane, J. (ed), *Civil society and the state*, London: Verso pp.381-398; Keane, J. (1988) *Democracy and civil society*, London: Verso; Keane, J. (ed.) (1988) Civil society and the state: new European perspectives London: Verso.

9.   Narsoo, M. "Civil society: A contested terrain" in *Work in Progress*, 76, July/August, 1991.

10. Arthur, C.J. (ed) in Marx, K. and Engels, F. *The German Ideology*, London: Lawrence and Wishart, (1970).

11. in McLellan, D. (ed) (1977) *Karl Marx: selected writings*, London: Oxford University press p.30.

12. *Ibid.*, p.45.

13. *Ibid.*, p.57.

14. According to Hunt (in Jessop, B. and Malcolm-Brown, C. (1990) *Karl Marx's social and political thought: critical assessments*, London: Routledge) development of the use of this concept in Marx's works can be divided into the following stages: i. The early stage prior to 1943 (before Marx embarked on economic studies in Paris), where "the concept is counterposed to the 'state' and is absolutely central to his analyses . . . His understanding of the concept is basically Hegelian, although the inverts the civil society-state relation in a typically Feurbachian fashion" ii. The transitional stage where Marx embarks on economic studies and begins to theorise the distorting or 'ideological' nature of the concept, but, according to Hunt, Marx cannot yet account for its essential content. At this stage, 'civil society' is equal to social relations in general. iii. The nature stage starting in the late 1850s, where mode of production is firmly analyzed as the basis of society, and the concept is given its full meaning (pp. 21-22).

15. *Ibid.*

16. *Ibid.* – emphases added.

17. Althusser, L. and Balibar, E. (1968) *Reading Capital*, London: Verso, p.162 – emphasis in original.

18. Hoare, !. and Smith, G.N. (1971) (eds) *Selections from the prison notebooks of Antonio Gramsci*, London: Lawrence and Wishart, p.12.

19. *Ibid.*, p.235.

20. *Ibid.*, pp.159-160.

21. Important as it is to critically examine the notion of 'democratic socialism', this issue is a subject on its own that require a separate intervention.

22. Glaser, D. (1990) "Putting democracy back into democratic socialism" in *Work in progress*, 65, April, 1990, p.30.

23. Swilling, M. "Socialism, democracy and civil society: the case for associational socialism" in *Work in Progress*, 76, July/August, 1991, pp.21-22.
24. *Ibid.*, p.36.
25. See Nzimande, B. and Sikhosana, M. *op.cit.*
26. Embodied in the notion of political parties as class parties is the fact that political parties can and do represent a coalition of classes or fractions of classes.
27. Mayekiso, Mzwanele "Working Class Civil Society: Why we need it, and how we get it" in *African Communist*, 2nd Quarter, 1992.
28. *Ibid*, p.33
29. Glaser, 1990 p.67
30. Marx in *The German Ideology*, in McLellan, 1975 p.215.
31. Wood, E. "The uses and abuses of 'civil society'" in *Socialist Register*, 1990, p.3.
32. Quoted in *ibid*, p.157 — emphasis in Kautsky's original pamphlet.
33. Lenin, *ibid.*, pp.158-159.
34. An alternative conceptualisation to 'civil society' is developed in chapter 3 in this volume. That alternative conceptualisation is developed within the context of the current South African situation.

Part 2: Case Studies

3

'Civil Society', Mass Organisations and the National Liberation Movement in South Africa

Blade Nzimande
Mpume Sikhosana

Introduction

The question of building democracy (national and socialist) in post-apartheid South Africa top the political agenda as the end of apartheid neared. Debates around this question have also been resurrected in the light of certain international, regional (in particular Southern African) and local political and economic developments. These include the hegemony of the western capitalist countries in the global economy and politics, which has been deepened by the crisis in Eastern Europe, and the failure of the post-colonial state to deliver democracy and economic development in Africa.

In South Africa, the unbanning of the national liberation movement and other political organisations on February 2, 1990, sharpened the debates about building democracy. These debates have necessitated new forms of engagement both amongst members of the mass democratic movement as a whole, and with the apartheid regime. A number of strategic shifts on the relationship and role of various mass organisations *vis-a-vis* the national liberation movement and the post-apartheid state had become evident during this period.

This chapter aims to construct an alternative conceptualisation of the process of democratisation of the South African society, by paying particular attention to the immediate goal of building a national democracy, and relating this to the longer-term objective of building socialism in South Africa. It begins with a critical analysis of mass organisations under apartheid during the transition to democracy. It will critique some of the assumptions and practices relating to the question of building democracy that have emerged since February 1990. An attempt will also be made to explain the present transition period in the light of the debates about democracy. The paper argues for the urgent necessity of building organs of people's power as the only means of ensuring a national democracy as well as for laying the foundations for a rapid advance towards socialism. The notion of 'organs of people's power' is advanced as the most appropriate theoretical conceptualisation of the task of building the national liberation movement and democracy.

Mass Organisations, Apartheid and the Transition to Democracy in South Africa

South Africa has some of the most highly-developed mass organisations on the continent; they mushroomed in the late 1970s and were consolidated in the mid-1980s. The basis for the emergence of these organisations can be traced to the colonial-type subjugation of blacks in general and Africans in particular. Their emergence laid the conditions for the consolidation and strengthening of the national liberation and mass democratic movements inside the country. These organisations' programmes were directed clearly towards national liberation, democracy and the revolutionary transformation of the South African society.

The mass organisations developed a perspective characteristic of the national liberation movement (whose key components were the African National Congress (ANC) and the South African Communist Party (SACP)), that of working class leadership and mass-based organisation based on *mandate, accountability*, and *internal democracy*. The practical development of, and experimentation with, democracy through actual struggle also infused into the national liberation movement this democratic tradition under conditions of mass mobilisation. This was made possible by, and further strengthened, the relationship between armed struggle and the political underground and open mass and labour struggles.

Mass organisations (sometimes referred to as 'social movements') under colonial conditions tend to develop a very specific character, laying a basis for becoming organs of a democratic revolution. This is explained by Vilas on the grounds that struggles in 'Third-World' countries tend to articulate four main contradictions, viz. national, class, developmental and imperialist contradictions.[1] The gender dimension should be added to these. According to Vilas, this produces a situation of not only fundamental contradictions of exploitation and oppression, but also contradictory tendencies within these struggles themselves. Because of the nature of colonial/imperialist oppression, it is not easy to sell the illusion of the separation between state and 'civil society'. Therefore, in practice, mass struggles assume a political character, and political struggles take on social and civic dimensions. This is related to the crude and brutal nature of economic exploitation and political repression.

It was for reasons broadly similar to the above that mass organisations in South Africa grew rapidly in the post-1976 era and progressively mobilised around the demand for people's power. This marked a radical shift from the struggle during the first half of this century where the demands were centred around incorporation into the structures of the white ruling class. This development is aptly captured by Mashamba thus:

> to defend their gains and advance their struggles, people organised themselves and created alternative structures of power, organs of people's power, on all fronts of the struggle. So we saw the development of civic organisations, street committees, youth and student organisations, Students' Representative Councils (SRCs), Parent-Teacher-Students' Associations (PTSAs), teacher organisa- tions, women's organisations, village committees, crisis committees, people's courts, etc. Thus a further development in the concept of 'people's power' took place: the dominance of the 'monolithic' notion of 'people's power' as 'the supreme controlling power in the state' which has to be seized by the people via the instrumentality of their leading organisations — the ANC and allied organisations — was superseded by a 'dispersed' notion of 'people's power' that had to be seized via the instrumentality of the various organs of people's power in each and every front of the struggle as a matter of both tactical and strategic priority.[2]

This development, we would argue, gave the mass democratic movement both a social and a political character, as well as a very sophisticated understanding of social transformation. The wielding of state power was being understood not merely as the function of a government, but that of the people as a whole. Furthermore, implicit in the character of the mass organisations is the notion that revolutionary transformation incorporates both the seizure of state power as well as the transformation of the everyday conditions of the people such that they themselves are able to control their day-to-day lives.

Perhaps even more important in the development of mass organisations in South Africa was their understanding of the concept "people", both in theoretical discourse and practical political struggles. This was best summed by the United Democratic Front (UDF) thus:

we use the term ('the people') to distinguish between two major camps in our society — the enemy camp and the people's camp. The people's camp is made up of the overwhelming majority of South Africans — the black working class, the rural masses, the black petit bourgeoisie (traders), and black middle strata (clerks, teachers, nurses, intellectuals). The people's camp also includes several thousand whites who stand shoulder to shoulder in struggle with the majority . . . In this popular struggle, the UDF has identified the working class as the leading class . . . The workers are the key to the victory of the whole people's camp.[3]

This particular understanding facilitates a distinction between the various social forces constituting the people's camp and the leading role of the working class amongst the people. This expresses the internal contradictions within the people's camp, the understanding of what unites the people's camp and how the different class interests articulate or disarticulate within this camp. It was within this context, for instance, that the working class came to occupy a central role in the mass struggles of the 1980s in South Africa.

The above was put into practice in virtually all the structures of the mass democratic movement. With regard to workers, conditions in the factories, on the farms and the mines were always intertwined with, and related to, the political structures of white domination and the role of the apartheid state in reproducing conditions for the exploitation of the black working class in particular. Similarly with civics and street committees, their struggles related civic and social issues such as rent and services to the nature of state power and the exploitation of the working class. In fact, the climax in the development of the notion of 'people's power' was this character of the struggles.

Embedded within these struggles was a particular understanding of the relationship between mass organisations and the national liberation movement. As Mashamba notes above, the struggle was understood in its totality and not merely as the sole preserve of the national liberation movement. Perhaps even more important was the understanding that although the ANC was seen as the vanguard of the national liberation struggles, it in itself could not effect revolutionary change without the participation of mass organisations *as part of the national democratic revolution*. From the perspective of the ANC itself, the pillar of mass struggle was central to the final defeat of apartheid.

In the post-February 1990 period, there has been a radical shift in the conceptualisation of the mass struggles in South Africa, as well as the relationship between the apartheid state, mass organisations and the national liberation movement. It is important to explain why there had been such a shift in paradigm, since this shift has had an impact on the course of the struggle after February 1990.

The unbanning of political organisations in February, 1990, was a watershed in the history of the national liberation struggle in South Africa. It is important to contextualise this development in order to relate it to the question under discussion. South Africa is not the first country in which such developments have occurred. According to Vilas, there are many examples in Latin America of limited democratisation of previously repressive regimes.[4] Vilas describes these as 'democratic transitions' which are ". . . those non-revolutionary processes whereby some military dictatorships in South America have given ground on questions of political regimes based on the principle of universal suffrage".[5] Vilas identifies some key characteristics of these democratic transitions as including:

i. restricting the process of political change to the institutional sphere in the strictest sense;

They do not project into the economic sphere, nor do they provide a framework for any substantial changes in the level of access of subordinate groups to socio-economic resources — by income redistribution, creating employment, improving living conditions, etc;[6]

ii. leaving the power bases of the reforming regime, for example, the military, untouched, and limiting the cracking down on and prosecuting of perpetrators of crimes against liberation movements.

As Vilas further points out, the old regime tries to project itself as the liberator of the very masses it has been oppressing and continues to oppress. Over and above this, the old regime can succeed for a while to effect changes from above, particularly if the national liberation movement is not in a position to impose its own advanced alternatives. In the case of South Africa, one might add that the old regime was trying by all means to hang on to control of the economy. It had also launched a low-intensity warfare aimed at weakening the national liberation movement and demoralising the popular masses.

The situation described above, graphically represents the situation in South Africa. Although the type of "democratic transition" being effected by the South African ruling class was a direct product of the advance of the revolutionary struggle, the apartheid regime tried to project this process as its own initiative, thereby enabling it to lay claim to being the guarantor of a democratic transition.

Carefully managed, and depending on the strategy and tactics of the national liberation movement, this process of 'democratic transition' in South Africa could lead to the demobilisation of the mass organisations and the people as a whole, resulting in the isolation and weakening of ANC, SACP and COSATU. To a certain degree, there are elements of this in South Africa at present; a few examples might suffice here. The apartheid regime had tried by all means to depoliticise civic and socio-economic issues, such that the mass democratic movement had been weakened. It also tried to channel struggles through institutional mechanisms created between itself and the major components of the national liberation movement (for example, multiparty constitutional negotiations, the National Economic Forum, the National Education and Training Forum, and so on). The privatisation of key social services is aimed at creating a rupture between the nature of white minority rule and the provision of services like education, health, housing, and so on.

However, even more important in the strategy of the regime was its attempt to prolong the transition process. The longer this was prolonged, the more the mass and national liberation movements are weakened. Furthermore, the regime attempted to separate civic and socio-economic issues from political-constitutional questions. This was intended to have the effect of depoliticising civic and trade union struggles and ensuring that political struggles were channelled through the negotiation process only.

However, the regime's strategies were constantly contested, and their course of development was determined by the balance of forces at different conjunctures in the struggle.

The national liberation movement responded to the post-February 1990 developments quite correctly by adopting a strategic perspective with regard to the *transfer of power to the people as a whole* and, within this, seeing *negotiations as a site of struggle*. The content of this strategic perspective, we would argue, was threefold. Firstly, it enabled the national liberation movement to relate to the unbanning as a continuation of the national democratic revolution. Secondly, it kept the strategic objective of the transfer of power to the people in place whilst at the same time engaging the regime in negotiations. This was to act as a guarantee that the national liberation movement would not allow the struggle to be quarantined within the negotiations process; but, even more importantly, it would ensure that the masses and mass struggle were the elements driving the negotiation process itself. Thirdly, this perspective, if translated into a coherent political programme, would also ensure that if negotiations hit a snag, the struggle itself would be so advanced that other avenues for achieving the strategic objective would remain in place. For example, it allowed tactical flexibility to the movement, such that the movement could negotiate with the regime whilst at the same time not ruling out the possibility of a seizure of power if negotiations failed.

In the post-February 1990 era, the liberation struggle acquired a new dimension in the opening of the terrain of negotiations: As we have observed, the regime is tried to institutionalise political struggle and weaken the national liberation movement, while the national liberation movement used mass political struggle to strengthen its position in negotiations. However, this process creates certain contradictions within the national liberation struggle itself. A few of these will be highlighted in the next section.

Mass Organisations and the National Liberation Movement Post-February, 1990: A Critique of Some Strategic Shifts

It is within the context of the above analysis that some of the strategic shifts that have taken place or are developing within the mass democratic and national liberation movements post-February 1990 should be located. This is because whilst it is important to analyse these shifts and their implications, February 1990, itself needs to be explained, as was done briefly in the above discussion. Our contention therefore, is that whilst we recognise that February 1990 was an advance in terms of the totality of struggles against apartheid, it should also be seen as part of the apartheid regime's counter-revolutionary strategy.

In attempting to analyse the strategic and tactical shifts within mass organisations and the national liberation movement, this chapter will focus largely on civic organisations as the formations where these shifts have been most prevalent or articulated.

Prior to the unbanning of the national liberation movement and other political organisations, the broad mass democratic movement (mainly UDF-affiliated youth organisations, civic/community organisations, unions, and other internal anti-apartheid formations) and the civics in particular emerged as part of the banned liberation movement's internal campaign.[7] In a statement adopted by the Central Committee of the South African Communist Party (SACP) in November, 1979, it is noted, for instance, that:

> Although the overall leadership of our revolution can only come from our liberation front through its effective underground presence, the combination of legal with illegal activity and even the strengthening of the underground itself demand the encouragement and creation of legal and semi-legal forms of mass organisation. Talk of mass political mobilisation without special concentration on the task is empty talk . . . Properly directed, the continuing search for new ways of combining at national, regional and local levels, provides the revolution with yet another important foundation for the battles ahead[8]

This does not suggest that the civic and other mass formations are the property of the ANC and allied organisations. It does, however, suggest that the radical civic movement that emerged in black townships in the late 1970s arose out of certain objective historical circumstances, viz. colonialism of a special type.[9]

Thus, whilst civic organisations (henceforth civics) were created as a response by communities to the appalling living conditions in the black townships, during this period they were correctly characterised as organs of people's power through which, amongst other things, the transfer of political power, from the minority regime to the oppressed majority, would be expedited. Civics at this stage, therefore, were as concerned with bread-and-butter issues as they were with broader questions of political power. As Majola observed:

> the apartheid state . . . rests on the standing army, police, prisons, courts, community councils, bantustan administrations, spies — it is these organs that guarantee the rule of the racists and monopoly capitalists over our people . . . The true antithesis to the community councils and the bantustan administrations are the people's communes that are already springing up out of the mass uprising. The true antithesis to the apartheid regime itself is a people's republic. (. . . using the term "people's commune" to define the political essence of what has developed in the townships because the term "Committee" would be quite misleading, giving an impression of something like the "Soweto Committee of Ten". Cradora or the Vaal Civic Association, however, is not a mere committee but a political community of a people).[10]

One of the reasons civics became popular, albeit unevenly, was because they were able to take up local issues together with national struggles for political power. It was because of struggles on the ground that life was brought into the UDF as a national umbrella front. Further, the popularity of civics can be attributed to the fact that their political perspective was that of the national liberation movement — the perspective of a national democratic revolution. It was because of this that the civics were closely aligned to the ANC and other democratic formations.[11]

The unbanning of the national liberation movement and other organisations saw the mass democratic movement beginning to define its own autonomy, not only in relation to the regime but also to the national liberation movement. This was, however, not unrelated to the blurring of roles between the national liberation movement and mass organisations after February, 1990. As a result, some mass organisations felt 'threatened' by the internal legal re-emergence of the ANC in particular. This introduced tensions that were manifested through, inter alia, the rather hesitant and painful disappearance of the UDF from the political scene almost as quickly as it had been formed. These developments led to a much sharper distinction being made between political and mass organisations, which are now theoretically counterposed as 'state' and 'civil society'. This provided the basis upon which all the major mass-based formations were to define themselves in relation to the national liberation movement.

The new discourse of 'civil society' has arisen as a result of the above factors, and has also been underpinned by the collapse of Eastern European socialism, as well as by the theoretical confusion that usually accompanies rapid shifts in the political terrain. A number of positions — which we consider to be problematic — regarding the role of mass organisations (civics in particular) in relation to the national liberation struggle, the future national democratic state, and the building of socialism, began to emerge at this stage.

First, it was argued that since civics deal with bread-and-butter issues, such as rents, housing, roads, electricity, transport, and so on, they should focus on 'local/civic' issues, whilst political organisations — the ANC in particular — should focus on 'political' issues. An article in the ANC's mouthpiece, *Mayibuye*, whilst recognising that, "problems of rents and services could not be separated from apartheid power relationships", argued that after the unbanning of political organisations in February, 1990, ". . . the extent of their [civics] involvement in political struggles has changed somewhat with changes in society. Political organisations can now more openly take up political campaigns, and civics can more deliberately focus on day-to-day community issues."[12]

Secondly, and related to the above, is the argument that since civics are non-sectarian — they strive to represent and accommodate residents of all political persuasions — they should operate independently of political organisations and any future state. Proponents of this position further argue that this autonomy will ensure that civics are watchdogs for democracy.[13]

The third position is that civics and other mass formations are characterised as organs of 'civil society' rather than of people's power. The argument is that civics should form part of and strengthen an independent, vibrant 'civil society' to ensure and guarantee democracy[14] This change from the discourse of 'organs of people's power' to that of 'civil society' and 'social movements' is essentially a very serious theoretical and intellectual retreat, as will be argued in the next section.

With respect to the above shifts and propositions, it is important to note that there have not been any fundamental changes to the South African social formation since the late 1970s. We would argue that the changes that have taken place since 1990, substantial as they are, do not warrant a departure from the strategic orientation of the national liberation movement. Whilst there have been some changes on the political scene, for example, the unbanning of political organisations and the assumption of constitutional negotiations, colonialism of a special type is still intact; in other words, the politico-economic system still favours the white minority regime.

Against this background, we should be cautious of the first proposition above which says that political organisations which were unbanned should directly take up political issues, and that civics should take up community issues. Although the national liberation movement was contesting political power, this was not done abstractly, but by addressing the material conditions of people in their localities. Failure of the ANC, for instance, to take up 'civic' issues might weaken the ANC not only locally but nationally as well. Such a conception fall within the strategy of the regime to separate the ANC from its mass base.[15] It was not unusual to hear elements of the ruling class arguing, for example, that "politics should not enter education" or that "sports and politics do not mix".

There is no civic domain that is not political. Whilst this is true of all societies, the counterpoising of the 'civic' to the 'political' becomes even more problematic in oppressive colonial societies where the superior living conditions of the colonisers are directly attributable to their political dominance. The material conditions of the colonised cannot be dichotomised into 'civic' and 'political' realms.

The juxtaposition of the 'civic' and 'political' roles (as in the separation of 'civil society' and 'political society') is flawed in that it fails to analyse how the two articulate, and has also failed to inform the strategy and tactics of the national liberation movement vis-a-vis a revolutionary working relationship with civics. The lack of a visible mass impact on the negotiation process could be understood partly as a result of the growth of these reformist tendencies within the mass democratic movement. The present strategic objective of the mass democratic movement was the attainment of political power as the most critical component of the democratic process. The tactical question was how best to tackle bread-and-butter issues in order to advance the struggle for the transfer of power to the oppressed majority.

The other argument is that civics should be independent of political organizations and a post-apartheid democratic state, in order to play a 'watchdog' role. This has a number of shortcomings. Firstly, the independence and 'watchdog' role of civics was so over-emphasized as to neglect the question of *how to ensure political victory* for the national liberation movement and the question of *how the masses wield political power*, which is the essence of participatory democracy. This argument also assumes that the national liberation movement would accede to state power but neglects the possible nature of this state, the balance of forces within it and conditions under which it would exists. In other words, the state under a government of national unity is not seen as yet another arena where fierce contestation will take place. Civics, as with other mass formations, cannot fully realise their objectives unless a democratic state is in place. Conversely, the national liberation movement would only be able to democratize the state to the extent to which civics and other mass formations have advanced the struggle for democracy against apartheid in their sphere of operation.

Futhermore, the role of civics as 'watchdogs' for democracy assumes that civics are torch-bearers of democratic values and are themselves inherently democratic. This position is based on the notion of the so-called 'autonomous organs of civil society'. According to du Toit, two strands of thought can be discerned in this regard. One is the argument that democracy could best be achieved not only by transferring state power from the minority to the majority, but by limiting that power. In opposition to this view which entrusts democracy to formal liberal rights and the market forces, another which poses as more radical, pins its hopes on 'civil society' (defined as voluntary associations through which citizens influence public life). Accordingly, the more power it acquires, the more citizens will enjoy the power to exercise the rights which democracy promises.[16]

Whilst the former view is insufficient in that it accords no active and critical role to the masses (through their formations) in building democracy, the latter has narrowly conceived the question of building democracy only in terms of aloofness from the state, and not participation in it. Both these views are unable to deal with the question of transforming and democratising a popularly elected government. In an analysis of the problems that led to the toppling of Allende's popular government in Chile in 1973, Miliband argued that:

> . . . a new regime bent on fundamental changes in the economic, social and political structures must from the start begin to build and encourage the building of a network of organs of power, parallel to and complementing the state power, and constituting a solid infra-structure for the timely "mobilisation of the masses" and the effective direction of its actions. The forms which this assumes — workers' committees at their place of work, civic committees in districts and sub-districts, etc. — and the manner in which these organs "mesh" with the state may not be susceptible to blue-printing. But the need is there, and it is imperative that it should be met, in whatever forms are most appropriate.[17]

We should, therefore, start engaging the question of what type of state is wanted and how mass organisations should participate in such a state; in other words, how do we transfer power to the people rather than how we distance ourselves from the state. An autonomous 'civil society' does not equal democracy. The central question that faces us is how civics and other mass organisations become part of the national democratic revolution without at the same time sacrificing their independence.

Interestingly enough, in practice, it is only the labour movement that has been able to adopt a more sophisticated approach to this question. COSATU, for instance, whilst acting as an independent and autonomous force, is also a formal partner in the tripartite alliance of the ANC/SACP/COSATU. Thus, we would argue that it goes beyond a simplistic counterpoising of political and mass formations.

Building Democracy: Building Organs of People's Power

There are three very important premises from which to move if the issue of building democracy is to be tackled. Firstly, the relationship between the state and the so-called 'organs of civil society' is not dichotomous but *dialectical*. Secondly, the building of democracy cannot be abstracted from the conditions under which this task must be tackled. For instance, in South Africa, the immediate goal is the establishment of national democracy, which should then lay the foundations for a transition to socialism. This question is important in that it gives content to concepts deployed in our analysis. Thirdly, the process of building democracy is in the last instance a political process, whose realisation ultimately requires political leadership. If building democracy is a political process, it cannot exclude the very central issue of state power.

Given the above conceptualisation, it is not appropriate to talk about 'organs of civil society' but rather *organs of people's power* as the only organs that will ultimately guarantee a democracy, both in the phase of national democracy and in the phase of building socialism. There are three main reasons for advancing such an argument. Firstly, as pointed out earlier, the question of separating state and 'civil society' is theoretically very problematic. Secondly, the notion of 'organs of civil society' obscures and confuses a number of issues, including the failure to distinguish between the different types of 'organs of civil society' (for example, state institutions operating in wider society, right wing organisations, capitalist institutions, and democratic mass organisations). Thirdly, the notion of 'organs of civil society' obscures the wider contestations taking place in society, as well as the class character of these contestations.

A brief definition of our understanding of organs of people's power and the differences between them and 'social movements' is necessary at this stage. 'Social movements' bring together a number of social forces and even classes around a particular issue. They are, therefore, issue-based and can either be political, in the strictest sense of the word, or non-political. 'Social movements' do not necessarily aim to fundamentally transform society, but can be reformist or aimed at changing particular aspects of policy on the issue around which they are organised. As a result, they are subject to extreme fluctuations in their strengths and weaknesses, and often disappear as fast as they emerge.

Organs of people's power, on the other hand, may or may not develop out of 'social movements'. They are primarily about the fundamental and revolutionary transformation of society; in other words, they are about the transfer of power to the people and are directly concerned with the wielding of state power. Their social base can be the same as that of 'social movements', in that they should form the direct link between the state and the people in a national democracy and under socialism. In fact, organs of people's power are the form through which the people should exercise state power, as demonstrated succinctly by Mashamba. Organs of people's power have the following specific characteristics: a democratic project; fundamental transformation of society; accountability; and working class leadership. This is the essence of participatory democracy. The conceptualisation of civics, street committees, the National Education Coordinating Committee (NECC), people's courts, and so on as being merely 'social movements' is, therefore, problematic. Four problems related to this will be highlighted below.

Firstly, this indicates a historical understanding of the origins and intentions of these organs in the mid-1980s in South Africa. These organs were not merely 'social movements' but were specifically organs of people's power aimed at a revolutionary transformation of South African society and the establishment of people's power. To simply refer to them as 'social movements' is both a theoretical retreat and a reformist understanding of their role even during the phase of negotiations.

Secondly, the notion of 'social movements' as used by some sections of the 'left' is problematic in that it is a historical and abstract implantation of the notion of 'social movements' in advanced capitalist countries. The nature of 'social movements' that develop in countries under the yoke of colonialism, neo-colonialism and imperialism is fundamentally different to, for instance, the Green Movement in Europe or the Civil Rights Movement in the United States. The former tends to take on the character of organs of people's power and the latter tends to take the form of pressure groups. There is a radical distinction here.

Thirdly, the notion of 'social movements' is theoretically unwieldy in that it incorporates a wide range of social organisations and struggles. Some of what are referred to as 'social movements' are defensive and reactionary, whilst others are revolutionary. For example, 'social movements', ranging from Solidarity in Poland, to the mass upheavals in Eastern Europe, to the street committees and civics in South Africa, all tend to be lumped under the umbrella of 'social movement'. In some instances, these movements are short-term expressions of highly-localised social and political outbursts, and in others, they tend to endure and even cut across national boundaries. Furthermore, the problem with the notion of 'social movements' as guarantors of democracy or socialism, is that they tend to be regarded as inherently democratic, with the purposeful and directed goal of transforming society. This is always assumed but never demonstrated. In fact, such an assumption is a bland categorisation. Whilst some of these movements may be democratic and have a political objective, others are definitely not. For instance, the mass movements that have brought Yeltsin into power in Russia cannot be said to be innately democratic and accountable. These were largely defensive movements, mainly reacting to the bureaucracy in the Soviet Union. The popular expression of power capable of overthrowing regimes is not equivalent to a democratising project or discourse. Unless we are able to discern and distinguish between these, we fall into the trap of treating every 'social movement' as democratic and transformatory, by virtue of being a 'social movement'. This is indeed a dangerous romanticisation of 'social movements'!

A fourth problem in the conceptualisation of 'social movements', and perhaps a most serious theoretical omission, is the failure to relate 'social movements' to political or state power. This question is sharply posed by Andre Gunder Frank in the aftermath of the collapse of Eastern European regimes. He observes that:

> the problem of *state power* poses a difficult and partly novel challenge to the social movements and their relation with political parties and the state. The revolutions of 1989 in Eastern Europe were made by largely peaceful social movements that sought and achieved the downfall of governments and crumbling of state power, which they mostly did not want to replace themselves.[18]

One might quickly add here that not only were these movements unwilling to replace the old regimes, but they were incapable of doing so. Although Frank draws very weak conclusions from his vitally important observation, this is a classic illustration of the inseparable relationship between mass struggles and political power. To simply focus on 'social movements' or 'civil society' is an inadequate, one-sided, and incomplete basis for conceptualising the task of building democracy and socialism. Whilst democratic mass organisations are a necessary component in building democracy, they themselves cannot complete that process; hence the central importance of political leadership and organs of people's power to bridge this gap.

It should, however, be made clear here that our argument should not be read as meaning that all 'social movements' should be organs of people's power. The essential point is that the only guarantor to building both national democracy and socialist democracy (as opposed to bourgeois democracy) is the building of organs of people's power.

Let us then briefly situate the argument for the development of organs of people's power as the key to securing and strengthening national and socialist democracy. Struggles for democracy in colonial countries should always be located within the nature of colonialism. National oppression and colonialism tend to collapse what 'democratic socialists' would call 'civil society' and 'political life' in those social formations. Such a situation can be summed up in terms of the early works of Marx and Engels as the incomplete separation between 'civil society' and the state, unlike in bourgeois democracies of advanced capitalist countries. That is why national liberation movements in all 'Third World' countries, and even more so in Southern Africa, incorporate within them aspects of 'social movements', these 'movements' taking on a political form. It is this dialectical inter-penetration that tends to throw up organs of people's power and the closer working relationship between national liberation movements and such organs.

The development of organs of people's power and their relationship to the ANC in particular in the mid-1980s marked the highest expression of the inter-penetration of civic and political issues in apartheid South Africa. The following quote from an assessment of the nature of organs of people's power during the mid-1980s in South Africa illustrates this point:

the street/area committees — the structures of an embryonic People's Power — are not only restricted to playing this (civic/local issues — authors) kind of role, *but also has a far more directly or narrowly political dimension to them*. At the same time as they are taking up the grassroots issues described above, *they also form the units in and through which major political issues and strategies (eg. the consumer boycotts) are discussed and organised.* Thus *the street committee system is beginning not only to form the avenue through which people can begin to take greater and more democratic control of the immediate conditions of their existence, but they are also emerging as the form through which direct political action against the state and ruling bloc can be decided on and implemented.* Understanding this latter dimension is of crucial importance both in understanding *People's Power* correctly and, I would argue, in guiding the organisational dynamics unleashed recently to the greatest possible effect in welding the oppressed classes in South Africa into a *mass force capable both of effectively confronting the central state and its apparatuses, and of governing after power has been seized* (though the precise organisational forms will clearly alter dramatically between these different phases).[19]

A few points worth noting in the above quotation are the following: there is a close relationship between civic and political issues prior to February 2, 1990, whereas afterwards the pre-occupation has been with the separation of civic and political issues as a means of creating political space for the respective civic and political formations. In the process, there is a very real possibility of weakening the national democratic revolution.[20] It seems that arguments for 'organs of civil society' are now focusing on the terrain of struggle — 'civil society' — saying very little about the people's institutions that should inhabit and become dominant in this terrain. This is the major reason for the shift away from talking about organs of people's power to talking about 'organs of civil society'. *In fact, the conception of 'organs of people's power' expresses the unity of political and civic struggles in the era of the national democratic revolution.* The nature of 'civil society' that will develop is not dependent on making the terrain independent, but is dependent on the type of institutions which will be developed to contest and transform that very same 'civil society'. To talk of 'organs of civil society' without addressing the question of organs of people's power is to strip our struggle of its revolutionary content.

The conceptualisation of organs of people's power separates bourgeois from socialist democracy. This conception and approach to building democracy cuts across the rather problematic divide between 'civil society' and the state. Here, we are using the phrase of some of those who argue for a 'vibrant civil society', defining the nature and content of the types of 'organs of civil society' that should be developed; in other words, at the root of it, we are talking about building people's power.

The concept 'people's power' is rooted in our perspective of a national democratic revolution, where the people are not just an amorphous mass but are a people united to bring about a national democracy. This is where the significance of the process of building democracy as a political task lies. This democracy should have organs of people's power as its agency since it is only such organs which are capable of practically bridging the dichotomy of 'civil society' and the state, and can lay the basis for a longer-term transition to socialism.

In concluding this chapter, it must be pointed out that our major concern is that concepts which are used have direct political implications. For instance, the shift away from developing our understanding of organs of people's power and the new post-February 2, 1990, vocabulary ('organs of civil society'; an 'autonomous and vibrant civil society'; and so on) implies not merely a change in concepts but is perhaps a dangerous shift away from the perspective of a national democratic revolution to that of bourgeois democracy.

Although the concept of organs of people's power still requires further theoretical elaboration, this seems to be the most appropriate revolutionary perspective which should characterise approaches to building democracy. Perhaps even more important is to begin to point out the way in which a revolutionary socialist perspective should be directed. Organs of people's power should serve both as instruments for securing and deepening national democracy and as organs for the transition towards socialism. Of course, in the process, the nature and role of such organs will change as conditions determine, but they are the only structures that will ensure participatory democracy and counter any tendency towards a bourgeois-democratic settlement that might be found within the ranks of the national liberation movement. This is the route towards national and socialist democracy.

Notes

1. Vilas, C.M. (1986) *The Sandinista Revolution: National Liberation and Social Transformation in Central America*, New York: Monthly Review Press.
2. Mashamba, G. (1990) "A conceptual critique of the people's education discourse" *Research Report*, No. 3, Education Policy Unit, University of the Witwatersrand, pp. 11-12.
3. *Ibid.*, p.5
4. Vilas, C. (1989) "Revolution and democracy in Latin America" in *The Socialist Register*.
5. *Ibid.*, p.40.
6. *Ibid.*
7. The United Democratic Front (UDF), to which most if not all civic organisations were affiliated, adopted the Freedom Charter on the occasion of its fourth anniversary, as did the Congress of South African Trade Unions (COSATU) at its 1987 Congress.
8. Statement adopted at an augmented meeting of the Central Committee of the SACP in November, 1979, "Forward to people's power — the challenge ahead" in *The African Communist, 80,* 1st Quarter, 1980, p.18.
9. The present authors subscribe to the thesis of 'colonialism of a special type' (CST), i.e. the fundamental contradiction in South African society is class exploitation and the dominant one is

national oppression. According to *The Path to Power* (1989) CST is: ". . . a variant of capitalist rule in which the essential features of colonial domination in the imperialist epoch are maintained and even intensified. But there is one specific peculiarity: in South Africa the colonial ruling class with its white support base on the one hand, and the oppressed colonial majority on the other, are located within a single country"

10. Majola, S. (1986) "The beginnings of People's Power — discussion of the theory of state and revolution in South Africa" in *The African Communist*, 106, 3rd Quarter, 1986, p.57.

11. See Nzimande, B. and Sikhosana, M. "Civics are Part of the National Democratic Revolution" in *Mayibuye*, June, 1991, pp.37-38.

12. See "The Role of Civics" in *Mayibuye*, 3, December, 1990, p.32.

13. See *Ibid.*; Tsedu, M. (1991) "ANC Versus the Civics: Residents' Groups Determined to be Independent" in *Sowetan*, 21 June 1991.; Nkosi, D.T. (1991) "Civics and the ANC" in *Mayibuye*, November, 1991, p.33.; Mayekiso, Moses (1992) "Role of Civics in Society and Their Relationship with Political Parties and other Structures in Society" — Address to a SACHED/CAJ seminar by SANCO President Moses Mayekiso, 10 November, 1992.

14. See Swilling, M. (1991) "Socialism, Democracy and Sivil Cociety: The Case for Associational Socialism" in *Work in Progress*, 76, July/August, 1991, pp.20-23; Mayekiso, Mzwanele (1992) "Hands off the Civics and Civil Society" in *Work in Progress*, 81, April, 1992, p.21; Mayekiso, Mzwanele "Working Class Civil Society: Why We Need It, and How We Get It" in *The African Communist*, 129, 2nd Quarter, 1992, pp.33-40; Mayekiso, Moses. op. cit.

15. See Nzimande, B. and Sikhosana, M., *op. cit.*, p.39.

16. Du Toit, A. Cited in Friedman, S. (1992) "Civil Society and the Legacy of Apartheid" in *Die Suid Afrikaan*, February/March, 1992.

17. Miliband, R. "The Coup in Chile" in *The Socialist Register*, 1973.

18. Frank, A.G. (1990) "East European Revolution of 1989: Lessons for Democratic Social Movements (and Socialists)" in *Economic and Political Weekly* 3 February 1990, p.252 — emphasis in the original.

19. White, R. (1986) "A Tide Has Risen. A Breach Has Occurred: Towards an Assessment of the Strategic Value of the Consumer Boycotts" in *South African Labour Bulletin*, Vol. 11.5, 1986, p.92 — emphases added.

20. See Nzimande and Sikhosana, *op. cit.*

4

Social Movements and Democratic Struggles in Swaziland

Ray Russon

Introduction

Social movements are a very significant element of civil society in any given social setting. Social movements in post-colonial societies have come about both as a result of particular experiences and a direct expression of certain demands to governments which over time felt little duty to consult or seek mandate on a number of national issues.

To understand the nature and stature of social movements in post-colonial societies one has to analyze the dialectical relationship between the state and civil society. Mandaza (1991:12) stated that the analysis of the social process in Africa requires that we take into account the relationship between state and civil society not as diametrically opposed forces, but as factors that impinge upon one another – almost dialectically related.

The dialectical nature of the relationship between the state and civil society has over time been marked by a growing gap between the two. At independence, state and civil society celebrated the triumph over colonialism. Over the years this unity in triumph started to break as the state started asserting itself as master over civil society by depriving it of its rights and powers of influence.

It is within this context that social movements as an organised portion of civil society have to be seen in post-colonial Africa. The fundamental question to be kept in sight in any attempt to understand social movements is whether these movements representing various factions and fractions of the rich, middle, poor, students, workers, farmers, women etc. are an attempt to reassert civil society over the state.

As a starting point, it is important to have an intuitive understanding of the state as an entity, its history and its composition.

The Colonial Context

British colonial policy was forced to become a little more "benign"or "progressive" as a result of the struggles of the colonised in Africa. This was as a result of the telling effects of the Second World War on British imperialism forcing it to change its colonial policy towards the extension and development of *Indirect Rule* combined with greater investment.

Loosely defined, Indirect Rule refers to allowing a certain degree of administrative control in the hands of a leading identifiable group amongst the colonised.

Territories like Swaziland, for example, were sorely neglected prior to the policy of Indirect Rule ushered in by the post-World War 2 era. Swaziland started experiencing an increased British presence after World War 2 which was followed by increased investment through the Colonial Development Corporation (CDC).

British imperialism had found a formula through indirect rule, one that would be more lucrative and least troublesome in its scramble for firm control over its colonies. In the case of Swaziland the British kept on hoping that some valuable minerals would be discovered and were at the same time worried about the continued attempt by the Boers in the Transvaal to annex Swaziland.

Indirect rule made the British appear more friendly to the Swazis as compared to the Boers. Indirect rule in Swaziland required a degree of social re-organisation in terms of identifiable structures and categories with specified duties and obligations. The underlying principle in this re-organisation was the notion of colour which Kuper (1971:286) defined as an ideological aspect of colonialism in Swaziland.

The re-organisation of Swazi society on colour lines found expression in three different categories, i.e. the white settlers, the indigenous Swazis and the so-called coloured or Euro-African as they were called during the colonial period (these are people of mixed descent). It is on the basis of this re-organisation that the emergence of social movements during this period in Swaziland can be understood.

The Nationalist Movement and the Independence Struggle

The politics of national liberation in Swaziland was largely inspired by political events in South Africa as some South African exiles settled in Swaziland and started organising themselves. This became evident in the political ideals and slogans of the emerging political parties for example the raised thump and the slogan *Ilizwe Elethu* (the country is ours) used by the Swaziland Progressive Party (later renamed the Ngwane National Liberatory Congress).

Before 1960, there had been very little organised political activity in Swaziland. It was the statement by Sobhuza II in May 1959 that set the struggle for independence in motion. Sobhuza II had made reference to the wish of the Swazi people to have more in terms of land and mineral rights. Reading the uncertainty of changing events, the European Advisory Council (EAC) and the United Settler Association (USA) proposed a multi-racial advisory committee which Sobhuza II rejected in favour of a legislative council with the qualification that Swazis were to choose their representatives using methods familiar to them and that representation would be on a 50-50 basis, i.e., between the whites and Swazis.

Applying itself to the changing political climate in Swaziland, the growing Swazi middle class was quick to find a role for itself under the guise of the Swaziland Progressive Association under the leadership of John June Nquku, a teacher who had been its president since 1945. The SPA was transformed into a political party in July 1960 without the consent of the Swazi National Council (SNC), to which it was now affiliated. This is a case in point to indicate the transformation of a social movement into a political party in response to a changing political scenario.

The new SPA going under the name the Swaziland Progressive Party (SPP), was to become one of the three major players in the politics of independence in Swaziland together with the USA and the SNC. It should be noted here, that all these three organisations had prior to this period acted as social movements standing for socio-economic rights and privileges of their members.

As the process of constitutional negotiations started unfolding in the late sixties guided in principle by the propositions of Sobhuza II a 50-50 representation and different methods of choosing representatives to the Legislative Council, the SPP issued a manifesto containing the following cardinal points:

1. a non-racial policy which would bring about democratic enfranchisement for all persons in Swaziland irrespective of race, colour or creed;
2. opposition to the incorporation of Swaziland into South Africa; and
3. complete integration in every walk of life and the ending of racial discrimination in all its forms.

The SPP manifesto showed a clear rejection of Sobhuza's proposition of 50-50 representation and different methods of choosing representatives and in essence, it marked a break away from the tribal framework. Seeing his power being challenged and the possibility of the division of his constituency Sobhuza II was quick to co-opt the SPP leadership namely J.J. Nquku, Dr Ambrose P. Zwane and O.M. Mabuza in the constitutional committee as members of the SNC.

The full constitutional committee comprised 26 members, including representatives of the Colonial Administration, the EAC and USA, the SNC and the Swaziland Combined Executive Association. The committee sat for the first time on November 4, 1960, but did not sit again until February 17, 1961 because of the traditional dance ritual *incwala*. With the connivance of the EAC/USA the committee's discussions were to proceed within the framework of Sobhuza II's proposal. This proved to be a fateful decision for the shaky alliance built between the SNC and the SPP leadership as J.J. Nquku minced no words in his rejection of this.

This irked the SNC which denounced Nquku for being inimical to Swazi traditions of respect of tribal authority and suspended him from the Committee. In protest against Nquku's expulsion, Zwane and Mabuza resigned from the Committee in June 1961 stating that they would be false to their convictions if they (the SPP) were to give the public a misleading impression that they had a hand in shaping a new constitution where they were not allowed to speak out their minds (Stevens 1971:336).

The SPP standing on its own tried to negotiate a seat in the Constitutional Committee with the Resident Commissioner to no avail and decided to enlist the services of a constitutional expert from the University of Cape Town, Dennis V. Cohen, a Professor of Comparative Law. With his assistance they listed their own constitutional proposals which amongst others included:

> the establishment of a Legislative Council with provision for a common voters' roll including Swazi, Whites and Coloured and allowing for universal adult suffrage (Stevens 337 *op. cit.*).

This provision appealed to the Coloured community who then sought an alliance with the SPP on political matters through their Euro-African Welfare Association (EWA). In the political arena the EWA became marginalised and was wholly swallowed up in the ranks of the SPP because it would no longer stand on its own due to its minority in numerical terms. The fold of the 1961 saw an imminent split in the SPP as its leader Nquku was deposed. He was accused of being dictatorial because of his refusal to hold elections and of being a poor administrator. In February the following year, Zwane was elected in his place with Dumisa Dlamini as the new Secretary-General. Since a small group remained loyal to him, Nquku continued as president of the other faction of the SPP. In August 1962, Nquku's executive split into two again after accusing him of misappropriation of funds and elected K.V. Samketi in his place. Nquku refused to step down and in essence three parties existed under the name SPP. To avoid continued confusion in the name, Dr Zwane announced a new name for his faction in May 1963 as the Ngwane National Liberatory Congress (NNLC) (see Stevens R.P. *op. cit.*).

The split in the opposition cost it a lot especially at such a critical period of constitutional talks. For example, such confusion was harnessed by the colonial administration in arrangements for constitutional talks in London in 1963 whereby they made available only one air ticket for the opposition and purposely gave the air ticket to the weakest group, the Nquku faction of the SPP.

The changing political scenario opened the flood gates for the emergence of more political parties in Swaziland. The Swaziland Democratic Party (SDP), organised in March 1962 under the leadership of Simon Sishayi Nxumalo and Dr Allen Nxumalo made its political programme known in May the same year. Rejecting the constitutional proposals of the EAC/SNC alliance and the policies of Pan Africanism advocated by the NNLC, the SDP advocated a qualified franchise until people had acquired sufficient literacy levels to understand politics. It further rejected racial segregation and advocated a one Swazi nationality and citizenship for all under a unified system of government, law and taxation (Stevens R.P. *op. cit.*: 340). Rejecting apartheid and 'assimilado' policies of South Africa and Mozambique respectively, the SDP hoped to maintain friendly relations with these countries. It rejected communism and extreme nationalism as detrimental for the country and opted for a constitutional monarchy under the protection of Great Britain (Steven, *op. cit.*: 340).

The SDP received its financial backing and guidance from the South African Liberal Party especially its members who had immigrated into Swaziland.

On the constitutional discourse, the SDP found itself leaning more towards the submissions made by the NLC progressives and a formal alliance was worked out just before the London constitutional talks.

This alliance was further strengthened with the formation of the Mbandzeni National Convention which shall be discussed below.

The life of the SDP was cut short as its leadership crossed carpet to join the newly formed SNC Party, the Imbokodvo National Movement, a grouping they had rejected at first.

July 1962 saw the emergence of another political party, the Mbandzeni National Convention (MNC) a product of an amalgamation of two least known organisations, the Mbandzeni Party led by Clifford Nkosi and the Convention Movement led by Dr. George Msibi. The new party, MNC, had Msibi as its president.

In its political charter released in January 1963, the MNC advocated for the supremacy of the Swazi Nation with some modernisation of traditional authority. It emphasized "restoration" rather than independence arguing that the Swazis never lost their independence.

As the struggle for independence started gaining momentum, the Ngwenyama and his SNC started counting their misfortunes especially as the emergent political parties started finding common ground to wage their struggle against colonialism and opposed some of the ideals posited by him.

Rallying political support around the SNC was proving difficult as these political parties took a sizeable section of the Swazis. As a result a Broederbond member and advocate by the name of Van Weik de Vries came in handy to advise the Ngwenyama to form a political party. The Imbokodvo National Movement (INM) was formed on April 16, 1964 by the SNC.

The INM was formed after a successful referendum on a clause about political party elections entrenched in the 1964 Legislative Council Constitution which the SNC rejected. The referendum was organised by the SNC and held in few areas to decide whether Swazis wanted political parties or not. Political parties were represented by the symbol of a reindeer (an animal foreign to Southern Africa to depict the fact that indeed political parties were foreign) while the anti-party sentiment was represented by the symbol of a lion (an animal that is well known and represents royalty in Swaziland). In essence the referendum became one of choice between the Ngwenyama (King) and those who did not want him. The result of the vote was obvious as people voted for the more familiar lion.

The nation was soon after the referendum summoned to the royal kraal where Sobhuza II announced his victory. Sobhuza then suggested that the name of the new movement should be the "ROCK" *IMBOKODVO NATIONAL MOVEMENT* (INM) affectionately known as *Imbokodvo* The launching of the INM was significant in setting the dividing line between liberal and traditional reform in such a way that the incipient and fragile unity amongst the liberal parties started showing cracks. The leadership of the Democratic Party was approached by the Ingwenyama and asked to cross carpet into the ranks of the INM. Without consulting the party membership on the ground the leadership succumbed, putting an end to the very short and impact-free history of the Democratic Party. The Mbandzeni National Convention led by George Msibi suffered a similar fate leaving the NNLC as the only viable opposition since the SPP factions had also become ineffectual.

The difficulty in reaching a compromise on a suitable independence constitution between the traditionalists and the progressives saw the British imposing a Westminster-type constitution for Swaziland's independence in 1967. This constitution had a provision for a Bill of Rights and allowed for a multi-party polity. This constitution was, however, criticised by both the traditionalists and progressives. The traditionalists opposed it because it allowed for one person one vote, political parties and certain liberties which they felt would undermine traditional authority. They agreed to accept it arguing that they would amend it after independence by arguing that "even a bride is made to look better by her in-laws after she is wedded".

The progressives on the other hand felt that the constitution allowed too much of an upper hand for the king who appointed certain members of parliament, ministers and the prime minister gave him too many privileges for example, mineral royalties, etc. Elections were held in 1967 with a landslide victory for the INM leaving the traditionalists with a high degree of complacency with the new independence polity. The opposition had no seat in parliament and everything rolled under the *Imbokodvo* (Rock) without question. The scales started tilting and the elections in 1972 gave the divided NNLC three seats in parliament. The NNLC would have done much better if it was not for its internal power struggle resulting from the intransigence of Dr A.P. Zwane who refused to have a woman elected by the Congress as Secretary General. The NNLC however, managed three seats in parliament under the candidature of Dr. Ambrose P. Zwane, Thomas Bhekindlela Ngwenya and Mageja Masilela.

The presence of the opposition in parliament made the traditionalists feel threatened and they started a court battle to unseat one member of the opposition Thomas B. Ngwenya arguing that he was not a Swazi citizen. After failing to unseat him through legal channels they approached the King and advised him to repeal the independence constitution which had all of a sudden become unsuitable and un-Swazi. The repeal of the constitution was done unprofessionally and unconstitutionally.

Political parties were banned, a state of emergency declared and the meagre civil rights enshrined in the constitution removed. Independence had ended for the progressives and many Swazi people while it had just started for the traditionalist. Sobhuza II, the hero who had brought independence to Swaziland in a bloodless struggle with a stroke of a pen, as goes one of his praise songs, had taken it away the same way. Now that political parties had been banned they had to choose between dissolving or operating from the underground. The INM which was the ruling party continued to operate de facto with its manifesto remaining as the guiding force for government policy and its leadership forming the cabinet and dominating the civil service.

The NNLC on the other hand refused to go down without a fight but having suffered a split in 1972 just before the elections it was too weak to offer any meaningful resistance. Its leadership was harassed, detained without trial, forced into exile and refused employment. It eventually started showing signs of disintegration especially when its leader Dr A.P. Zwane returned from exile cap in hand. Despite his continuous claim that the NNLC was still alive and well undercover, the party remained inactive and unorganised except for his lone voice.

The Proscription of Political Parties and Emergency Rule

The banning of political parties left civil society at the total mercy of the state and the former could only make its aspirations and sentiments known through social movements such as trade unions.

The atmosphere left by the repeal of the constitution in 1973 ushered in an era of fear, intimidation, uncertainty and suspicion. Even social movements suffered from this hangover for a long while, trade unions for example, were smashed and suffered from a culture of subservience.

The year 1978 saw some slight political changes following the teachers' strike of 1977, as parliament was re-introduced under a new so-called traditional system of election called *Tinkhundla*, which was largely undemocratic. *Tinkhundla*, directly translated means a public meeting place in its singular form and as a political system it allowed for an election of an electoral college which then chooses members of parliament. The Prime Minister and all cabinet ministers are hand-picked by the King. Open political debate and political parties were however, still not permitted; nor was the exercise of civil liberties.

This unsatisfactory change could, to some extent, explain the formation of a radical political party in the late 1970s calling itself the Ngwane Socialist Revolutionary Party (NgwasoRep) led by Thomas Magagula. NgwasoRep proposed a socialist alternative more under the influence of African nationalism. Its leader soon went into self-imposed exile but had severe problems in newly independent Mozambique. NgwasoRep did not make its presence felt both within and outside Swaziland until its leader returned "cap in hand" in 1989.

Sobhuza II ruled relatively trouble-free until his death in August 1982. After his death there was some political turbulence as power struggles within the Royal Family ensued. Some young people had already anticipated such turbulence and had come together to form themselves into a political party in the winter of 1983.

Declaring its manifesto and programme of action after its first congress on January 1, 1985 the People's United Democratic Movement (PUDEMO) committed itself to setting up mass structures on the ground. Its programme of action identified all categories of the Swazi people and for workers declared that:

> where trade unions do not exist go out and create them, and where they exist go out and strengthen them (Pudemo 1985).

It went on to call for the formation of organisations for women, youth and civics while for students it identified the Swaziland National Union of Students (SNUS) as the vehicle for uniting students.

PUDEMO laid a great deal of emphasis on the proliferation of mass structures or social movements as one form of struggle to pressurise the government. Organisations linked to this mass based programme include amongst others, the Swaziland Nation Association of Civil Servants (SNACS), Swaziland National Union of Students (SNUS), Swaziland Youth Congress (SWAYOCO), University of Swaziland Workers Union (UNISWAWU) Swaziland National Association of Unemployed People (SNAUP), Swaziland National Association of Rent Payers (SNARP), Swaziland Congress of Trade Unions (SWACOYU), Human Rights Association of Swaziland (HUMARAS) and a number of other youth and women's organisations. It is during this period that we find a major wrangle between the state and civil society organised in its many structures as social movements.

Political pressure was brought to bear on the government by political parties operating from the underground especially PUDEMO. After holding its historic Congress in SOWETO in February 1992, PUDEMO returned to Swaziland and un-banned itself inciting a considerable amount of national enthusiasm. A few months later, probably responding to the national enthusiasm two political parties announced themselves i.e., the Swaziland National Front (SWANAFRO) and the Swaziland United Party (SUP). However, both parties have not made a felt presence over and above announcing their leadership.

The Labour Movement and the Independence Struggle

The Catchpole report on labour legislation in Swaziland released in May 1960 set the ground for the proliferation of trade unions by stating that:

> There are no organisations of workers and the task of representing complaints and grievances to employers, which is normally the function of trade unions, is undertaken by *Ndunas* (traditional supervisors) appointed by the Swazi National Council and allocated by them to particular employers . . . . Their task is to resolve any complaints, grievances and minor disputes which arise including any problems concerning earnings (cited from Fransman, 1982:59).

The Catchpole report was itself not some form of benevolence on the part of the state, but it was a direct result of concern on the part of capital and the state, regarding the growing number of a permanent industrialised labour force together with the winds of nationalism and change blowing throughout the continent. It was felt that an unorganised and oppressed labour force was more susceptible to political influence.

The banning of the liberation movements in South Africa together with the Southern African Communist Party (SACP) and the South African Congress of Trade Unions (SACTU) saw an increasing presence of South African exiles in Swaziland. Most of these exiles had seen that the power of organised labour in South Africa and their influence in the development of the labour movement in Swaziland could not be understated.

The Pulp and Timber Workers Union (PTWU) became Swaziland's first trade union. It was formed in March 1962 and registered on October 25, 1962 with the objective of, among others, improving the working conditions, payment and promotion prospects of Swazis (see Fransman 1982:61). This therefore shows that trade unionism is a fairly new phenomenon in Swaziland although industrial activity dates back to the 1950s. This can partly be explained by the use of the *Nduna* system which became a sore spot for workers after a while, as shall be discussed below. The Catchpole report had warned against the lack of representative structures for workers as un-conducive for good industrial relations, and when strikes exploded in 1962 there was no reluctance to register trade unions. Between 1962 and 1965 there were a total of 15 registered trade unions in the Country.

Labour Unrest

Barely a month after the formation of the first trade union, Swaziland suffered a wave of strikes beginning with one called by the PTWU. The strike was as a result of the intransigence of the Usutu Pulp Company in meeting a minimum wage demand and the dismissal of two union members. The strike was a major success commanding a one hundred percent stay-away by mill workers together with a small number of forest workers. During the strike the mill was kept going by the white staff. The workers received wage increases after they agreed to resume duty (Fransman *op. cit.*:62).

A significant aspect of the strike like all the subsequent ones was its political content. The demand for the promotion of Swazis was a clear challenge of colonial policies of racialism. In challenging this policy the union was actually challenging the ideological aspect of British colonialism (Kuper, 1971:286).

The politicisation of the unions is directly related to the programmes of political parties in Swaziland especially the Progressive Party later known as the NNLC and the Swaziland Democratic Party which helped organise and supported trade unions. The wave of strikes continued in 1963 beginning on February 28 when 600 employees of a railway constructing company to carry iron ore to the Mozambican downed tools for just one day for better wages. In the same year, 1963, a very significant strike took place at Ubombo Ranches challenging both the SNC traditionalist industrial dispute-handling mechanism with the *induna* system and the deep-seated contradictions of colonial capital and administration.

Ubombo Ranches was started in 1949 as a cattle ranching company which later started producing rice and in 1957 grew sugar cane for the first time. The commitment to sugar cane grew as the annual quota was increased to 40 000 tons necessitating the construction of a sugar mill.

As the Company expanded, labour increased and a restructuring was necessary. A new field manager P.A. Andries was appointed in 1961 for this purpose and was quick to endorse the task system. Fransman

(1982:65-6) captures events leading to the strike in the following paragraph:

> Following the restructuring there was trouble with workers because of the allegedly unreasonable measure of their task and on two separate occasions the labourers refused to go to work. When the retiring General Manager, Mr. Szokolay, handed over to his successor he stated that his biggest worry had been the African labour and that the disturbing influence of growing political activity in the around the estate would certainly lead to trouble.

This simmering discontent amongst the workers, particularly the weeders, irrigators and cane cutters who were, in terms of pay, the less fortunate classes of labour continued and in January 20, 1963 a large meeting of workers was called. Significantly this meeting was addressed by Mr. Dumisa Dlamini, the Secretary of what was then the Zwane wing of the SPP (later to be known as the NNLC) and by Frank Groening, a local member of the party. The following day, a mass march led by Dumisa Dlamini and Frank Groening was staged and three demands were presented to the General Manager. The first demand was a minimum of R30 per month for all workers. Secondly, the dismissal of three supervisors was demanded: Andries; the Field Manager, Percival; who was in charge of the Labour Department and also the Compound Manager, and Gizane Gamedze. Lastly the re-engagement of two Swazi employees, who had been dismissed was demanded. Other subsidiary demands accompanied these, for example, living conditions in the compounds.

On January 28, the management replied and rejected the main demands but agreed to some of the subsidiary demands. On March 18, a total strike on the sugar estate and the cattle ranch, including office staff and domestic servants took place. This took the form of daily orderly processions led by leaders of the SPP waving the Party's flag. The strike ended on March 27 pending the outcome of an official enquiry that had been ordered by management.

At the end of the strike, the Ingwenyama was actually drawn in to make a direct intervention when he called 40 employees to a meeting attended among others, by the Resident Commissioner Brian Marwick. The Ingwenyama dismissed the notion of cheap labour as unfair but went on to dismiss the strike as foreign and, not in line with Swazi tradition.

Strike action did not end with the Ubombo Ranches strike but continued to jolt both capital and the colonial administration. On March 29, 1963, about 150 saw-mill workers went on strike at Peak Timbers demanding, amongst other things, higher wages. Other strikes of less significance took place between March and May 1963 with the most significant being one at Havelock Asbestos Mine on May 20. The leadership of the NNLC, Dumisa Dlamini and Mcdonald Maseko led about 1 500 strikers demanding among other things, one pound a day (R2) which had now become a general NNLC demand. Talks held between the 21st-23rd of May failed to break the strike (Fransman, 1982:69).

The Ingwenyama found himself at the centre of the controversy by sending a telegram to the striking workers stating that:

> No true Swazis would talk to me through the strike. If any misunderstanding existed, arrangements for delegates to visits royal headquarters should have been made through *Mntwanenkosi* (prince) Msitsela (who had been appointed by the SNC as Labour Officer to the Mine) (cited from Fransman 1982:69).

The King's message was ignored by the workers and this did a lot to dent the image of traditional authority.

On June 9, the NNLC resolved to mobilise a national stay-away in support of the striking workers at Havelock and to demand the release of the strike leaders who had just been arrested. It was also hoped that this action would force the government to endorse the R2 per day demand. The R2 per day demand was now tabled by the NNLC as a national demand and transformed into political capital. With full control of the Labour Movement, on the R2 per day demand, the NNLC moved into full political arena and rejected the British White Paper on the Constitution issued the previous month on the grounds that it was racialist and undemocratic (*Ibid*:69).

The King was asked by the Resident Commissioner to send his regiments to break the strike in Mbabane and to assist the police in "restoring order". However, as a later confidential committee of inquiry was to point out: "the Ngwenyama proved to be unwilling or unable to assert his authority over his own regiment" (*Ibid*:70).

On June 13, another strike broke out at Ubombo Ranches when 1 700 workers protested against the delay in the progress of inquiry into the March strike and went on to demand R2 per day instead of the R30 per month they had demanded prior and the withdrawal of the British

Government's constitutional proposals. The King was called in to intervene once more but to no avail (Fransman 1982:71).

> The situation was now getting out of control by the end of the year more than 66 000 days of labour time had been "lost" and one estimate of the total cost of the "civil disturbance" was put at R1.7 million. Doubts also grew as to whether the local police force numbering 350 were adequate to the task. The Resident Commissioner then requested external assistance and on June 16 an airlift of the First Battalion Gordon Highlanders stationed in Kenya was completed *(Ibid: 70)*.

Many strikers and leaders of the labour movement together with leaders of the NNLC were arrested and charged for public violence or its incitement, conducting illegal strike action (under the Industrial Conciliation and Settlement Proclamation) and intimidation.

The wave of strikes left an air of uncertainty, confusion and defeat within capital, the state and the SNC. The failure of striking workers to abide by the King's directives aroused more hostility towards organised labour from the traditionalists, while capital on the other hand remained divided with some dismissing trade unionism while others felt it was necessary. The labour movement suffered some set-backs as the Colonial Administration continued with its *high-handedness* although spontaneous strike action continued in selected areas like Manzini and Sidvokodvo.

The SNC which had formed itself into the INM and was fresh from a convincing win in the election of the Legislative Council in 1964 softened its position on trade unions. They instead preferred a trade union movement that would allow for the *"nduna* system" in order to make sure that it remains under the control and influence of the SNC. The INM then made an attempt to form what was to be known as the Amalgamated National Union of Swaziland which was rejected by both workers, employers and the state which opposed attempts of the SNC to exercise a direct influence in labour relations.

The Colonial Administration moved ahead and prevented the control of unions by political parties and non-citizens from leading a trade union. These measures did neutralise the strength of the Labour Movement and its alliances in such a way that by 1966, for example, only 595 man-days compared to 66 000 man-days of labour in 1963 were lost and only 3 strikes involving 280 persons took place. It is however, true that the labour movement played a very significant role in the build up to independence by exalting the opposition, NNLC, and remaining as a lingering threat at all times in the period of transition.

The Labour Movement After Independence

Regardless of the fact that the labour movement was a major actor in the struggle for independence — by expressing some political demands in their strike actions and remaining the necessary threat and muscle for action — the post-independence regime was highly suspicious of trade unions. The reason for this is easily discernible more so because traditionalists through their INM were now in power.

The hostility towards trade unionism dates as far back as the period of strikes when the striking workers at Havelock defied a telegraphic message from the King ordering them to stop the strike and send representatives to talk with him. This together with the repeated demand to remove the *Nduna*, an appointee of the SNC was viewed as a disparaging attack on traditional authority and the King. Reporting in 1964 on *Methods of Regulating Wages in Swaziland,* Whitson captured such hostility as follows:

> The most unfortunate and, to my mind regrettable difficulty however, arises from the attitude of the Swazi National Council towards trade unions (cited in Simelane 1981).

Another factor that fuelled the hostility was the alliance between the workers and the major opposition, the NNLC, which continued to be a threat to traditional supremacy. The INM had no well defined policy on labour except for control which had been deprecated by the Colonial Administration whilst the opposition had mobilised the workers around issues that matter most. The strike action of 1962 and 1965 proved beyond any reasonable doubt that an organised work-force commanded a power to reckon with. The Swazi rulers were therefore, set on doing everything within their might to control the embryonic organisation of the working class (Simelane *op. cit.*:6).

Although trade unions were now legally permitted under the *Trade Unions and Employers' Organisations Law NO. 12* of 1966, the INM on coming to power at independence through a land-slide victory at the polls, embarked on a campaign to discourage trade unionism in favour of an alternative policy. First and foremost, the labour portfolio was brought directly under the Deputy Prime Minister to exert more control over it. Secondly, utterances and statements from this office in particular were anti-trade unionism denounced unionism as "foreign to the Swazi way of life". Thirdly and most importantly, an alternative model based on the *Nduna* System of the colonial times was introduced known as *Ndabazabantu*. The *Ndabazabantu* system was, for all intents and purposes, to take the place of a union in the work place representing workers on matters ranging from grievances to conditions of work including the negotiation of wages whilst making sure that workers' demands were not excessive (Fransman, 1978).

> *The Ndabazabantu* was to instil in the workers the notion that whilst they were entitled to a 'reasonable' wage not far below what may be called a living wage, capital was entitled to its profit (*Ibid.*).

Simelane defines that policy as having had negative effects on the evolution of union organisation in Swaziland to such an extent that by the turn of the 1970s decade there were only seven registered trade unions, three of which drew their membership from Government employees. The Government had actually refused to recognise these unions setting a bad precedence for other employers.

At the initiative of the teachers' union, the seven unions came together for the purpose of forming a national centre. This resulted in the birth of the Swaziland Federation of Trade Unions (SFTU) in October 1971. The teachers however, together with the civil servants union, elected to remain outside the Federation, with the former still resisting affiliation whilst the latter following its rebirth in 1986.

The declaration of a State of Emergency on April 12, 1973 had a serious effect on the already weakened labour movement in Swaziland. The *King's Proclamation* which brought forth the State of Emergency, banned political parties and all other bodies or organisations which caused "national unrest" and all meetings of a political nature. All such meetings required a written permission from the Commissioner of Police who was at liberty to refuse whenever he felt that a meeting might lead to what he perceived as "national unrest".

Although the Proclamation had made reference to meetings of a political nature the police demanded a police permit for any form of gathering except for church services. Even where a permit was granted, police would be present taking notes and if ever they believed that the meeting was becoming political they were at liberty to stop it. Although not banned by the *King's Proclamation* of April 12, 1973, trade unions were top of the list of organisations to be monitored, and if need be, to be banned if they refused to tow the line. So the trade unions had to make a choice between being functional and be banned for life or to remain nominal. The SFTU eventually registered in 1973 could itself not do anything to organise the trade unions and as a result remained inactive. The paralysing effect of the *King's Proclamation* to the development of the labour movement in Swaziland was the denial of the right to assemble. However, this would be challenged later by the Swaziland Manufacturing and Allied Workers' Union (SMAWU) at the Industrial Court which ruled that unions need not apply for a permit to hold meetings.

On the whole therefore, trade union organisation was at its weakest in the 1970s, but this did not, however, mean that workers' grievances could be submerged forever as spontaneous protests and strike action continued to take place. This proved the weakness and inappropriateness of the *Ndabazabantu* system which actually became the bone of contention amongst the workers. Catchpole had warned strongly against the absence of a machinery for negotiation or communication between employer and employee and had observed the ineffectiveness of the "*Nduna* System" upon which the *Ndabazabantu* system was modelled. In effect, the Swaziland Government, was trying to reverse historic events to the period of the early 1960s and indeed succeeded in inciting a volatile atmosphere for labour relations. The epitome of such a process was the outbreak in October 1977 of a teacher's strike followed by a mass uprising of students countrywide. The strike was primarily wage-related and secondarily political as there were reports of students tearing the national flag, singing political songs and stoning government cars. The teachers' union was subsequently banished.

The government was suddenly woken up from a long reverie about total control of labour through the *Ndabazabantu* system and the Works Councils which were preferred by employers. Something had to be done and quickly, about both the political and industrial relations systems in the country. An International Labour Organisation (ILO) team was requested to find a better industrial machinery for labour relations while a deputation was sent around the world to find a "suitable" constitutional order. In 1978 the *Establishment of Parliament Order* was proclaimed setting up a bi-cameral parliament to be elected through a relay system of election known as *Tinkhundla*.

On the labour front, the *Ndabazabantu* system could not be revamped but the Works Council's system, it was felt, could work alongside the permission to form free trade unions. Works Councils although desired, could do little to improve industrial relations as the Labour Department in its 1979 report, observed that the lack of strong workers' organisations is the primary cause of the weakness of the system:

The councils are dominated by employers since they are better trained, more experienced and better informed that the workers (cited in Simelani, *op. cit.*: 9).

Clearly, there was a need for strong trade unions.

In 1980 therefore, the Swaziland Government enacted *The Industrial Relations Act* and *The Employment Act*. The former allowed for the establishment of industrial unions instead of trade unions and Works Councils. Works Councils are the most favoured by the Act because it allowed for their formation in every industry only six months after it came into force. The intention here was to allow the Works Councils to be firmly entrenched in such a way that workers would not see the need to form industrial unions which were much more difficult to form. A Works Council only requires an agreement in writing of only six employees to gain recognition from an employer whilst an industrial union requires a 40 per cent paid up membership of workers in that particular industry, an onerous task indeed. To register an industrial union with the Labour Commissioner requires an agreement in writing of six workers but this does not permit the union to represent or negotiate on behalf of the workers until it gains recognition from the employer. This has resulted in most unions being titular and unable to deliver the goods whilst struggling to obtain the 40 per cent membership. By the time the 40 per cent membership is obtained a large number of the members are not fully up to date with their membership fees and employers never fail to bring this up at recognition. Most cases on recognition end up decided by the court because employers always find reason, no matter how nebulous, to refuse recognition.

The 1980s witnessed increased confidence on the part of workers in term of organising themselves so much so that by the end of the decade seventeen unions had been registered. The Union of Teachers re-emerged as an Association of Teachers. The civil servants' union was also revived. The re-emergence of political groupings although operating undercover saw an active policy towards the organisation of trade unions. PUDEMO, for example, went out to create unions and strengthen them and examples have already been cited above. An attempt by workers clearly persuaded by democratic ideals expounded by the democratic movement to register another national body for unions i.e. the Swaziland Congress of Trade Unions (SWACOTU) was obviated by the Labour Department arguing that it is politically inspired. The Labour Department was made aware of the *Convention on Freedom of Association* which had been ratified by Swaziland but continued to resist demonstrating the air of suspicion and uncertainty which still hangs over the labour movement in Swaziland.

Youth Movements

Although young people have always been organised into some regiments to serve traditional authority these regiments cannot really be of much essence in our discussion of social movements here. Nonetheless a brief overview would suffice. The regimentation was done in terms of age and gender with the underlying factor being the type of duty to be performed for royalty or the nation. The young men who had not met with the other sex are organised for purposes of gathering a shrub used to build a byre for the traditional ritual of *incwala*. The young girls are organised for purposes of gathering reed for building a byre for the Queen Mother. These two occasions take place only once a year on separate times of the year though.

Social movements as understood in our view would therefore not embrace these regiments. The youth movement I will attempt to draw into this discussion is the Swaziland Students Union (SSU), which emerged during the early 1960s as Swaziland was gearing up for constitutional talks. The SSU which was later to be known as the Swaziland National Union of Students (SNUS) was formed by university students from the Pius XIII College in Basutoland (now Lesotho) and remained largely a student elite type of organisation which rarely made its presence significant outside university and college circles. The Students' Union made its existence felt when it directly challenged the racialist tendencies of the Colonial Administration and endorsed a political programme with similar constitutional demands as the progressives. Its leader Timothy Zwane (not related to the NNLC Dr. A.P. Zwane) rejected any form of traditional representation in the constitutional talks (Stevens 1971:339).

It is this disparaging attack on traditionalism that won the Students' Union some hostility from the SNC although not openly expressed. Except for being a rattle bag, the Students' Union did not make a significant input and it slowly became swallowed up in the ranks of the NNLC Youth Wing. Although having been a strong and possibly the only vocal opponent of the State of Emergency, the SNUS elected to remain on the University campuses.

The post-Sobhuza era saw a lot of political turbulence as infighting in the Royal Family took place. The SNUS re-organised itself under the guidance of the new democratic movement (PUDEMO) and started setting up branches in the other colleges such as the William Pitcher Teacher Training College, Institute of Health Sciences, Ngwane Teacher Training College, Swaziland College of Technology and some of the schools in the towns. The students were rallied out into the streets, under the leadership of university students, to protest the ousting of the Queen Regent Dzeliwe and the Prime Minister Prince Mabandla Dlamini, and at the same time demanding the release of all political detainees held under the 60 days detention without trial order. About 40 students were arrested and charged for unlawful demonstration but were acquitted by the court. A second demonstration was arranged in the capital, Mbabane, where another group of students was arrested and charged but acquitted by the court.

The students had become a strong force to reckon with, and in an attempt to break the students' capacity, the cabal in power clandestinely organised some students from the University for a secret trip to Kenya for an undisclosed mission. On their return, the students at the University expelled them from campus after setting on fire one dormitory occupied by one of them. The Minister for Education started a campaign denouncing the national union of students SNUS as illegal and hurriedly organised a few students to form an alternative called Swaziland National Association of Students which was rejected in all quarters.

SNUS achieved its objective of campaigning for the ousting of the cabal in power known as *Liqoqo* under the leadership of Prince Mfanasibili. The post-coronation era for which the students had fought so much for brought no meaningful changes as the State continued its campaign against SNUS as illegal. SNUS continued its struggle on different terrain now directing its efforts towards student grievances and demanding free education for all. A mass student meeting was called by SNUS in Manzini in March 1990 and in response the State deployed armed security personnel to disband. A number of students were injured in the process and the student leaders arrested although they were later released SNUS still remains a very significant organisation for student mobilisation for a number of different ends except for the one hurdle that it is not recognised by the government.

There has been a number of other different youth organisations with different intents and purposes, for example, the Swaziland Boy Scouts, Swaziland Girl Guides, Swaziland Workcamps Association and a number of self help project based organisations. All these organisations were called together by the Directorate of Sports and Culture in 1987 to form the Swaziland National Youth Council (SNYC) which became an umbrella body for all youth organisations. The SNYC is a body that is financed by the State and therefore finds it difficult to be critical of the hand that feeds it. In all essence, it has become an organisation to promote self-help projects outside of which it is incapacitated. In its own right, however, the SNYC has slowly been able to fill the gap of a youth organ between the State and the youth on the ground. It was only recently that it encountered some form of competition when the Swaziland Youth Congress (SWAYOCO) was launched. At its launching through a prayer meeting which the state defined as a disguise for a political rally, one guest speaker (the present author), the leadership and some attendants who were suspected to be linked with PUDEMO were arrested and charged for holding an illegal political meeting but later acquitted by the court. It is true that political utterances were made, political songs sung and slogans chanted as young people danced the *toyi toyi* which has become a symbol of protest against apartheid in South Africa.

SWAYOCO had a clear political programme from its inception. Its constitution made it clear that it was to mobilise progressive young people to stand up for their rights, both economically and politically. It embarked on clean-up campaigns in the townships and launched branch committees. The momentum was great as young people ranging from the ages of between 6 and 30 years took to the streets singing songs against the State and its leaders.

The state's hostility towards this organisation was clear and it came out strongly arguing that SWAYOCO was illegal because it was not registered. The leadership of SWAYOCO made a mockery of this stating that there was no legislation that required such an organisation to be registered and that the government was using the *Registration of Patents and Deeds* to register organisations, which was not obligatory. SWAYOCO organised a long march for February 2, 1992 which the State opposed arguing that if ever it took place people would be hurt. The SWAYOCO leadership insisted that the government ban of the march would be defied. The Prime Minister came in timeously to diffuse the situation and allowed the march to go ahead. The march started in Mbabane to Manzini, a distance of about 45 kilometres. The members escorted by large numbers of police officers grew larger and larger as the march proceeded towards Manzini. At the assembly point in Manzini there were over two thousand young people who were addressed by the SWAYOCO leadership and, amongst others, the present author.

SWAYOCO made its stand on the process to renew the Tinkhundla very clear. They marched to the Review Committee's offices and denounced the whole process as a waste of time and resources. SWAYOCO constitutes the strongest of social movements to confront the State directly in Swaziland.

Women's Movements

Women in Swaziland have for a long time been subjugated, dominated and treated as children. During the struggle against colonialism, women had no role to play whatsoever both in traditional, progressive and settler circles. A case in point was the split in the NNLC in 1972 following the election of a woman as its Secretary-General. The President Dr. A.P. Zwane refused to accept her arguing that a woman was not the 'right material' for the struggle against colonialism. It is possibly for this reason that the NNLC never had a Women's Wing but only a Youth Wing.

The only organisation that was created by the traditionalists as some kind of a women's regiment was *Lutsango LwaboMake* (translated to mean Women's Kraal). The organisation was dominated by the wives of traditionalists and its primary role was to educate women about respecting authority, tradition and men. It represented elderly women who did not fall under the regiment of young girls *(ingabisa)* who served the purposes of gathering reed.

This organisation has been the major stumbling block for the emergence of a representative women's organisation. Whenever such an attempt is made, the defunct *Lutsango* comes up to reassert itself with the support of the male traditionalists and the Queen Mother, to crush any such organisation. A good example is an attempt by a group of women to celebrate the International Women's Day in 1991. The Queen Mother hurriedly summoned them to the Royal Kraal and told them that they are not supposed to organise anything about women without her consent since she was the chief patron for women.

Lutsango has actually proclaimed itself more than just a regiment but a mother body for all women's organisations. Organisations that have been allowed to flourish and have received the blessing of *Lutsango* are, self-help women's organisations, which do not challenge male domination nor tradition. Most women's organisations are forced to bow down to the might of *Lutsango* because it is the only route for them to get any funding from government and even some donors.

Attempts to infiltrate *Lutsango* by democratic forces have proved futile and attempts to destroy and displace it even more difficult.

PUDEMO and the SFTU have women's wings but their impact is still to be seen.

One organisation which has just come up, which might challenge at least one aspect of male domination, is the Swaziland Action Group Against Abuse (SWAGAA) which is dominated by women in its leadership. This organisation has the potential to directly challenge male violence against children and women in particular.

Civic Organisations

Civic organisations together with non-governmental organisations (NGOs) in Swaziland are a recent phenomenon. However, NGOs are less of social movements in the adopted understanding of the concept in this book. This is because most NGOs are organised on the basis of a top-down approach by a few individuals who purport to be representing a certain sentiment with no objective of mobilising large numbers of people as members but instead these individuals act to meet certain needs. NGOs have however proliferated enormously in Swaziland and they presently have a National Assembly for NGOs with the support of the government.

Civic organisations have emerged from the people on the ground as a result of certain problems and neglect on the part of the State. The first of such civics was the Rate-Payers Association which emanated from different areas, at different times, without a national coordinating centre. These have been able to push the Town Councils like Manzini to improve services such as roads and lighting. The strongest of these include the neglected township known as Ngwane Park which has effectively used the weapon of refusing to pay rates until some of its demands are met. Since 1990 this association has been putting relentless pressure on the Manzini Town Council to improve services such as lighting and urban roads. The town council has since acceded to the pressure.

The successes scored by the Ngwane Park Rate-Payers Association has seen the proliferation of similar associations in a number of townships to such an extent that there now is a move to form a national coordinating body.

Rent-payers' association are presently on the road to proliferation as well following the formation of a mother body of rent payers the Swaziland National Association of Rent Payers (SNARP) launched in June 1991. This association has effectively put relentless pressure on the government to come up with a policy on housing and rentals and according to its president, Alfred Mabila, it is through the efforts of

SNARP that the King created a ministry of Housing and Town Development. Slowly it has been able to set up branches in Manzini and Mbabane where there are two promising rent payers associations representing tenants occupying apartments run by a parastatal body, The National Housing Board. Recently these two associations took the Housing Board to court for an injunction to stop a rent increase which was a success. Among its objectives SNARP is campaigning for the right of every citizen to have a roof above his/her head, security of tenure and a reasonable standard of living.

Another civic organisation to mention here is the Swaziland Consumers Association which is presently involved in raising people's consciousness regarding their rights and consumer-related hazards. This organisation has developed a good working relationship with the Rent-Payers' Association and they both have space on the local radio to broadcast about their policies, etc. Yet another organisation which emerged in an attempt to organise unemployed people in 1989 was the Swaziland National Association of Unemployed People (SNAUP). This organisation started off well and was promising to be a useful vehicle to campaign for unemployed people especially to the young who constitute about 59 percent of the unemployed population in Swaziland.

The state started having suspicions of this organisation and frustrated all its attempts to hold meetings. Every time a meeting was arranged the police would be there to disperse everyone and on June 11, 1991 its leader Kuseni Dlamini, a 19 year old young man was arrested together with other thirteen people who were or had been involved in some form of social movement. They were charged with a total of thirteen counts which included high treason and sedition. This move on the part of the State was aimed at crippling most social movements including unions, for example, the Association of Civil Servants to which the accused had been linked. The trial took about five months and the accused were acquitted.

References

Bonner, P., *Kings, Commoners and Concessionaires*, Johannesburg, 1983.

Catchpole, F.C., 'Report on Labour Legislation in Swaziland' (unpublished), 1961.

Crush, J., 'The Colonial Division of Space: The Significance of the Swaziland Partition' in, *The International Journal of African Historical Studies,* Volume 13.

Fransman, M., 'The State and Development in Swaziland'. PhD thesis, University of Sussex (unpublished), 1978.

----- 1982: 'Labour Capital and the State in Swaziland 1962-7' in *Southern African Labour Bulletin (SALB)*, Vol. 7 No. 6/7, 1982.

Government of Swaziland, *Population Census,* Government Printer Mbabane, 1986.

Kuper, Hilda, *The Swazi: A South African Kingdom*. New York.

----- *Uniform of Colour*. University of Witwatersrand Press. Johannesburg, 1963.

----- Sobhuza *II, Ngwenyama and King of Swaziland,* Duckworth, London, 1978.

Lynd, G. F., *Politics of African Trade Unionism,* New York, 1978.

Longman, John, 'The Swazi Coup' in *South African Outlook* 103 (1224).

Macartney, W.J.A., 'The Independence Constitution of Swaziland' in *The Parliamentarian: Journal of the Parliaments of the Commonwealth* July, 1978.

Mandaza, I., 'The State and Democracy in Southern Africa: Towards a Conceptual Framework' in *SAPEM* Vol. 4 No. 9, 1990.

Marvin, John 1973: 'King Sobhuza II of Swaziland' in *Optima* June.

PUDEMO, Programme of Action.

Russon, R.A., "Youth and Politics in Swaziland" in *Economic Digest* Vol. 3 No. 1 March 1998.

Simelane, N.G., 'Evolving Role of Trade Unions in Swaziland' (unpublished), 1981.

Spence, J. E., 'British Policy Towards the High Commission Territories' in *The Journal of Modern African Studies* Vol. 2 No. 2, 1964.

Watter, L., "Reflections on Youth Movements" in Manning P.K. (ed); *Youth: Divergent Perspectives*, John Wiley and Sons Inc N.Y., 1973.

Stevens, R.P., *Lesotho, Botswana and Swaziland,* London, 1967.

Ndwandwe, S. S., *Politics in Swaziland, Johannesburg 1960 to 1968*.

Sachikonye, L., 'Democracy, Civil Society and the State: Social Movements in Southern Africa' in *SAPEM* Vol. 4 No. 9, 1991.

Zwane, A. P., Interview on the Political History of Swaziland, 1992.

5

War, Adjustment and Civil Society in Mozambique

Eugenio Macamo

Introduction

This chapter assesses some of social movements in Mozambique from a broad perspective. The argument is that these social movements serve as significant elements in the development of democratic governance in societies such as Mozambique and can play a significant role in the society's endeavour for social and economic progress (Mamdani *et al.* *1988*). For them to be able to do so, however, they need to remain autonomous and broadly participatory on the one hand, and to grow and expand their influence without losing their roots on the other.

We begin by contextualising this chapter by briefly outlining several empirical and theoretical issues. Mozambique is a country where a multi-party system has been only established for three years. Although it is a highly interesting case, there is still very little relevant academic literature, because the process is a recent one. The few written materials there are on the process of democratisation are rather theoretical, tending toward generalisation and based on virtually no original field work. This sometimes leads to a number of rather optimistic, extremely idealistic and voluntarist positions. The most important development though is that most Mozambican intellectuals now favour a more open social and political framework.

Secondly, due to the fact that Mozambique is in a transitional phase from a one-party system to multi-party system, many social forces are still at elementary stages of organisation. Nevertheless, some of them are more spontaneous while others operate in some sort of partnership with state institutions such as the ruling party, Frelimo. In some instances they are emerging strongly assisted in the initial phase by people who were in exile or defectors from Frelimo. Some movements are the product of independent initiative while others are supported by NGO's. Some are fighting to survive within the new framework because the state or the party had assumed greater control of their projects and designs.

Thirdly, consequently as part of this analysis, it is necessary to outline briefly the kind of democratic institutions the government and the party have tried to put in place in Mozambique after independence, and the more negative aspects of Mozambican democracy relating to its shortcomings in the field of economic development.

The nationalist vocabulary of the first generation coming from the national liberation movement has dissipated and given way to a new and imported discourse. Structural adjustment, real prices, debt re-scheduling, reduced wages and social expenditures are the new creed.

Fourthly, in an assessment of social movements in Mozambique, a series of problems such as arise the nature and content of the institutional framework, the vitality of the traditional political culture and the manner in which the political field is delineated by the actors with access to it (Mafeje, 1991). The role of social movements depends on the way power is organised and institutionalised; for example, in the case of Mozambique, the nature of the presidential power (the confusion between the incumbent and the institution) and the relationship between the state and the ruling party.

Finally, it should not be lost sight of that Mozambique from independence to 1992 was a country politically, economically and socially affected by the war. This means that the people could not move all over the country because it was not safe and that economic activities could not take place between the cities and the countryside.

Our presentation in the remainder of this chapter is necessarily sketchy. The first and second sections locate historically the question of state, civil society and democratisation in Africa and in Mozambique in particular. The third section explores the conditions under which the democratisation process is taking place: structural adjustment, the war aftermath, ethno-regionalist aspects and the emerging parties. The fourth section assesses the capacity of those social forces and classes involved in the democratisation process. In the fifth section we analyse briefly case-studies of social movements that have emerged in the country namely the students and religious movements. The role of entrepreneurs in the process of social and economic development is also explored. To what extent are entrepreneurs able to promote social change in the society? The open policy question is: how best to maximise the development potential of the existing entrepreneurship in Mozambique in order to achieve development and democracy? Finally, this chapter examines some constraints that the new social movements are facing internally and externally.

Civil Society

Civil Society has been defined as "an arena where manifold social movements . . . and civic organisations from all classes . . . attempt to constitute themselves in an ensemble of arrangements so that they can express themselves and advance their interests" (Bratton, 1989). Bayart indicated that civil society should not be viewed as a separate arena unlinked to the state, and that there is a dynamic, complex and ambivalent (though not necessarily conflict-ridden) relation between the state and the society (Bayart, 1983). Civil society, as distinct from society in general — although the two have all too frequently been used synonymously in recent literature — refers to that segment of society that interacts with the state, influences the state, and yet is distinct from the state (Chazan, 1992).

The main features of the civil society in Mozambique, and in some other countries in Africa compared to Europe, centre on that they are not nearly as strongly organised. The fact that the civil society was weakly constructed in our country does not mean that it does not exist. In fact, in the rural areas it often works and develops side by side with the state.

Historical Background

The analysis of state and civil society and the process of democratisation in Mozambique should be located historically within the broad debate on the nature of the pre-colonial and colonial systems in Africa.

The extent to which pre-colonial political systems exhibited more or less democratic or predominantly authoritarian features is once again the topic of heated debates. These debates also took place just after independence. According to some of the first African political leaders (Senghor, Nyerere, Nkrumah), pre-colonial Africa was almost ubiquitously steeped in democratic traditions (Buijtenhuijs *et. al.*, 1993). Some African social scientists like Ayitte and to a lesser degree Kodjo, formulate rather idealised descriptions of the traditional political systems, sometimes giving the impression that they represent a specifically African form of democracy (Ayitte, 1990; Kodjo, 1990). As far as the colonial legacy is concerned, most authors agree that the colonial governmental tradition was based upon "autocracy, centralisation and paternalism" (Sandbrook, 1988).

The independence movements in Africa were confronted with demands made by French and English colonisers that a parliamentary democracy, following the Gaullist and Westminster model respectively, be instituted as a prerequisite for independence. In Mozambique, however, the political arena after independence was determined by the fact that the people fought for national liberation from the Portuguese colonial rule.

The colonial state — in particular the Portuguese one — had to take the dynamics of African society into consideration and that the colonial regime was constantly confronted with the fundamental dilemma between legitimacy and capitalist accumulation: how far could one go in allowing for capitalist accumulation without losing all legitimacy in the eyes of the colonised people?

Furthermore, in order to comprehend the political situation in independent Mozambique, we should first address the matter of the African state because soon after independence there was a strong belief within the ruling elites in the scope for social engineering processes. Moreover, there were very high expectations about the role the state would play as the prime mover in all development efforts. However, due to the many constraints that the state was faced with in the fulfilment of its task, it soon became clear that state had not quite developed in the direction that was originally anticipated. Moreover, at the advent of independence in Mozambique, there was no substantive indigenous bourgeoisie in Mozambique and state power was appropriated by the ruling party.

Theoretically, at first, it is important to note that the state gives the impression of being an authoritarian leviathan, and to a certain degree this is indeed the case whereby in the political situation in Mozambique, the ruling party made effort to maintain control over the state apparatus. There was an effort made by the ruling party to establish a sort of hegemony over the state and society.

Frelimo's governance rested on two pillars: the idealisation of the nature and role of the state; and the construction of a nation and of the national unity as a unique and most important objective, completely ignoring all the factors of differences and beliefs: languages, social and economic formations at different stages, development and particular political interests of certain social groups. These objectives were partly achieved by establishing a network of "dynamising groups" working in close collaboration with Frelimo.

This aspect brings us to the role of civil society. Attempts were made to incorporate such organisations as trade unions, women's, youth, student associations amongst others into the state or party system. This created problems because at the same time the state was in fact weak by any conventional measure of institutional capacity. The government had limited material means, it was poorly organised and administered.

In this sort of "paternalistic" democracy, through the dynamising groups established by the ruling party "the process of empowerment rose not from the bottom but rather trickled down from the top".

Mass organisations that were intended to mobilise various interest groups in support of Frelimo objectives, and for communication between the party and the population were carefully supervised by the party. The main organisations were, the Mozambique Women's Organisation (OMM), the Mozambique Youth Organisation (OJM), the Organisation of Mozambican Workers (OTM). The OMM worked for the integration of women into political and economic life, and for the emancipation of women from their subordinate role. The OJM, aimed at mobilising youth for Frelimo policies, was involved in training programmes, and in organising recreational activities. The OTM, was supposed to form an arm of the party to organise the labour processes, and not only to be concerned with workers benefits but to increase productivity, and encourage worker's participation in planning and decision-making.

The War as the Main Constraint in Mozambique

The civil war was the main political, social and economic constraint in the process of democratisation in Mozambique. The devastating effects of the war are also abundantly documented in reports from the United Nations and other sources. During the period 1980-88 Mozambique suffered a loss in transit traffic revenue of approximately US$1,5 billion, a similar loss in export trade revenues, and a loss in domestic agricultural production to an estimated US$1,25 billion. With GDP at approximately half of what could reasonably be expected without the war, the total loss of GDP for the whole period 1980-88 can be added up to the substantial figure of US$15 billion, according to a United Nations estimate.

The impact of war on the rural population was aggravated in 1983-1985 by serious drought conditions. Thus began a period which has continued up to 1992 with growing numbers of refugees seeking protection from war and starvation. By 1989, the situation was indeed alarming. One million Mozambicans were estimated to be living in refugee camps in neighbouring countries, mostly in Malawi and Zimbabwe. Internally, the number of displaced people totalled 1,7 million. Another 2,9 million were considered to be affected by the war in as much as they could not provide for themselves. In sum, 4,6 million people, or every third Mozambican, was thus dependent upon aid for the basic necessities of life (AIM, 1992).

The most important factor, in the Mozambican case, to ensure the democratisation process was the need for peace. Without it no progressive measures could be undertaken either by the government nor by our society.

The United Nations Security Council approved a request from Secretary General Boutros Ghali for a force of about 7 500 men to be sent to Mozambique to assist in implementing the peace accord between the government and Renamo (*ibid*). The UNOMoz was expected to cost at least US$331 million. The UN Under Secretary-General, James Jonah, stated that Boutros Ghali was fully committed to the Mozambique operation, and that the UN was "making efforts to avoid an Angola-type outcome" (South Scan, 1993).

As Mozambique was at war during almost 30 years, many people are refugees or displaced people within the country and the problems include the destruction of the infrastructure, the wanton pillaging, the social and economic disruption of the country · and the severe traumatisation of the people as a result of the war. To what extent will it be possible to allow these people to take part in the process of democratisation and elections in the country? The UN High Commission for Refugees (UNHCR) will soon have to undertake its largest operation in Africa to date when it repatriated nearly 1.5 million Mozambicans (*ibid*). This was done before elections to allow them to vote; however, the operation is expected to take at least three years to complete. The emerging parties and all social organisations were tasked to find urgent measures ·to facilitate the reintegration of returning refugees, displaced persons and demobilised soldiers in order to allow the people to participate fully in the process of democratisation and development of our society.

Effects of the Economic Recovery Programme

Under the pressure of day-to-day reality, *the relationship between democracy and development* is once again being debated in Mozambique as in other African countries. Once again, Mozambique is facing a big dilemma: whether it is feasible to translate democratic ideals and principles into practice under poor economic conditions, in some areas even poorer than when it first became independent.

The question is therefore whether democracy is a prerequisite for development, or development a prerequisite for democracy? The main difference is that today Mozambique has learned from its experiences obtained in the last 20 years of independence. In some quarters, a crucial relationship between political liberalisation and successful economic rehabilitation has been posited making it feasible to link political requirements to economic aid, as is now an integral component of the policy of Western donor nations (World Bank, 1989).

But another important position in this debate is expressed by the Secretary of the Organisation of African Unity (OAU), Salim Ahmed Salim, who argued that "while Africa must democratise, our efforts will be hamstrung by the non-democratic international economic system in which we operate" (Quoted in Buijtenhuijs *et. al. op. cit.*).

The Mozambique government as part of adjustment is on a deliberate policy to curb public expenditure in order to reduce the budget deficit. The measures have clearly adverse effects on the social services, such as housing, health, education, amongst others, that have to be reduced substantially. It should be noted that the highly and densely populated cities like Maputo and Beira suffer from inadequate service facilities especially health and education. The largest cost relates to medical facilities where certain services have now to be paid for. All these economic realities coupled with a high and growing inequality in income distribution, obviously suggest a trend towards increasing misery of large sections of the urban population.

As a result, the people, living standards markedly deteriorated. In Mozambique today the costs on human life do not only affect so much the low income groups but the middle class as well.

There is need to provide education and other skills that will enable most Mozambicans to participate effectively and meaningfully in society. The imposition of policies with adverse effects on significant sections of the population requires a certain constellation of social forces to ensure that the policies stick. And yet if the current wave of policies are to stick or to be reversed, it is essential to understand their political underpinnings. It means that the social basis and political implications of new package of Economic Recovery Programme (ERP) should be taken into consideration.

The structural adjustment programme is not only an economic intervention. It has also brought social and political implications. The social and political structure in Mozambique is changing. More specifically, to what extent are new policies encouraging capitalist production relations, and social forces linked to the external financial support? (Hermele, 1989).

There is a new "coalition" that the ERP brought about: a new type of relations between classes. The old alliance between peasants and workers has been superseded or replaced by the alliance between bureaucrats and technocrats with international capital. This means that internally a new national bourgeoisie is rising, with peasants and other social classes being marginalised. Nevertheless, it should always be borne in mind the fact that the networks involved are plastic and rest on unstable foundations.

The Role of Ethno-Regionalist Aspects

Another question relates to the importance of the ethno-regionalist factor in the nature of social movements and their political competition? The question of ethnicity is a topic that has been written about and one that warrants careful scrutiny (Macamo, 1992). In the earlier studies, there was confusion as to the use of such concepts as tribe, race and ethnic group and even today there is very little consensus about what the central features are of the ethnic group. The reason why ethnicity is still a relevant issue in the civil society and plays a role in the process of democratisation is that in the long-term view of Mozambican or African political history, the colonial and post-colonial eras are seen as a relatively short period, during which traditional African structures have certainly not disappeared. This view emphasises the large extent to which traditional structures inform present-day reality. Without insight into these structures, the contemporary situation cannot be comprehended.

Ethnic groups and identities have not remained completely static even after independence. On the contrary, they are subject to change, and that they are not isolated phenomena but components of a much larger whole, the modern state, in which they develop and manifest themselves in interaction with other groups of a comparable nature (*ibid*). In fact, ethnic groups are not always monolithic blocs; they often split up into various clientilistic networks led by keenly competing political "forces". The ethno-regionalist dimension in the organisation of social movements is associated with political logic, like for example, ethnic proportioning within the government, the party, etc. Such political calculations, largely influenced by ethnicity, are important especially as they are often determined by the leadership of social forces.

Despite the difficulty of defining ethnicity and the polemics on the concept, even today in Mozambique the rivalry for scarce government jobs and development funding is perceived by many people in ethnic terms, and ethnicity thus remains an integral factor in the Mozambican political life. For example, people continue questioning why southerners are in high positions in government and therefore enjoy greater economic and political standards and why the city of Beira, being located in the centre of Mozambique is not the capital of the country.

Emerging Political Parties

There were 31 opposition parties in Mozambique in 1991 (Macamo, 1993). In general, the opposition groups do not yet represent a markedly alternative view of society; the social movements had no clearly formulated programmes (AIM, 1993). Some of them usually confined themselves to vague slogans about more "freedom" and "economic development" without developing concrete programmes. Others have not developed programs which appeal to emerging social groupings (*ibid*). They appeal either on the basis of minor ethnic identifications or religious values which are irrelevant to the social context. Yet others have been developed by people who no longer have any link with grassroots support. Other groups make promises that in practice they will not be able to keep (Mozambican Government, 1991). Unless and until the opposition groups draw up a more coherent programme with respect to economic democratization, there will be little or no structural change after elections, given that the present economic reconstruction programme is neither coherent nor well thought-out.

Entrepreneurs: Development and Democracy

Peter Anyang' Nyong'o pointed out that we must acknowledge that there is still a quest and thirst among the African popular masses for two things — on the one hand, political freedom and on the other hand, socio-economic progress. These two needs cannot be separated. People do not want political freedom first and then socio-economic progress later. They want both socio-economic progress and freedom today (Anyang' Nyong'o, 1992). Given our past history and the performance of our society today, the open question is; what is the role of entrepreneurs in the process of social and economic development? To what extent are entrepreneurs able to promote social change in the society? Do they link development and democracy in our country?

Mozambique is dominated by the structural adjustment programme and a new social and economic force is emerging — the entrepreneurs. The World Bank believes that generally they raise the level of popular participation in the community. It means, that it is expected that small and medium enterprises can contribute to competition within the society and improve the people's economic welfare.

Small entrepreneurs on the other hand are thought to be a seed-bed of talent and efficiency. Our entrepreneurs in Mozambique, however, suffer from a wide variety of constraints and handicaps that inhibit them to become more active. They are weak and unstable. Access to capital, credit and markets are not readily open to them. The operating environment is discouraging. Crippling bureaucracy on the one hand, and corruption among the state functionaries on the other, further add to the burden of entrepreneurial endeavour.

It is important to note that there is a difference between the process of class formation and class structure of the former Portuguese colonies and other countries dominated by white settlers in Southern Africa. The difference is in the fact that in Mozambique, for example, there is no white bourgeoisie. At independence, about 90 percent of the 250 000 Portuguese who lived in Mozambique left the country (Frieling, 1987). Another source of difference is in the fact that "colonial regulations nearly completely denied the African population access to educational and medical facilities. Settlement of the African population was restricted. Furthermore, Africans were not allowed to trade or carry out commercial activities" (*ibid*). In this context, the entrepreneurs emerge as one possible alternative that can be seen as a social class able to introduce progressive social change and contribute to the social-economic development of the country. The main questions to be analysed are as follows: do they have a wide social base that could be mobilised as a social movement towards a programme of progressive social change? Are they interested objectively in process of accumulation which could improve the economic situation of the country or are they only "lumpen bourgeoisie" interested in self-consumption and corruption? Do they have a nationalist approach regarding the process of accumulation?

The Maputo entrepreneurs' informal sector is partly of a different character because of different economic conditions prevailing in the country, namely, the social-political and economic crisis in Mozambique. After independence strict regulations regarding the informal sector were kept in force until 1986. Until 1987 the government of Mozambique did not explicitly include entrepreneurs in their development plans. But recently — and particularly — after the introduction of ERP this attitude is changing. In contrast to the situation in West Africa or South Asia, is its very weak and shallow production base, which in a way reflects the smallness and under-development of the country's manufacturing sector. Furthermore, manufacturing activities are heavily concentrated around Maputo and Beira.

There are some historical reasons why entrepreneurship is still under-developed in Mozambique: Owing to the (until recently) heavily centralised control of the economy, it was difficult for small entrepreneurs to exist in the informal sector without licensing because of the difficulties in obtaining raw materials and other inputs (previously obtained by showing tax payments).

Historically, Mozambique as well as other labour reserve countries in Southern Africa exported labour to South African mines and farms. This was a kind of release valve for the potentially unemployed which inhibited the emergence of the type of informal sector common in other parts of Africa. Another fact is the decline of small-scale business during the first post-independence decade where many skilled workers and artisans left Mozambique for other countries. This skill drain has adversely affected the development of the formal economy and limited the productive capacity of the informal sector. Finally, the capital base of small entrepreneurs — whether operating in the formal or informal sector — is extremely low. The economic marginalisation of small private entrepreneurs for a decade since independence eroded their capital base to a mere fraction of what it was. Then, despite recognition given to small business in 1983, during the 4th Congress of Frelimo, and regular reiterations about the importance of small enterprise, entrepreneurs found it difficult to acquire credit and, until recently, almost impossible to obtain foreign exchange (Vletter, 1992).

Social Movements in Mozambique

Firstly, the working class is still relatively small in Mozambique. Most of the workers have not become completely proletarianised: they still have land rights in the peasant sector and often maintain close ties with their region of birth. This is the reality in many parts of Mozambique particularly in the central and northern regions of the country. In the southern region, the level of proletarianisation has already advanced much further due to the proximity to mines in South Africa.

The army of workers is concentrated in the cities of Maputo and Beira where they are employed in strategically important sectors of the economy. They maintain close ties with the lower segments of the urban population. Furthermore, they are organised into trade unions. However, due to its close relationship to the state from the beginning, after independence, they never were 'radical'. On the contrary, they tended to be 'reformist' and have tried to promote the economic interests of their members within the status quo. More recently, however, a number of factors such as the acute economic crisis have heated conditions of conflicts with the regime, which has demanded more and more sacrifices from the workers in the developmental process.

Secondly, peasants constitute the large majority of the population in Mozambique. There is usually a large extent of differentiation in this respect, ranging from poor peasants to some agri-businessmen. In Mozambique, land was expropriated at an early stage by white Portuguese colonists and foreign capital and so there are large numbers of peasants who have little or no land and could survive by engaging completely or partially in wage labour on larger plantations. They were discriminated by the state as regards the supply of inputs, credit and agrarian services. In addition, the state often plays an instrumental role in the expropriation of their land by way of land reform laws.

Finally, women in Mozambique are politically and socially discriminated that in certain cases, women then opted for the most radical forms of politically action. In our case women were directly involved in the armed struggle for the national liberation. We do believe that no true democracy can exist as long, in particularly, rural women are treated almost as "slaves".

The Student's Movement

A larger segment of the younger generation in the cities have been involved and are campaigning for democratisation. Given that around 60 percent of Mozambique's population consist of youth it is important therefore to know how are they coping with the crisis (Azevedo, 1984).

The establishment of social and welfare services has been used by many governments as an effective way to winning the support of the masses particularly those people living in the urban areas.

However, the reduction of public expenditure in the social sector, therefore, in Mozambique as in many other countries contribute to the alienation of the masses from the government in power. Due to the crisis which affected, first of all, the economy of Mozambique, the party started to lose its influence. The first strike that was held in Mozambique after independence was organised by the students at Eduardo Mondlane University in May 1990. There were general reasons common for the social-economic sectors. These general reasons have to do with the consequences of the war; the deterioration of social conditions, the socio-economic crisis and the increasing cost of living. Coming to the specific reasons, the government was not able to improve the amount of the scholarships; the conditions in the residence for students; the quality of the food given to the students. Taken in account all those questions, in May 1990, the students together decided:

> not to return to the classes; not to take any meals; to organise themselves in a social organisation separated from the youth organisation.

Our main point is to see to what extent that event had contributed to the process of democratisation of the civil society in Mozambique. This strike became a political movement towards more and active participation of social forces in the process of democratisation and accountability. One of the reasons why the students' movement existed was the fact that it was flexible and practical. It was based on the real needs, interests and knowledge of the students involved. In the beginning the authorities did not know how to react as strikes were not foreseen in the former constitution. Strikes, therefore, were neither legal or illegal. That was the clearest sign that a new phase had dawned in Mozambique.

Church-State Relationship and Civil Society in Mozambique

Quite a separate role has been played by the churches which are linked to large segments of the population. They have combined the struggle for their own religious and cultural identity with political demands. The churches can be useful in terms of interpreting democratic ideas for the people at the base, in raising consciousness and perhaps even in mobilising the people and in creating political solidarity.

It is important to devote attention to the African religions. The literature barely mentions these religions. And yet there is good reason to assume that these religions have always exerted quite a bit of influence on political developments and still continue to do so. We analyse the question of religious movements under the context of their relations to the state.

In the development of church-state relations in Mozambique there seems to be two distinct phases. The first phase from 1975-1982 and the second from 1983 up to the present. During the first phase the relationship between church and state was very tense and often unfriendly. This was especially true of the relationship between the Catholic Church and the state. In the second phase the relationship between church and state became much more relaxed and cordial. The aim of this section is therefore to explain the reasons for this change in relationship between church and state and to look at possibilities of participation of the church in the civil society in this process of national reconciliation and construction for the future.

The Attitude of the Frelimo Government Towards the Church in Mozambique: 1975-1982

When the Frelimo government came into power in 1975, the relationship between state and church in Mozambique deteriorated sharply. This deterioration was not only caused by the policies of the newly formed state, but also by past actions on the part of the church. During the colonial era, the Portuguese government treated the Roman Catholic Church as the official church of Mozambique. The Roman Catholic Church was therefore seen by Frelimo supporters as a collaborator of the colonialist regime. This image of the Catholic Church was further strengthened in the minds of Frelimo supporters when the Catholic Church denied a request by Frelimo to minister to them in their bush camps during their guerilla warfare against the colonialist regime. This resulted in severe antagonism against the Catholic Church especially by the leadership of Frelimo. In the euphoria following their successful struggle against colonialism, they declared that they had achieved victory without the assistance of the church or God.

In this regard, it is important to distinguish between the attitude of the state and the attitude of the party. The state in its constitution granted freedom of religious belief. This was explicitly stated in article 19 which states that the state and the church must be totally separated. The implication of this article was that the state would not interfere in the activities of the church. The Minister of Justice also confirmed on more than one occasion that the freedom to worship is defined in the constitution and that the state would not discriminate against any religious group.

The party however, had a different approach. It was interested in gaining and exerting the hegemony on Mozambican society as a whole. The party therefore saw the church as a potential opponent which could block the hegemony of the party. Furthermore, the party also exposed scientific socialism. Part of what they understood under this concept was that party members should only be guided by rationality with adherence to the traditional African religions viewed as a form of obscurantism that could not be reconciled with their scientific socialism. The fact that Mozambique was a one-party state led to such a fusion between party and state that the distinction between the 'non-religious' attitude of the state and the 'anti-religious attitude of the party could not be maintained. The anti-religious attitude of the party was in the end also adhered to the state. This explains why the state scrapped all religious holidays from the calendar, scrapped all religious education for the school curriculum, nationalised church property and persecuted a number of church leaders.

The Change in Attitude of the Frelimo Government Towards the Church: 1982-1991

In the development of church-state relations since the end of 1982, it is possible to distinguish between two distinct phases. The first phase started at the end of 1982 while the second phase began in 1987.

1982-1986

By December 1982 the Frelimo government had changed its hostile attitude towards the church and was trying to win its good-will and cooperation. In December that year, the government called the different churches in Mozambique together for deliberations. There are a number of explanations for this turnabout in attitude of the government which we will now discuss.

The first factor which forced the government to change its relationship with the church was the vital role that churches were playing in the Mozambican society. The changed attitude of the Frelimo government was brought about in part by the fact that they had no other option except to acknowledge the role of the church. The churches were playing such an important role in the society that the state could simply no longer afford a hostile relationship with the church. In order to substantiate this claim, let us look to the role that the churches were and still are playing in Mozambique.

This discussion of the vital role that the churches are playing, should not be seen as an attempt to excuse its churches of their misconduct in the past or even in the present. It would be folly to deny that the church had done much to fuel the atheistic attitude adopted by the Frelimo government. However, the image of the church that Frelimo portrayed when it came into power in 1975, was not a true reflection of the church in Mozambique. There was another side to the story about the role of the church in the society.

Although it could not be denied that there were strong links between some leaders in the Catholic Church and the colonial regime, it was not true that the whole of the Catholic Church supported colonialism. There were also leaders within the Catholic Church who opposed the colonial regime. In addition the Catholic Church was not the only influential church in the society; the Protestants and Muslims were also major players as far as religion was concerned. None of these two though could be accused of being collaborators of the colonial regime. The Muslims were treated as the enemies of the colonial regime.

The Portuguese colonial government stated more than once that their objectives were on the one hand, to evangelise and civilise the population and on the other hand, to fight Islam. The Protestants also played a vital role in fighting colonial imperialism. They were pioneers in the national awakening of the native population of Mozambique. They started ministering and teaching to the population in their native languages and thus gave them respect for their native languages and culture. In this regard they made a valuable contribution to the rehabilitation of the personal and national self-respect and dignity of the Mozambique population (Celula, 1987).

Instead of being collaborators of the colonial regime or later the Frelimo regime, they earned themselves the reputation of being protectors of basic human rights and dignity of the native population. Good examples of protestants who played a leading role in opposing the colonial government include Eduardo Mondlane who was the first President for Frelimo as well as Zebedias Manganhela, a pastor is the Protestant Church, who was killed by the security police of the colonial government, because they suspected him of raising funds for Frelimo. Also the Catholic Church had changed its act after the independence of Mozambique by appointing native people into the top positions of the hierarchy of the church in Mozambique thus becoming more attuned to the aspirations and needs of the native population.

Besides that it was simply not true that all the churches were collaborators of the colonial regime; the different churches also played an important role in providing the population with basic social services. In a society where social services were deteriorating because of the civil war being fought in the country, the churches were and are playing an increasingly important role in the social sphere. They were and are involved in food supply, education and health care. In this regard the churches were rendering services to the local population which the government would have liked to do itself, but was no longer capable of doing, because of the war and the economic crisis it was experiencing.

A further reason why the state could no longer afford the poor relationship with the churches was due to the fact that the churches were in a position to relieve the economic crisis of the country to some extent. All the major churches were in a position to channel funds via the contacts with the international religious community to Mozambique.

A further consideration which forced the government to enter into more friendly relations with the churches was that the churches very often had a better infrastructure in the rural areas than the state. The mobility of the state and its functionaries was severely restricted as a result of the civil war in the country. The largest part of the country was either under the control of Renamo or otherwise it was not safe for the representatives of the state to be seen there. The churches on the other hand did not have this problem. Although the war also had a detrimental effect on their activities, they still were in a position where they had access to all parts of the country. This resulted in a situation where the churches had a superior infrastructure in the country compared to the government. The state often had no other option than making use of the infrastructure of the churches when it wished to communicate or supply social services to the population in the rural areas. The churches were better positioned to address the needs of the population than the state.

Overall, the dire state of the economy was a decisive factor in the shift of policy towards the church. Production was on the decline and the country was plagued by a drought. This resulted in a dispersal of the population as well as generally worsening social conditions. These conditions forced the government to acknowledge the discrepancy between their political ideals and the socio-economic reality. This in turn forced them to reconsider their political approach in general. They became more willing to consult with other groups that they earlier considered as their ideological opponents and enemies. In this regard they became willing to consider the contribution that the churches could make in solving the political and economical crisis that state was facing. The Nkomati-Accord of 1983 with the apartheid government in South

Africa was another illustration of their willingness to cooperate with people and groups that they earlier rejected.

Another contributing factor was the war waged against the government by Renamo. Renamo was gradually acquiring more control over the land and people. Therefore the war was not only a military problem, but also a political problem. The government was forced to find an internal political solution to end the war that was crippling the country. In order to reach a solution they were forced to seek the cooperation of the different groups in the country, because it was impossible for any one group to bring an unilateral end to the war.

The outcome of the deliberations that took place at the end of 1982 was the reinstatement of Christmas as a public holiday as well as much improved relations between state and church. Another result of this conference was the establishment of the Department for Religious Affairs which was responsible for the relations between the church and the state. This conference thus introduced a new style of interaction which became a powerful instrument in the improvement of relations between church and state.

1987-1991

The factors discussed above remained valid and influential after 1986. Also the crisis of the Frelimo government that gave rise to the changes that occurred in 1982 was still continuing when President Samora Machel died in a plane accident in 1986. His successor, Joaquim Chissano, realised that his government was incapable of ending the war through direct military force. He therefore believed that the solution to the war must be found through political and diplomatic means. Furthermore, he also inherited a negative balance of payment from his predecessor. He realised that he could not depend on the socialist countries of the Eastern-Bloc for help in this regard, because they were struggling with their own economic crisis. This prompted him to turn to the West and the Middle East for help.

They were willing to give him relief aid for his ailing economy, but only on very specific conditions. Some of the conditions that they demanded from state were a new constitution based on a liberal democracy, a more market-orientated economy and improved relations between church and state.

The Frelimo government reacted to these demands by introducing the structural adjustment programme (SAP) which was aimed at restructuring the economy along market economy lines. They also started working on the formulation of a new constitution for

Mozambique. In the process of writing a new constitution, they invited a wide variety of interest groups to participate in this process.

Amongst these groups which they invited to participate in the writing of the new constitution were the different churches in Mozambique. A measure to improve their relations with the churches was to invite the Pope to visit Mozambique, which he did in 1987. Besides this, they also started to return the property of the churches, granted them permission to erect new buildings, which was forbidden up to that time. Religious believers were also allowed to join the Frelimo Party and to fill any position within the Party. The President, the Minister of Justice and Director of the Department of Religious Affairs also started to attend ceremonies and church services of the different religious communities. Through these and other measures, the dialogue between state and church was further improved.

By 1991 the state's relations towards the churches had improved so drastically that some of the church leaders in Mozambique even voiced concern that the relationship had become too friendly. These leaders were concerned that the state, in its attempt to win the goodwill of the churches, was indeed co-opting the churches to such an extent that they were losing their prophetic call and initial distance towards the state.

The Role of the Church in the Restructuring of the Mozambican Society

There is, however, consensus between the state and the churches that the churches in Mozambique have a very important role to play in the restructuring of the society — a society plagued by serious problems, such as civil war, poverty, illiteracy, unemployment, a soaring crime rate and many more problems. In this concluding section we shall focus on the areas in which the churches can make a contribution towards the rebuilding of Mozambique.

The first and most important task of the churches in Mozambique was to bring an end to the civil war. All the churches realised that this was their top priority, because the rebuilding of Mozambican society was an idle dream as long as the war prevailed. The churches fortunately were in a position where they could mediate between the warring parties. In the past they had been playing an important role in urging the warring parties into negotiations with each other. It seems that the churches are seen by both parties as a credible and reliable mediator. This, of course, is a good indicator that the church will also in future be able to play its role as peace maker.

A second and equally important task for the churches is the rehabilitation of the morality of the population. The war in combination with the severe poverty that the population has experienced over nearly two decades, had an eroding effect on morality in the country. Respect for human life had diminished and crime had become a way of life for many people, especially youngsters. In Mozambique one can hear many sorry tales of thirteen-year old children who have already killed a dozen or more people often for very minor reasons. People who have nothing to eat often have to steal food in order to survive. There are also bands of criminals who are exploiting this situation and for whom crime has become a way of life. The state is quite explicit about the fact that it could not on its own stem this tide of criminality or rebuild the morality of the society. Without a steep decline in criminality and a corresponding rise in morality, they know that a new political dispensation will have very little practical effect. They are therefore urging the churches to do their utmost to restore morality in the country.

The churches generally are more than willing to perform this task, not in order to please the government in the first place, but because they see it as an authentic task of the church. In all of the churches there is a commitment to rebuild the family, church and community life. Once integrity and morality has been restored to a certain extent in these spheres, the foundation for a more morally responsible society has been laid.

Education and social services is a another area where the churches will have to continue to play an important role. In both of these areas there is such a huge backlog that it is impossible for the present or a future government to cope on its own. The churches have to a certain extent, the personnel, the money and the will to assist the government in this task. It seems that church schools will in future once again become a familiar sight in Mozambique. There is even an indication that one of the churches might start their own university in the not-too-distant future.

Finally, the churches could also play a role in the economic rebuilding of the society. Internally, they could create working opportunities for the mass of unemployed people in the country. Externally, they could use their influence in international religious and ecumenical organisations to bring the living conditions of the Mozambican people to world attention. In this way they can initiate development projects and channel international funds to Mozambique.

References

Association pour la Promotion des Recherches et Etudes Foncieres en Afrique, Paris, decembre 1992, pp. 295-303.

Ayitte, G.B.N., "La democratie en Afrique Precoloniale" *Afrique 2000*, No. 2 (1990), pp. 39-75.

Bayart, J.F., "La Revanche des Societes Africanines" *Politique Africaine*, No.11, September 1983, pp.99.

Bratton, M., "Beyond the State: Civil Society and Assocational Life in Africa", *World Politics*, Vol. 41, No. 3, April 1989, pp. 417.

Buijtenhuijs, Rob. Rijnierse, Elly "Democratisation in Sub-Saharan Africa" 1989-1992. Research Reports 1993/51. African Studies Centre, Leiden, pp.5.

Carta Pastoral dos Bispos de Mocambique, in *Boletim da Celula* No.37, Junho, 1987.

Chazan, N., "Africa's Democratic Challenge: Strengthening Civil Society and the State" *World Policy Journal*, Spring 1992, pp.281.

Diouf.C.M., Diouf M. "Statutory Political Successions: Mechanisms of Power Transfer in Africa". Working Paper, Codesria 1/90.

Hermele, Kenneth, "Structural Adjustment and Political Alliances in Angola, Guinea-Bissau and Mozambique" pp.1-18, AKUT Uppsala, 1989.

Kodjo, E., "L'OAU *et la* democratie" *Jeune Afrique* No. 1542, du 18-24 Juillet 1990.

Le Roy, E., "Good Governance on l'exigence d'autorites gestionnaires, in: E. Le roy (ed) *La Mobilisation de la terre dans les strategies de development rural en Afrique noire francophones.*

Macamo, Eugenio., "Political Parties Problems in Power and Opposition — The Case of Mozambique", Eastern and Southern African Universities Research Programme (ESAURP) Conference on Political Parties in the Transition to Multi-party Democracy in Eastern and Southern Africa, Arusha, June 1993, pp. 1-21.

Macamo, Eugenio., "Internal Conflicts, Peace and Development in Africa — The Case Study of Mozambique" AAS, Nairobi, 1992.

Mafeje, Archie, "African Households and Prospects for Agricultural Revival in Sub-Saharan Africa". Working Paper No. 2/91 Codesria, pp. 1-41.

Mamdami M., Mkandawire T. and Wamba dia Wamba, "Social Movements, Social Transformation and the Struggle for Democracy in Africa". Codesria Working Paper No.1, pp. 1-26, 1988.

Nyong'o, Peter Anyang'., "The Quest for a Popular Democratic National State" in Africa Demos — Bulletin of the African Governance Program. The Carter Center of Emory University, p.8 Vol.II No.2, February, 1992.

"Peace Agreement signed" in AIM Mozambique News Agency Monthly. N. 195 October pp. 4-8, 1992.

"Regulamento Para a Formacao e Actividade dos Partidos Politicos" pp. 1-17, Imprensa Nacional de Mocambique 1991, Maputo.

Sandbrook, R., (1988), "Liberal Democracy in Africa: A Socialist Revisionist Perspective", Canadian Journal of African Studies, Vol.22 No.2 pp. 240-267.

Rahmoto, Dessalegn. "Peasant Organisations in Africa: Constraint and Potentials". Working Paper No. 1/91.

"Relatoria do Comte Central do Partido Frelimo" Coleccao 6. Congresso, pp. 1-80, Maputo, 1991.

Interviews Were Conducted in Maputo With the Following People

Job Chambala	—	Head of State Department of Religious Affairs
Iray Baptista	—	Department of Anthropology, at Eduardo Mondlane University
Boaventura Zitha	—	Administrator, Christian Ecumenical Organisation.
Salimo Omar	—	Secretary-General of Islamic Ecumenical Organisation.
Rafael Chivale	—	Head of Igreja 12 Apostolas de Africa.
William Humbane	—	United Methodist Church
Teoodio Wate	—	Faculty of Law, Eduardo Mondlane University.
Shafurdine H. Khan	—	Mozambique's Ambassador to Zambia
Joaquim Antonio Mabuiangue	—	Monsenhor Catholic Church.

6

The Movement for Multi-Party Democracy in Zambia: Some Lessons in Democratic Transition

Donald Chanda

Introduction

After its October 1991 elections Zambia witnessed a change of power from the ruling party, the United National Independence Party (UNIP), to the Movement for Multi-Party Democracy (MMD) in a peaceful manner. Today it stands as an example for constitutional transfer of power in the emerging plural politics in Africa, and provides some lessons and hope for new democratic institutions imbued with a new political culture.

This chapter outlines the politics of opposition to UNIP's one-party state that characterised the preceding two decades, and the political and economic problems that crystallised in the formation of *de facto* opposition party in 1990. It discusses the fresh demands on the political process and constitutional change, the emerging institutional democratic changes and practices particularly as they relate to the media, the judiciary and national political parties.

Democratic Necessity

Democratic theory and practice from the ancient Greek city states to the famous convention in Philadelphia in 1776 have always been about empowering people to rule themselves. People must be able to come together and discuss their affairs, publicly and freely. They must be able to create certain regulations that affect them all, certain institutions that serve them equally, certain actions which give them the most accessible opportunities to get what they want as individuals and as groups, to satisfy their needs and wants.

Although in practice we tend to divide between governors and the governed, it should be on condition that those who govern should derive their power and authority to do so on a daily plebiscite, a daily empowerment of the state's public officers by the people, to enable them to carry out certain public duties. Public accountability to the people, on the part of those officers entrusted with state functions is the cornerstone of democratic practice. Since the public system of accountability and transparency make one of the central pillars of democratic rule, without accountability and transparency in public service, the state will quickly lose the people's confidence. The state will experience a breakdown in its functions. It is therefore the duty of the people to review the constitution, public regulations, institutions and public officers entrusted to run the state system and change them accordingly. Decisions on public policy therefore should never be left to a small group of loyal party officials or the president's companions. If this is done, then it cannot be democracy.

The Democratic Element in Anti-Colonial Struggles

When the first African welfare society, Mwenzo African Welfare Society, was formed in 1912 in Zambia by Donald Siwale and others they were expressing a birth-right of freedom to exercise certain rights and liberties as Africans in their own land. They were telling the colonial authorities that the Africans too had a right to lead their own organisations to serve them as Africans. Among the key objectives of the society was to ask the white colonial administration to give a voice of representation on the governing bodies of the colonial state system, to the Africans, so that problems affecting the Africans could be heard and attended to. In essence, this was a very political act.

It questioned the undemocratic colonial system, though in a very mild way. This kind of political demand on the imposed colonial system was understandable given the nature of resistance against colonialism from Africans at that time. As time went on, several other African welfare societies were formed in various provinces. It did not take long before the colonial government was forced to recognise the societies as a force in the system of running public affairs.

In 1948, the *Federation of Welfare Societies* was formed and its key purpose was to represent African interests in the nation. A more explicit political body was later to be formed as the Northern Rhodesia African Congress. This metamorphosis was necessary in the light of the political developments in the country and pivoted the welfare societies, with their representative role into a political force with demands on the state system. The Congress underwent a quick political transformation especially due to the labour protests against exploitation on the copper mines. By 1951, African political consciousness against the unjust, undemocratic colonial rule transformed the congress into a more politically charged body, the African National Congress. The demands on the state were equally political; they did not limit themselves to representation on state organs but challenged the constitution on which Africans were ruled and demanded changes in the constitution to enshrine African rights. Above all, the new Congress challenged the colonial rule itself and called for an African self-government.

Toward the end of the 1950s the colonial system felt endangered, while the ANC pressed more and more for a majority-rule government. Political change had to occur to usher in a new system of rule. Some of the effects of these changes were that the ANC itself split between those who wanted immediate independence for Africans and those who preferred a gradual transfer. It was out of the more militant wing which demanded independence that the United National Independence Party (UNIP) was born. UNIP pressed for constitutional changes that led to independence in 1964, with the ANC as an opposition party.

The One-Party State

UNIP ruled Zambia with the ANC in opposition between 1964 and 1972. Two other parties had been formed, one in 1966 the United Party, led by the late Nalumino Mundia but this party was banned by UNIP because it was accused of being violent. The other party, the United Progressive Party (UPP) was formed in 1971, following tribal feuds within UNIP. From the time of tribal accusations in UNIP, in 1968 and 1970, following elections in the Central Committee, Kaunda and UNIP did not hold democratic elections as a way of deciding who should hold public office. Instead Kaunda chose to use the system of tribal balancing, a system whereby he picked individuals of his choice from major language groups, whom he argued represented their tribes. This system was used to keep Kaunda and his party in power until 2 November, 1991, when he was voted out of power.

When the UPP proved a formidable challenge to UNIP, Kaunda quickly accused the party of violence and argued that it was his national duty to preserve peace. He first arrested all UPP supporters except its leader, Simon Kapwepwe, the former Vice President. In February 1972 he banned the UPP and arrested Kapwepwe.

During the same month he introduced the one-party state. At a press conference held at State House on 25 February 1972 he said:

> I have decided to meet you today to make public the decision of my Cabinet that Zambia should become a One-Party Participatory Democracy and that practical steps should now be taken to bring this about. The first of these steps is to appoint a National Commission to deal with the subject.

When the Commission finally reported in October 1972, it made several recommendations which included a limited term of office of the President, but many of these were left out by the time of final enactment of the one-party state on 13 December, 1972. Clause 4 of the Republican constitution forbade the creation of any other party except UNIP.

The Opposition to the One-Party State in Zambia

The fact that the one-party state was imposed by the leadership on the people of Zambia was the greatest problem to its establishment and continuation. Various people, independently or in groups refused, by one form of expression or the other to accept the infringement on their rights and freedoms, like the freedom to form political parties, which the one-party state brought about. It also limited the political choices the Zambian citizenry could make.

The most consistent and organised opposition to the decisions of the one-party state has been expressed by the trade unions and the student bodies as groups. Many individuals especially those that had served the party and among the intelligentsia were also consistently critical of the one-party idea and its practice. The trade union movement, the Zambia Congress of Trade Unions (ZCTU) opposed the economic policies that the one-party system imposed, as well as the political machinations that came with such policies. In addition to calling for better economic policies to serve workers, the unions opposed Party Councils at places of work and the absorption of unions into a wing of the ruling party — UNIP. Although co-optation of some individual trade union leaders was possible, the trade union as a whole never compromised its original position against the one-party rule. Trade union leaders who respected and constantly served the workers' constituency therefore remained opposed to the one-party system. The Zambian President Chiluba, who was then Chairman of ZCTU found himself in that position, and it was from that same position that he became the President of the MMD, the ruling party today.

The student unions, especially the University of Zambia student union remained opposed to one-party rule from its inception. In fact, many student union leaders in 1971 and 1972 were accused of belonging to the UPP opposition party. Except for the few who were co-opted into the ruling party, the mainstream student body remained a watchdog for the ordinary people's interests and against oppressive state policies. Indeed, the June 1990 food riots, which preceeded the coup attempt, were sparked off by University students who wanted to demonstrate against a government decision to increase the price of mealie-meal.

The church, through its preaching remained a consistent voice against economic policies that left people in misery, and constantly reminded the government about its insensitivity to the poor and underprivileged. At the same time, the church pointed out the glaring differences between the privileged groups which included top government officials, and the underprivileged in terms of material and national resource allocations.

Various other individuals, among them former government officials and the intelligentsia also consistently (although not united at first) pointed out to the conspicuous consumption of national resources by a few privileged elements. They pointed out to the mediocrity that had crept in the top government officials and the fact that the President had surrounded himself with a coterie of "yes men", who were turning him into a semi-God as such making himself and his party accountable to no one (Daniel Lisulo, a former prime minister, quoted in the *Times of Zambia*, 25th August 1987).

In the wake of mounting political and economic problems especially after the fall of communist regimes in Eastern Europe 1989, the ruling party had to find ways of legitimising its continued hold over power. Thus in March 1990 the ruling party called for a National Convention, asking people to contribute in terms of what they thought the political and economic order in the country could be. The conference was opened by the then President Kenneth Kaunda who flatly stated that Zambian system of government could not be compared to that of Eastern Europe, because it had already gone past that. He added that comparing the two would be insane, emphasizing that Zambia would remain a single-party participatory democracy.

Virtually everyone else, apart from party members came out in support of multi-party democracy. These included Humphrey Mulemba, a former UNIP secretary-general, former ministers like Arthur and Sikota Wina, Vernon Mwaanga and the ZCTU President, Mr. Frederick Chiluba. In fact, Sikota Wina, one of the key 'fighters' during the nationalist struggle asked Kaunda to step down and remain an elder statesman. He added that the party supremacy had produced one of the most notable dictatorships on the continent, which had virtually suppressed all freedoms.

Kaunda and his party were unyielding. He called those who were calling for a multi-party system, disgruntled malcontents, and 'drug pushers' who now wanted to confuse the people. The call for multi-party politics, however, continued. Many people seized whatever opportunity they had to call for multi-party politics. Thus, when the food riots came in June 1990, everybody blamed the poor government policies. By the end of that week which had been characterised by food rioting, there was an attempted coup though it was not well coordinated. The food riots left many people dead but the government did not reverse the decision over the price increases, although it was left shaken. These events together challenged the government legitimacy in holding on to power, when its policies were in conflict with people's interests. Under these circumstances, a group of people decided to come together and force the government into multi-party politics, so that people could have an alternative for another government.

The Birth of Movement for Multi-Party Democracy (MMD)

July 20-21 1990 represented a turning point in Zambian history. Various groups of people and individuals gathered together at a conference for "Multi-Party Option". Among the key speakers were former ministers such as Mr. Wina who was also chairman of the Conference, Mr. Mwaanga and Mr. Kashita; the ZCTU was represented by its president, Mr. Chiluba and its general secretary Mr. Newstead Zimba. The Economic Association of Zambia was represented by Mr. Lewanika and Mr. Chitala, while the church and the academic community had people like Reverend Mumpanshya, Dr. Angel Mwenda and the president author.

There were two major outcomes of the conference. Firstly, it overcame fear of the ruling regime and spoke independently of what it thought the country needed. In fact a National Interim Committee was formed as well as other operational committees to spearhead the call for multi-party politics. Thus a *de facto* opposition party was formed although it was constitutionally illegal at that time. The resultant Movement for Multi-Party Democracy (MMD), became a *de facto* party until 17th December, 1990, when clause 4 of the Constitution was amended and the bill signed by the then President allowing the formation of other parties. Between July and December 1990, The MMD fought several legal constitutional battles discussed below.

The second outcome of the conference was the unity of purpose that it brought. For the first time, all the isolated voices for the multi-party came together: the intelligentsia, the workers, the businessmen, the church, even representatives from far-flung villages. One delegate stated that the composition of the conference represented the nation.

This unity of purpose was very important because each group came in and played its much needed role in the struggle against the ruling party. Briefly the following groups constituted the MMD.

The Intelligentsia: They were independent groups of people and individuals with the ability to interpret the national policies, articulate new ones and needs for the people. The group led the critique of the UNIP policies, and explained why the economy was in such a wrong shape.

The Businessmen: Their interest lay in promoting productivity of their own businesses and national wealth at large. They needed a supportive state system for their investments. This business atmosphere was lacking under the ruling government, so an alternative state system was important to them. They were practically involved, especially in financing MMD organisational and campaign activities.

The Workers: Under trade unions, they have been the most organised group and most consistent in fighting against exploitation. They have always been calling for fair economic policies that would reduce their suffering. They provided the organisational mechanism to MMD, as well as lent it the unflinching voice against the ruling regime.

The Small-Scale Producers, Informal Sector Producers and the Unemployed: Their survival has always depended on the sale of 'little' items they can lay hands on. They are constantly looking for new opportunities, and an alternative party seemed to offer that new opportunity, although many of them were also manipulated and threatened by the ruling party. They have been a very frustrated and abused group economically and politically. Although they are very susceptible to manipulation, they are mobile and the best group for organisation on the ground. Their numbers and support constituted an asset to MMD.

The Peasant Subsistence Producers: Extremely frustrated by the neglect of their working environment, the ravages of astronomical prices and dilapidated infrastructure, the majority in this group were looking for an alternative system, that would at least give them a new promise. They were very clear about their needs, although not about national needs and policies. MMD spoke about their needs and provided new promises. The ruling government could not sustain its renewed promises and often simply intimidated them.

The strength in MMD lay in the fact that it incorporated all interest groups in all corners of the country, and it provided new promises with a new alternative. The crucial question however, would the new alternative and new promises work?

The Struggle Against the Ruling Party: Some Lessons

The MMD demanded that, among other things, the nation should revert to a multi-party system of government so that Zambians should get the option to choose a party of their choice to rule them for a mandated period. The MMD challenged the ruling party to legitimise its continued rule, since people looked overtly resistant to the ruling party and its policies. For this, the MMD called for a national referendum for the people to choose between a one-party system and a multi-party system before December 1990. Under pressure the ruling party yielded to the call, and the electoral commission was asked to allocate voting symbols on which people could choose. The ruling party was given a foot, representing continued one-party system while the MMD was given a raised index figure with a thumb, for multi-party. Although the MMD had called for referendum by December, the ruling party said it was not possible until August 1991.

A Fresh Register of Voters

Realising that apathy has characterised elections during the one party era, the MMD called for a fresh register of voters, so that many more people and especially the previously under-aged who had now become eligible could now vote. The electoral commission embarked on the registration exercise in October 1990. Many more people registered since a dim hope was growing that their vote would be significant in the then emerging political process.

Constitutional Changes

The MMD called for constitutional changes, arguing that the nation had not brought single party to the country by referendum in 1972 and that a referendum would mean that people will first vote for it, then for general elections again. They argued that, this would be expensive for the nation. The MMD called on the ruling party to have a constitutional change through parliament, just like it had brought in single party rule through a cabinet decision. Under pressure the ruling party introduced the constitutional amendment bill in parliament which was later passed, allowing for the formation of other parties, other than the ruling party. The President signed the bill on 17th December 1990. Before that, the MMD had organised national rallies advocating for multi-party democracy. The MMD would hold a rally only after the police authorised a rally in that district. In some cases such rallies were refused. In fact the first attempt to hold a National Convention by the

MMD to elect its national leadership failed because the ruling party blocked them from using a conference venue.

The Constitutional and Delimitation Commissions

When the multi-party bill became law in December 1990, there was need to review and change the entire constitution so that it would be in line with new multi-party politics. For this the President appointed a constitutional commission headed by a solicitor-general to go around provinces and take people's views on a new constitution. The President also appointed two members of MMD (the Chairman and the Secretary) to serve on the Commission, but the MMD refused.

At the same time, a Delimitation Commission was set up to review the constituencies with the view to increase the number of parliamentary seats from 125 to 150. The idea was to accommodate the increased population and the plural politics of the new era. The increased number of the constituencies was welcomed by many Zambians, except that there were many administrative issues that came with it especially regarding the registered voters and polling stations. It was not uncommon during the voting time that many names were misplaced from the original polling station registers. And some people could not vote as a result of this.

The constitutional commission drafted the report and presented it to the President. By June 1991, the government announced the new constitution which gave the President extensive powers over the legislature and even the judiciary. Among the contentious points was that the President would appoint ministers outside Parliament. The Constitution was rejected by MMD. Even though the bill was presented in Parliament, the debate in Parliament was halted until the MMD and the ruling party met to discuss the contentious points in the constitutional bill. After the agreement and consequent signing by the President of the ruling party and MMD, then the constitutional bill was passed in Parliament with those amendments.

Freedom of the Media

The re-introduction of multi-party democracy did not only allow people to form or belong to the political parties of their choice, but freed people to voice their opinions on the nature and organisation of the state. It freed civic associations to express their views and demands on the state. Above all it unshackled the media, through which the people now expressed their views and opinions without fear, and the censorship that characterised the one-party era. Multi-party democracy has created an independent press which has acted as a vehicle for free expression and exchange of ideas, which is a necessary element in a democratic process. In fact, a number of independent newspapers and newsletters have sprung up which depict independent views.

This freedom of the press did not come without struggle. At a press conference in November 1990, President Kaunda instructed the two national newspapers not to cover the opposition parties, and parastatal companies not to advertise in private newspapers especially the *Mirror*, a church-based paper. However, the MMD took the case to court on constitutional grounds arguing that the decision infringed on rights of individuals and groups. The court under Judge Musumali ruled that it was unconstitutional for the President to restrict media coverage of opposition parties. The most important aspect of this judgement was that the custodian of the constitution of the republic was told by the court that he was violating the Constitution that he had sworn to uphold. This pointed to the emerging democratic practice not only of the press but the independence of the judiciary. Even the much government-controlled radio and TV finally carried advertisements and messages of the opposition parties. When there appeared a bias by TV and *Times of Zambia* newspaper, the Press Association of Zambia (an association of journalists) petitioned the managing directors and obtained a court injunction that restrained the two managing directors from working until after elections. Although the Supreme court overruled the decision later, the effect was felt.

Independence of the Judiciary

The emerging practice of independence of the judiciary has played a very critical role in Zambia's democratic transition. Two cases will suffice in explaining this role. The first one was over MMD's legality to hold rallies between July and December 1990, when it was not constitutional to do so. The MMD took the matter to court. In its ruling the court held that, although it was constitutionally illegal for people to form other parties, the MMD was not a party but a group of people expressing their rights over national issues. And that on the basis of human and constitutional rights they should be allowed to lobby for multi-party democracy.

The greatest test case, however, was the one that involved the MPs who crossed from UNIP to the MMD. UNIP took the matter to court saying that since the MPs had been voted to Parliament on a UNIP ticket, they should be expelled from Parliament since they were no longer members of UNIP. But the court ruled that the MPs would remain in Parliament as independent candidates until Parliament was dissolved.

The MMD Convention

In February 1991, the MMD held its national convention. The elections were conducted in a democratic manner. For example, the Presidency was contested by four people; Mr. Wina, then the National Interim Committee Chairman; Mr. Chiluba, then Vice Chairman; Mr. Mulemba, former UNIP Secretary General and Mr. Shamwana, a former Judge and treason convict. The results of MMD presidential elections were hailed as very democratic and non-tribal by the majority of people and the international press, including the BBC. This was also demonstrated by the fact the those who lost the elections took it as a democratic choice of the people; they have continued to serve the party actively up to this day. In fact, Mr. Wina and Mr. Mulemba were in Chiluba's first Cabinet. There were charges of tribal voting, but these were expected since for almost three decades the ruling party and its President had preached that Zambia was a collection of fragile tribal groups which would collapse if he Kaunda was out of power. This was the basis on which his tribal balancing rule was founded.

The results of that democratic convention were a real pointer to the emerging democracy. MMD produced a team of leaders at the convention which was national and politically balanced in character. It carried both the "old" and "new" blood in politics. It incorporated all the groups of people by democratic election. It represented the social forces that wanted to see change in Zambia. To many Zambians, it provided new light of how leaders could be elected as opposed from the selection practices under UNIP and its President, where leaders were chosen on the basis of the tribe and those who knew them, rather than people who they were supposed to serve. The MMD proved that the democratic alternative worked.

The Opposition Campaign

The MMD started off on a weak note in terms of the resources and the machinery with which to campaign compared to the ruling party UNIP. But this very weakness especially the realisation was to be turned into strength. The MMD left no options untried. It used all the resources at hand which largely came with the good-will of the people. The people of Zambia were also ready to listen to an alternative voice since they had suffered so much political fatigue under UNIP and were prepared to change. The MMD, therefore, was on an offensive campaign to show itself to the people as the only viable option with a programme that would in future restore confidence and improve life in the country. It also never took matters for granted, it scrutinised every trick the ruling party made, and exposed all the ills, past and present, that UNIP made. It maintained this vigilance, and always remained alert against the ruling party. For example, the MMD called for the monitoring of elections by international observer groups and the clarification of procedures for voting, including the approval of the list of voters. It also made sure that arrangements were made to enable those who had lost national identity cards to get certificates to vote. Without the insistence of the MMD on international observers, whose role is stated below, probably the election results would have told a different story in that by administrative manipulation by the ruling party could have rigged elections.

The All-Party Conference and the Inter-Party Working Group

Like the church which arranged the joint UNIP — MMD meeting over the constitution referred to earlier, on a non-partisan ticket, the University of Zambia students took the initiative and arranged an inter-party conference at Mulungushi International Conference Centre. It should be noted that the ruling party had invited all opposition parties to State House earlier. The MMD declined to accept this invitation and called for a neutral meeting place, hence the all-party conference.

The greatest benefit from this conference was the creation of a sense of responsibility and national accountability in each party. It also taught the parties that the diversity of parties was not, and should not be, a deterrent to unity and national interest. It brought about the spirit of unity in diversity.

The all-party conference, apart from laying down the principles of national unity, brought together all the presidents of all parties. It also created a working structure, the inter-party committee, which was chaired by the MMD. The party secretaries from all parties made up this working group which was to take up all issues regarding party rivalries and handling of national assets by all parties. In fact, the UNIP-MMD meeting over the constitutional bill was itself a by-product of the all-party conference spirit, which was arranged by the church this time. The other result of the meeting was that it created a 'hot line' between President Kaunda and Frederick Chiluba.

The International and National Independent Election Monitoring Group

The MMD pioneered the call for international election observers. Although UNIP first objected to it, it had to agree finally and the observers from well known institutions like the Carter Centre, the Commonwealth, the OAU and other bodies came to Zambia. First, many of them had advance parties which studied the administrative procedures of the elections and helped in finalising the procedures of the elections where it was necessary. During the election day, they played a very active role in ensuring that voting procedures were followed; and their presence prevented vote-rigging in many respects. For example, on the morning of voting former US President Carter physically visited a sample of polling stations in Lusaka, and ensured that all boxes and other materials were inspected before voting started.

Parallel to international election monitoring groups, local groups were constituted comprising non-partisan bodies like the church, the student bodies and individuals who independently helped in the conducting of free and fair elections in the country. These groups constituted the *Zambia Elections Monitoring Committee*.

It must be noted that all the monitoring groups played a very crucial role in supporting the administrative duties of the election commission, the body responsible for elections. Their significance did not end on election day; the results were to be authenticated by all groups and their reports mattered in the judgement and later acceptance of election results by all parties. Indeed when more than 50% of the election results came, the various monitoring groups submitted their reports. Their reports all concluded that by far the elections were conducted in a free and fair atmosphere and that the results were acceptable to all monitoring groups. They noted the administrative problem associated with some misplaced names on the register on polling day, but these did not make a significant contribution to affect election results.

The Election Results and Power Hand-Over

The ruling party, UNIP, was defeated by the opposition MMD by a very large margin. UNIP got 25 of the 150 Parliamentary seats while the MMD had 125 seats. This represented 83,3% of the vote won by the MMD. In fact the Presidential vote had the same convincing picture of score by large margins except for one province, the Eastern Province of Zambia. So clear was the victory that on November 2, after the MMD President had more than 75% of the vote, he was sworn in by the Chief Justice as the new President of the Republic of Zambia. Two hours prior to that, the outgoing UNIP President addressed the nation accepting defeat and promised to lead the opposition so that it would challenge the MMD in the next elections after five years. The outgoing President noted that many sections of the community, notably women, did not vote, and that reasons should be established as to why that was so. It should be noted that 45.4% of the eligible voting population actually voted. This result, however, asserted people's power and demystified the office of Presidency, which was being built on a personality, rather than the office. Mr. Chiluba, the current President has even gone further in demystifying the office by adopting the simple title of 'Mr. Chiluba'.

Conclusion

No social phenomenon is incidental nor occurs instantaneously. The Zambian case, as I have illustrated above took shape over space and time in a process of change. New ideas, institutions, and practices have characterised each stage of the social phenomenon, because no phenomenon such as a democratic transition can exist in a vacuum. Certain external and internal pre-conditions determine its dynamics.

One, lesson among the many, seems to be that multi-party politics came to Zambia at a time when the ruling party had the legality but not legitimacy to rule. That is why even though the MMD operated illegally between July and December 1990, the ruling party could not act strongly against it. The conditions were ripe to challenge the ruling party. The political changes in the international context were definitely 'influential too in making the atmosphere conducive for change in Zambia.

MMD rose to power through the provision of a legitimate alternative. People were prepared for change and all the MMD had to do was to present itself as the legitimate alliance of people who provided that alternative. People had suffered severe poverty and political fatigue under UNIP rule and its never changing leadership.

The question we have to ask ourselves, however, is: does a democratic transition such as the Zambian one, explain the maturity of a diversified petty bourgeois class, alternating in state power, under a new political culture? Or does it indeed mark a new stage in political state organisation where the people's role is more respected, more representative, more authoritative thereby marking a new level of state organisation and political consciousness? One would like to believe the latter, but a belief is not enough.

References

Chitala, D. and Lewanika, A. *The Hour Has Come; Proceedings of the First Multi-Party Conference.*

Diop Monar Coumba, and Diuf, Mamador, *Statutory Political Successions; Mechanisms of Power Transfer in Africa* (working paper 1/90)., Dakar, Codesria, 1990.

Hall, Richard, *A History of Zambia,* Lusaka, Longman, Zambia, 1969.

Hall, Richard, *The High Price of Principles,* New York; Africana Publishing Corporation, 1969.

Kasom Francis, *The Press in Zambia.,* Multi Media Publishers Lusaka., 1986

Kaunda, K. D., Zambia Shall Be Free, London Heinemann, 1962.

Mazrui, Ali, The Africans; A Triple Heritage, London: BBC Publications, 1986.

Notes from several court cases, newspapers and press conference.

7

State and Social Movements in Zimbabwe

Lloyd M. Sachikonye

Introduction

From the mid-1980s, a fuller picture began to emerge of the character of the Zimbabwe state and its authoritarian tendencies towards certain social movements. In this chapter, we seek to explain the basis of the authoritarianism which represented the state's response to struggles by labour and students for improved working conditions, democratisation and academic freedom respectively. We assess the social basis and agendas (such as they are) of these two social movements, and their relative strengths and limitations. Finally, the chapter will examine the potential impact of these social movements on the political process in Zimbabwe in the remainder of the 1990s.

Social Movements Before and After Independence

As we observed in chapter 1, current political discourse has usefully focused on previously neglected concepts and those forces which constitute civil society and their relations with the state. There has occurred an overdue shift from an emphasis on the state and its related political institutions to other social actors whose role impinge on the democratisation process while also checking the aggrandisement of the economic and political processes by the state.

In Africa, it was in the upsurge of anti-colonial struggles that social movements such as labour, student, religious, youth and peasant movements played a determinant role in swelling the nationalist movement for independence. The nationalist movement therefore became the dominant social movement which articulated the social interests of these movements. To the extent that the nationalist movement provided ideological expression to anti-colonialism and articulated a vision of an independent nation-state, it proved to be a unifying social force. However, as we already argued in chapter 1, the nationalist movement was also an unstable coalition. The demobilisation of the various social movements on the morrow of independence had negative consequences for the development of democratic institutions and practices in most countries in Africa. Monolithic one-party systems and authoritarian personal rule characterised the political systems till the winds of democratic change began to blow in the 1980s.

Zimbabwe was not an exception to the general trend of the demobilisation of social movements at independence, even though it never formally authorised the installation of a one-party state. As in other African countries, the tendency was for the state to seek the co-opt those key movements such as labour, student and peasant movements onto the state apparatus. In that way, the autonomy of these movements would be compromised and neutralised. Yet we saw how complex the relationship between the state and civil society (of which social movements are constituent organs) is. The post-independence expansion in public sector employment and in education directly contributed to the enlargement of the working-class and of the student population. Similarly, increased state credit and technical services provided a boost to peasant agriculture. At the same time, however, the state and party apparatus became well-high indistinguishable as local government structures were established in the districts, village wards and former townships.

Of course, the process of the co-optation of social movements by the nationalist movement was not a simple one. Many of the social struggles prior to independence were inevitably politicised whether these related to the land question, working conditions, access to housing, education or social services.

A major feature in the early forms of Zimbabwean nationalism was the fusion of urban and rural-based struggles particularly in the 1940s and 1950s. The anti-colonial movement during this phase drew upon common grievances concerning land expropriation, livestock destocking, poor working conditions and wages and general social oppression faced by the peasant and working classes. It was an awareness of the potential strength and radicality of the worker-peasant demands and possibility of a class alliance that the colonial state sought to co-opt rural traditional authorities, the chiefs, and to repress the trade union movement. The popular base of such labour organisations as the Reformed Industrial Commercial Union (RICU) African Workers' Voice Association (AWVA) organised by well-known nationalists such as Masotsha Ndlovu, Charles Mzingeli and Benjamin Burombo testified to the resonance of the urban-rural protest movement. In the latter phase of nationalism, from the 1960s onwards, the formerly strong urban-rural dimension of the movement began to weaken as it became largely dominated by a petit-bourgeois leadership based in the towns. As occurred during other nationalist struggles elsewhere in Africa:

> without the mass pressure that surged into the streets of colonial cities and made its impact felt even in remote corners of the bush, the educated elite would have remained upon the sidelines of everyday life, genuinely feared and tolerated by colonial officials of a liberal sort, or else jeeringly ignored and pushed aside by officials of another kind. As it was, the activists were given power by the pressure of a social struggle (Davidson, 1992:166).

In this conceptualisation, nationalism was a broad integrative social movement which increasingly became centralised within an elite centred within the petit-bourgeoisie. This would have long-term consequences for the broad-based democratic nature of the movement.

Trade unionists were prominent actors in the nationalist movement. Labour struggles gave a boost to nationalism and groomed some unionists for eventual leadership:

> nationalism entered a new phase with the reorganisation of the old African National Congress which had much support from union leaders. Four of the five top executive members of the ANC were union leaders including J.Z. Moyo, Reuben Jamela and J.T. Maluleke who were detained during the 1959 emergency (Zimbabwe Government, 1976: 17).

Joshua Nkomo who would later head the Zimbabwe African People's Union (ZAPU) had cut his teeth in union politics in the Rhodesia Railways African Workers' Union. A notable figure in the trade union movement at that juncture has observed that:

> a long-awaited relationship began to flourish between former trade unionists, now in politics, and those that remained in the trade union movements. Most union leaders were young and tended to be more radical than some political leaders. In consequence, union leaders shared the radical views of the youth wing of the party rather than those of the mainstream politicians (Chigwedere, 1978).

The youth movement itself found powerful expression in the Youth League from which major figures such as the late George Nyandoro and James Chikerema emerged to assume prominent positions in the nationalist movement. Similarly, student union politics particularly in the 1960s and 1970s assumed an explicit nationalist favour. The exiled wings of the nationalist movement — ZANU and ZAPU — continued to be swelled by student emigres. In the armed struggle itself, school-leavers were a major force as trained cadres.

Of course, other social forces such as church-based organisations, community associations and cooperatives were also important actors in the nationalist movement. However, as the countdown to independence became closer, the nationalist movement sought to hegemonise its position in political and ideological terms. Attempts were made to co-opt the trade union movement, an attempt which partly succeeded but led to the fracturing of the movement. The African Trade Union Congress (ATUC) and the National African Federation of Unions (NAFU) were explicitly linked to ZANU and ZAPU respectively. Within the nationalist parties themselves, the socialist tendencies consisting largely of younger but radically — inclined cadres in the March 11 movement (in ZAPU) and in the Zimbabwe People's Army drawn from both ZANU and ZAPU) were soon isolated to pre-empt any challenge to the nationalist 'old guard' leadership. The radicalisation of the nationalist movement was substituted by socialist rhetoric which was left untranslated into a programme. The structures established in rural areas during the liberation struggle did not survive; they were subordinated to the interests of the nationalist parties. No independent peasant organisation survived or emerged, as even the Zimbabwe National Farmers' Union (ZNFU) and the National Farmers' Association of Zimbabwe were linked to the ruling party. Furthermore, as Louis Masuko shows clearly in his chapter in this volume most cooperatives (with a few exceptions) were related both to the party and state in terms of material support and planning. The youth and women were mobilised through Youth and Women's Leagues respectively.

At independence, therefore, the position of formerly active social movements was not very robust nor reflecting autonomy. This reflected the considerable headway by the nationalist movement — now transformed into a ruling elite — in exerting its hegemony over the Zimbabwean society. The post-independence state now sought to sponsor a national labour centre, the Zimbabwe Congress of Trade Union (ZCTU), as the umbrella organisation for the labour movement, in spite of the existence of other centres with considerably greater union membership. With the significant capacity at its disposal, it expanded public sector employment, rewarding party membership in the process. State structures such as ministries catering specifically for cooperatives, women, youth, higher education, peasants in need of resettlement amongst others were established to dispense patronage and exert hegemony. The major newspapers and broadcast media were subsumed under the state, with only a few monthly and weekly newspapers and magazines remaining independently owned. Steadily, the city, town and district councils were brought under party control. Exceptions to the organisations subsumed by the state were the churches and industrial associations in commercial and industrial sectors and large-scale agriculture.

This is the broad context in which we can examine relations between the state and certain social movements. It is a context in which the grip of the state on civil society is considerable. However, the process of the aggrandisement of political control by the state over a range of civil society institutions goes back to the era of the nationalist struggle as we observed above. Of course, the relationship between the state and civil society, between the state and social movements, is not static but a dynamic one as we shall see in the next two sections..

State and the Labour Movement: Phase of an Uneasy Pact

The structural features of the labour movement need to be spelt out albeit briefly in order to assess its relations with the post-colonial state. The movement has its basis in a working-class of 1,1 million, which approximately constitutes 10% of the total population. The relatively small size of the working-class is an index of the limited level of industrialisation in Zimbabwe. More profound than the size of the working class is the partial character of the proletarianisation process itself. The migrant labour system upon which commercial agriculture, mining and the domestic service sector drew during the greater part of the colonial period was not completely demolished at independence. The oscillation of migrant workers between capitalist industry and the peasant agricultural sector contributed to the ambiguity and ambivalence in their worker consciousness. In practical terms, grinding urban poverty compensated slightly by the retention of close family links with even poorer subsistence peasant farming undermined the financial base of any permanent organisational effort.[1] When added to the massive relative surplus population, this poverty:

> greatly increased job insecurity and mitigated against trade unionism particularly amongst the most oppressed, isolated and vulnerable segments of the black workforce — those in capitalist agriculture, rural commerce and industry and in white households' domestic service.[2]

One estimation in 1990 was that up to two-thirds of the 1,1 million workers retained links with the peasant sector in terms of access to land. Their incomes needed to be augmented by food production, if not cash crop production; on retirement, the peasant sector provided minimal levels of subsistence and welfare. The legacy of the migrant labour system and the semi-proletarianisation which resulted for a significant proportion of the Zimbabwe working-class need to be borne in mind when evaluating the labour movement's capacity for self-assertion and autonomy.

In addition, the Zimbabwe labour movement could not be said to have defined a distinct working-class political project at independence. Its demands tended to be diffuse but revolved around improvement in working conditions now that independence had been attained. Presumably, it could not have been otherwise. As one analyst observed about African labour movements, their struggles have mostly had:

> a populist rather than a proletarian character and that there struggles have very often focused on the contradiction between the state and the common people rather than on the contradiction between capital and labour and that they have had a lot to do with human and civil rights, with human dignity, and, in some cases, with cultural identity.[3]

Thus before and after independence, working-class action was never a matter of the working class alone but relied heavily on moral and sometimes also material and political support from other strata particularly the self-employed in the informal sector and the peasantry. In Zimbabwe, the labour movement focused not simply on income policies but on racism in industrial relations; a number of industrial strikes were triggered off by racist managerial regimes. At the same time, consumer issues and land redistribution featured prominently in statements by the labour movement leadership.

How then can the relations between the labour movement and the post-colonial state be characterised? The relations were partly determined by the changing class composition of that state with the entry of an African petit-bourgeoisie into the highest echelons of government, the bureaucracy, the judiciary and the expanding parastatal sector. Economically, the emergent bourgeoisie was weak but it saw the state as one avenue of accumulation. The continuity of capitalism and of the state structures which guaranteed it, was ensured and the reconciliation policy was a compromise with the white and international bourgeoisie. Briefly, this is the broad context in which the then Prime Minister Mugabe summarised his analysis in these concise terms:

> the country is based on free enterprise and is therefore capitalist. We have to accept that we will not bring about an immediate disruption of the economy; we can work in gradual phases . . . The trade union movement is very weak in this country. It has always been, and it is necessary to promote a unitary movement rather than a multiplicity of national movements.[4]

The rationale for heavy state intervention in the industrial relations was therefore ostensibly to rectify the weakness of the labour movement. True the labour movement at independence was fractured, as we observed above, and amongst its fractions were some which courted state intervention. This is the specific context in which relations between the labour movement and the state evolved in the first five years of independence.

State-labour relations were generally free of controversy and conflict during this period but were regulated by the policies formulated at independence to mediate capital-labour relations. It was relations between capital and labour which were characterised by bitter conflicts expressed in numerous strikes at independence. As we have discussed elsewhere in some detail, confrontation at the workplace in 1980-82 was a common feature in labour relations.[5] The pact that eventually defused the capital-labour conflict in 1980-82 essentially entailed direct state intervention in wage determination (through statutory minimum wages), monitoring of retrenchments and unfair labour practices (through statutory provisions on lay-off procedures) and promotion of intra-firm communication between workers and management (through workers' committees). The high-profile state intervention was ensured by the relatively weak organisational and political status of the trade union movement, which we have sought to explain above.

Subsequently, pervasive state intervention in the regulation of labour relations during this early post-independence period has been variously and somewhat uncritically interpreted as "progressive" or "benignly paternalist". Early government emphasis on the reconstitution of splinter unions into large industrial unions and on the restructuring of the national labour movement into the Zimbabwe Congress of Trade Unions (ZCTU) demonstrated the direct stake of the state in the domestication of the labour movement. Socialist rhetoric camouflaged the state objective of stabilising of labour relations through rooting out militant unionism and the draconian handling of strikes. It was not uncommon to hear on May Day rallies statements from ministers referring to the ZANU-PF government as "a workers' government"; there were also expressed such platitudes as "free trade unionism means the freedom of the workers unite rather than be divided, sub-divided and exploited by capital".[6] At the same time, politicians did not hesitate to wield the state machinery to quell industrial action and to warn unions not to "rock the boat". In a scathing attack on striking teachers and nurses in October 1981, Mugabe was quoted as remarking that:

> if by choosing to strike they want to blackmail the Government, then the Government has no sympathy for their cause and will not hesitate to take drastic steps as punishment for their unjustifiable negligence of duty and disloyalty to the state . . .. We would rather start from scratch than make do with irresponsible nurses and teachers.[7]

The tough stance was translated into draconian handling of strikes, principally the arrest of strikers and their prosecution in court under the *Industrial Conciliation Act* or the *Law and Order Maintenance Act*. During the early 1980s, arrested strikers included not only teachers and nurses but also railway workers, miners and bus drivers. The resort to coercive state methods to subdue workers represented continuity of the colonial-state's repressive "labour regime". Beneath the veil of populist-socialist rhetoric lurked an authoritarian state with a propensity to utilise coercion to safeguard conditions for capitalist accumulation. Even on the question of wages, the state did not play a disinterested role. Two interpretations were made to justify minimum wages increases: firstly to remove "exploitation and discrimination in pay" on the grounds of social justice and equity and secondly, to spur "efficiency and productivity".[8]

However, the mediatory role of the state in capital-labour conflicts left the impression that the state was an ally of the working-class. Its exhortations to the unions to restructure and centralise their operations suggested that the state was 'pro-working class'. Yet a different interpretation of the rationale and objectives of the state's role is not only possible but necessary. The basic structures of the colonial state were still intact; the post-colonial state was required, as we observed above, to continue regulating a regime of capitalist accumulation. The overall framework of its economic and social policy guaranteed the essential features of that regime of accumulation.[9] The "growth with equity" policy, the policy of increased state participation in the economy and social redistribution measures (education and health expenditure) did not represent a fundamental break with the existent regime of accumulation. The state provided crucial support to the bourgeoisie in 1980-1982 when the colonial labour regime became vulnerable to proletarian assault through widespread strikes.

From the view-point of industrialists, the formation of strong industrial unions was not incompatible with their economic interests. It was acknowledged that "well organised and enlightened trade unions will foster good negotiation procedures making government interference in such aspects as minimum wages unnecessary".[10] In the absence of a strong, efficient trade union movement it had been necessary for the state to intervene in industrial relations.

Finally, there appeared to exist some congruence of perspectives between the labour movement leadership and the state on the diagnosis of the labour relations crisis of 1980-82. The weak influence of the labour movement leadership was confirmed in the response of the then ZCTU Secretary-General, the late Albert Mugabe, who admitted that the widespread strikes of 1980-82 were organised spontaneously outside its ambit. Echoing basic agreement with the position of the state and the bourgeoisie, Mugabe stated that:

> Strikes do more harm than good. We don't need to retard economic progress by arranging strikes . . .. There are some bad eggs in the union movement. The minister talks from a position of knowledge. There are some people in the movement who go out looking for difficulties, and try to be difficult. We will watch them closely and discourage striking as much as we can.[11]

Increasingly, the central labour federation (ZCTU) was seen as the principal vehicle for the de-radicalisation of working-class struggle whose major expression was plant-based industrial action. However, there were limits to the extent that the ZCTU could exert its leverage on individual unions in the resolution of spontaneous plant-based strikes.

At this juncture, we may draw a useful comparison with the role of a Zambian trade union in the labour relations crisis which hit the mining industry in the late 1960s. Michael Burawoy observed that the mine workers' union concurred with management that there was an alleged problem of discipline in the mines and that "the problem of educating today's youth in the facts of life was real, and they would continue their struggle to make them realise that paper qualifications alone did not make useful citizens".[12] The union failed to recognise the significance of the transition from colonial to post-colonial production politics; it merely reiterated the government view that striking workers were undisciplined and irresponsible.13 In this particular Zambian case, the state not only identified its interests with those of mining capital but also upheld a despotic regulation of production akin to the colonial pattern.

In Zimbabwe, there existed between 1980 and 1985 a corporatist pact of alliance between the state, capital and the national labour centre but not necessarily with individual unions on labour issues, principally on the question of repression of strikes. It was a pact in which the labour movement was the weaker partner. The definition and implementation of statutory minimum wages and related labour legislation were largely the preserve of the state. So was the drawing up of the paternalistic *Labour Relations Act* in 1985 which retained some of the authoritarian aspects of the superseded *Industrial Conciliation Act*. The provision of this new Act proscribed strike action in most sectors of the economy. These sectors were christened "essential services" in which the workers' basic right to withdraw labour to enforce their negotiating position was curbed. In addition to its preponderant role in the determination of labour conditions generally, the state sought to co-opt the labour movement in much more formal terms. There was a thinly disguised view within the ruling ZANU-PF party that, like in Tanzania, Mozambique and Angola, the labour movement should be grafted onto its structures as one of its mass organisations alongside the youth and women's leagues. Internal maladministration within the ZCTU provided a 'propitious' opportunity to the state to intervene more directly in the undermining of the national labour centre. The rationale for co-optation was spelt by a Minister of State for Political Affairs who stated that:

> because of our class position as a party and government, we expect the trade unions to operate within the parameters of our socialist objectives. Because of Zimbabwe's history of settler colonialism, most working people and peasantry had very little technical, scientific and managerial skills and their ideological consciousness was still too low.[14]

Some union leaders backed ZANU-PF's ideology such as it was:

> "there is no reason unions and government should disagree on the question of ideology".[15]

Thus the state defined its role as one of benign paternalism and ideological guidance to a weak and fragmented labour movement.

Through 'administrators' appointed by the state in 1984 to run the national centre, the labour movement leadership was side-lined in the run-up to the second congress of the ZCTU in the following year. Meanwhile, struggles for leadership began in earnest between the existing executive leadership which professed allegiance to ZANU-PF and a second fraction which advocated labour movement autonomy. The recession which was exacerbated by a severe drought in 1982-84 had a severe squeeze on workers' incomes; a state-imposed wage freeze compounded the slump in living standards. Previous sentiments expressed by some unions that "our government is taking the right direction by not adopting a capitalist system which has deprived the majority of our workers for a long time" now proved naively misplaced.

In sum, the first five years of independence witnessed a dominant state intervention in labour relations with a visible bias to the immediate interests of the bourgeoisie. The spirited, if fragmented, struggles of workers at the work-place were undermined by the tacit pact between state, bourgeoisie and the labour movement leadership to create stability in labour relations through the repression of strikes. The regulation of this labour regime was enhanced through the creation of workers' committees at work-places; this facilitated communication between management and workers without strengthening the organisational presence of the trade union. However, the co-optation of the ZCTU leadership rested on a shaky basis. There did not exist popular support in the unions for the co-opted leadership. As the ideological orientation of the ruling party became clearer notwithstanding the strident socialist rhetoric, there was a groundswell of opposition both to government economic and social policy and to the self-serving ZCTU leadership. In the next section we consider changes in relations between the state and the labour movement in the context of fundamental changes in economic and social polices from the mid-80s to the present.

Labour, Capital and State Relations in the Context of Economic Reform

The second half of the 1980s and early 1990s witnessed a revitalisation of the labour movement through its reorganisation following the 1985 ZCTU congress. This coincided with the adoption of economic liberalisation measures, a *volte face* in ZANU-PF's professed policy of socialism, and a retreat from social redistribution measures (provision of free education and health services, and funding for rural resettlement). The flirtation with socialist ideology had sat uneasily with the preservation of capitalist structures in the economy and the domestication of labour militancy. The adoption of an Investment Code in 1989 which envisaged de-regulation of labour conditions and presaged the implementation of a Economic Structural Adjustment Programme (ESAP) in 1990 created considerable tension between the state and the labour movement. It was inevitable that the fragile pact forged soon after independence between the state and labour would now break down. The pact succumbed to the pressure from the high tension which now characterised relations between these two institutions. This section outlines the implications of these developments for changes in relations between the state, capital and the labour movement. We have discussed elsewhere the background to the shift in economic policy in the late 1980s and the implications of that shift on the fortunes of the working class.[16] It was a shift from social redistribution measures and state participation in the economy to more *laissez faire* policies which were comprehensively incorporated into the ESAP measures sponsored by international financial institutions, principally the World Bank (WB) and the International Monetary Fund (IMF). The shift occurred in a context of the convergence of the interests of the dominant domestic forces (the bourgeoisie which now included some senior politicians and ministers) and international capital which had been consistently wary of the demagogic socialist rhetoric of the ZANU-PF government.

The leading architect of post-independence economic policy, Finance Minister Bernard Chidzero summarised the phases of accumulations since 1980 into four.[17] Briefly, the first phase which lasted between 1980 and 1982 was "a honeymoon period" in which minimum wages were introduced as well as controls over prices and other aspects of the economy. The second phase (1983-85) was "an exasperating one which coincided with nearly three years of drought, the sharp drop in commodity prices and recession" resulting in a significant squeeze on incomes and tighter controls on the remittance of profits. During the third phase 1986-87, a policy reversal was seen as paramount in order "to generate more wealth", "attract investment" and to discard measures which were "not conducive to profit-making".[18] The fourth phase which began in 1988 is this current phase of adjustment or "ESAP" in short.

The accumulation crisis in the mid-1980s was the outcome of a combination of domestic and external structural constraints, policy mistakes and climatic vagaries. The causes of the crisis were decidedly not simple. However, incoherent development planning, the absence of a balance between expenditure on productive and social sectors and the half-hearted pursuit of the objectives of equity and participation certainly contributed to the crisis.[19] Opposition from entrenched domestic forces and international capital included the withholding of investment, a form of an ideologically motivated economic embargo.

This compounded the crisis. Pressure on the state sought shifts in the regime of accumulation through increase of leverage of capital over labour. This is why the de-regulation of labour conditions was central in the Investment Code and ESAP. The state relented its preponderance in wage determination with the scrapping of minimum wages; it withdrew from the regulation of prices whose effect had been to cushion the working-class from high cost of living. Through the scrapping of free primary education except in rural areas and subsidies on health charges and on basic food commodities, the state avoided funding of the social consumption and reproduction of the working-class. The latter had to fend for itself on decreasing income levels in a context in which capital was provided with more leverage in the determination of profits and wages. The new regime of accumulation suited the bourgeoisie at the expense of the labour movement which grumbled bitterly.

How can we explain this marked shift in economic and social policy? Part of the explanation relates to divisions within the state on ideology and development strategy. Some fractions within the ruling elite (concentrated in ZANU-PF and government) came out strongly in the second half of the 1980s against the lip-service to socialism and redistribution policies. These fractions of the petty bourgeois elite were in the process of transforming into a bourgeoisie proper through the utilisation of opportunities made possible by access to state resources. Their acquisitive tendencies contributed to a stalemate on the terms of a Leadership Code which sought to restrain those tendencies amongst ZANU-PF leaders.[20] The lengths to which this emergent bourgeoisie (which included some cabinet ministers) went to exploit advantages of accumulation opportunities provided through the state was their profiteering in the car racket known as the "Willowgate scandal" of 1988. Cars bought from a state-owned car assembly plant were later resold at higher prices which fetched substantial profits to this racketeering bourgeoisie. But even as early as 1982 and 1983, personal aggrandisement and corruption by some politicians had provoked public demonstrations by women and students. In 1988 and 1989, the critique by students and trade unions against the acquisitive tendencies of the politicians became sharper. The student movement condemned what it termed "monopolistic politics of domination, inefficiency, corruption and petit bourgeois primitive accumulation".[21] It was pointed out that the ZANU-PF leadership had in fact built economic alliances with the erstwhile settler bourgeoisie and international capitalists.[22]

This is the background against which we should assess the response of the labour movement and capital to the changed parameters and imperatives of accumulation. We consider the response of the labour movement with reference to specific issues concerning ideology, politics, collective bargaining, retrenchments, amendments to the Labour Relations Act and ESAP. Whereas in the first few years after independence, the labour movement broadly endorsed what existed as the 'socialist' policy of the regime, sharp criticism of its ideological inconsistency began to be made in the second half of the 1980s. The ZCTU began to express its scepticism over ZANU-PF's Marxist-Leninist credentials.[23] The less repressive of the ideologies from the labour movements's stand-. point was socialism which ZANU-PF was discarding in favour of full-blown capitalism. The continued espousal of socialism by the ZCTU put the movement and the ZANU-PF government at ideological loggerheads. More broadly, the labour movement criticised what it believed were authoritarian tendencies of the part of the state especially on the one-party state question. The ZCTU was forthright in its condemnation of the intention to instal a one-party state system soon after the 1990 general elections.[24] It also asserted its autonomy on political issues by refusing to endorse ZANU-PF in the 1990 elections.

The next major issue of contention between the state and the labour movement concerned wage bargaining with the phasing out of statutory minimum wages in 1989. In 1989-91, most unions proved skilful in wage negotiations with their employers in both the private and parastatal sectors. Within the context of the new labour regime, trade unions wrested considerable concessions from management through collective bargaining. Hitherto, state intervention in wage setting had tended to depress wage scales with the exception of several sectors such as agriculture and domestic service where workers' bargaining capacity was still low. The bone of contention over collective bargaining concerned the state's admonitions against high wage awards ostensibly because they fuelled inflation. In 1990-1991, pay awards ranged between 19 and 30 per cent in the private sector to which the state responded by advocating staggered payment of the increases. To reinforce the state's position on this issue, the Reserve Bank counselled that it was absolutely essential that wage and salary settlements negotiated in 1991 should not undermine ESAP:

> what is required is some social contract on the part of labour and employers over the next two years for SAP to succeed.[25]

Under such a contract, wage demands, dividend and profit declarations would have to be significantly scaled down with the employers supporting ESAP through re-investment of dividend and profit realisations and with workers accepting lower wage increases.[26] This assumed voluntarism was not forthcoming in a context in which the state sought to marginalise the labour movement in the socio-economic policy-making process. Indeed, the labour movement leadership criticised the state's double-standards on collective bargaining; the proposal to stagger wage increases was described as "an insult to the intellect of the working-class" which should "not be used as a scape-goat by other agencies in the management of the economy".[27] Through the Labour Relations Act provisions, the state still wielded considerable powers with respect to collective bargaining: the Minister of Labour could veto wage increases in "the interests of the economy or consumers".[28]

The new regime of accumulation inaugurated under ESAP envisaged widespread retrenchment of workers in both private and public sectors. At least, 26 000 jobs in the public sector and 20 000 in the private sector were to be axed. The rationale for the retrenchments in a context of high unemployment was a source of friction between the labour movement and the state. Reports of mass retrenchments became much more common: such diverse industries as mining, agriculture, manufacturing and the services reported cut-backs in jobs. The much-vaunted capacity of ESAP measures to create a significant number of additional jobs has not materialised. Scepticism persisted over the adequacy of the social dimension fund (SDF) to finance the re-training of retrenched workers or to provide them with reasonable amounts of start-up capital to facilitate their entry into the small-scale business and informal sectors. Thus, one of the more immediate and visible aspects of the new regime of accumulation is the substantial reduction of labour costs through lay-offs and tightening of the managerial supervision geared towards productivity. The vulnerability of workers has been underlined in the lay-offs which no longer require cumbersome procedures to implement. Worsening the conditions of employment security more generally was the catastrophic drought of 1992. Collective bargaining therefore concentrated more on the retention of that security than on wage improvements in a situation in which official inflation was 40 per cent in 1992.

To regulate the new labour regime, at both plant and national levels, the state amended the Labour Relations Act to strengthen managerial prerogatives in the process of enhanced de-regulation of labour conditions. First, the labour movement questioned the extensive powers which continued to be invested in the Minister of Labour. Those powers were stated to be "clearly inconsistent with spirit of ESAP" and should be removed or at the very least trimmed to that which is consistent with deregulation of labour relations".[29] Second, the movement lambasted the provisions which made it "practically and legally impossible to carry out a lawful strike".[30] We saw how heavy-handed the state has been in its repression of strikes; there would be no let-up to this approach under the new labour regime. Thirdly, and significantly so, the new amendments upheld the formation of splinter unions which the labour movement argued was "designed to divide workers" and therefore was "highly objectionable".[31] Finally, the ZCTU protested that the functions of the Employment Councils should not be usurped by plant-level Works Councils. The amendments sought to empower such councils with powers to engage in collective bargaining and in drawing up of codes of conduct. Their net effect was "to do away with trade unions and remain with councils which more often than not are heavily influenced by employers".[32] In spite of these strong objections, the state incorporated these amendments into the Labour Relations Act (LRA) and thus generated much anger and frustration within the union movement. Subsequently, the ZCTU abstained from joining Zimbabwe's tripartite delegation to the 1992 ILO meeting in Geneva; its members also walked out of a meeting with the Minister of Labour in Harare in June 1992. Instead, it organised a nation-wide demonstration (heavily repressed by the state) against both the LRA amendments and the austerity ESAP measures.

Finally, we must consider the uncompromising stance of the labour movement over the ESAP measures themselves. The ZCTU criticised the liberalisation measures (encapsulated in the Investment Code) which presaged ESAP. The Code intended to lure foreign investment was attacked for constituting capitulation to international capital by the state. Acutely aware of its marginalisation in the design of ESAP, the ZCTU leadership called for a "widespread and informed" debate on economic policy. It observed that ESAP measures would "hit hard" the poor and that:

we are told that these hardships are temporary and that if we tighten our belts we will be better off by 1995. But will we?[33]

This scepticism regarding the presumed benefits from ESAP has been more or less vindicated so far as the living standards of both the poor and working class continue to plummet. The new regime of accumulation has rolled away the earlier gains of workers, undermined employment security and placed more leverage in the hands of employers.

State and the Student movement in Early 1980s

We now assess relations between the state and student movement during the period 1980 to 1985. As elsewhere in Southern Africa, (the student uprising in 1976 in South Africa and the University of Zambia student protests in 1990 and 1991) the student movement has confronted the state on political issues pertaining to democracy, high-level corruption and university autonomy. On the attainment of independence, Zimbabwe also possessed a tradition of student radicalism which at the University of Zimbabwe was closely associated with the nationalist struggle for independence, as we have already observed.[34] The conflict between the state and students has long roots extending back to the 1950s and 1960s when there were perpetual clashes between them and the colonial regime. Students opposed the continued existence of the Central African Federation and participated in the nationalist struggle for independence. It was observed that:

the students could hardly remain unaffected by these events nor by the riots that took place in various parts of the country during this period. In October 1960, all African students took part in a total hunger strike in sympathy with their people who had been killed in a disturbance in a Harare township. Practically all African students were nationalists[35]

There followed the radicalisation of black student unionism in the aftermath of UDI in 1965. In the 1970s, huge numbers of students particularly from secondary schools and training colleges volunteered to go into exile to link up with the liberation movement and train as cadres. However, the significant role which students, apart from the peasantry, played in the execution of the liberation struggle still awaits to be fully written about. This is the brief historical background to our assessment of state-student relations in the early post-independence period.

Any analysis of the state-student relations should, however, be located in some broad conceptual framework. We will refer here to a framework developed elsewhere on the role of universities and students in the broad society (Miliband, 1969: Miles, 1973; Smith, 1974; Jacks, 1975; ESAURP, 1987). Concerning the relationship between a university and the state in advanced capitalist society, it has been argued that:

> on the whole, the university, as an institution, has seldom refused to serve the 'national purpose', as defined by the state, and has found it relatively easy to rationalise its acceptance in terms of its own proclaimed ideals. From this point of view, the notion that universities, as those who work within them, are centres of dissent is a piece of mythology. If anything, the university, including the majority of its teachers, has always tended, particularly in times of great national crisis, and precisely when acute moral issues were involved, to take a poor view of its staff and student dissenters, and quite often to help the state by acting against them.[36] (Miliband, *op. cit.*).

These sentiments are also reflected in a study of the growth and orientation of universities and student population in the United States.[37] It was pointed out that "reflecting the shifting class origins and status of students, this process of growth has taken place under the careful guidance of the representatives of capitalism on the boards of trustees of the universities" (*ibid.*). In their effort to remake the working class in the image of their own needs, those representatives had succeeded in re-organising the universities as an integral part of capitalist production. It was further argued forcefully that:

> most students are being prepared for supervisory and technical or scientific jobs not of their own choosing and serving not their own interests but the interests of the ruling class. The root of the oppression of students can be identified as the authoritarianism built into the structure of the universities which prevents students from exercising meaningful control over the purposes and final social results of their studies. This relationship of authoritarian control and alienated study is typified by the relationship between students and trustees, which is in the deepest sense a class relationship.[38]

These observations make inroads into the common view, much played upon, by the mass media, that universities are by definition anti-state. If in the context of advanced capitalism in which they supposedly are expected to process greater autonomy, universities have chose linkages with the state, those in developing societies such as Zimbabwe have a tighter dependency relationship with the state. We need to explore further how the dimensions of the state-university relationship bear on student movement politics.

At this point, we will review briefly the background to the pact between the students and the state in the first five years of independence. Like in the case of the labour movement, the student movement conceded the ideological high ground to the major ruling party (ZANU-PF) in the state. Amidst the euphoria of independence, the student movement was generally uncritical towards the new regime. Domestic issues regarding living and working conditions, within the university, and not national politics, occupied most students. In one case in which students did not initiate the denunciation of creeping corruption within the new ruling elite, they organised a demonstration to support President Mugabe's attack on the emerging acquisitive tendencies. Until 1986, little public criticism emerged from within the student movement on germane national issues such as the repression of strikes, the brutalities against the 'dissidents' and civilians in Matabeleland, the continuation of the state of emergency and the stalled land reform. It appeared as if the considerable social expenditure of the new regime on education and health and the Africanisation of the public service provided it with significant public support. Graduate employment was almost virtually guaranteed in the first five years of independence and university students were beneficiaries of such opportunities. The entry of graduating students into the privileged middle class steeped in the public service, the professions and in the private sector occurred. The state might have gone some way to co-opt the student movement if it had a sophisticated strategy. As it was, its main form of penetration was the ZANU-PF university student branch which would later become alienated from the party in the late 1980s. How and why did the "honeymoon" between the students and state come to an end in the second half of 1980s? This is the question we address in the next section.

Conflicts between the State and the Student Movement

We saw that growing social contradictions characterised Zimbabwe's political economy in the second half of the 1980s in a context of an ideological shift and drive towards economic liberalisation. The ruling elite was transforming into a bourgeoisie with a direct interest in capitalist accumulation. The limitation of independence had become plainly obvious: job creation proceeded very slowly, real wages became static, land reform stalled and authoritarian tendencies did not abate. It became difficult for new graduates to obtain jobs except in such scarce areas as engineering and technical fields and medicine. The state could not deliver on its promises. This was the context in which friction between the Mugabe government and the students became more pronounced. There was no systematic critique of state policies by students and here we will schematically discuss the issues on which the conflict, came to a head during the 1986-1992 period. First, there was state and press condemnation of the 1986 student demonstration, not organised against the state, but against Malawi and South Africa over the death of President Machel in a plane crash. Property belonging to the national air-lines of both countries was damaged. Those students arrested following the violence were, however, not charged. Nevertheless, there was a great deal of anxiety on the part of state authorities over the ready capacity of students to vent their anger at the alleged conspiracy by South Africa in the death of Machel. Henceforth, state authorities prohibited students from demonstrating in Harare's central city area until, for a short phase, in 1992.

Second, presumably the first direct scathing critique of the Mugabe government concerned corruption amongst the ZANU-PF leadership, particularly relating to a number of cabinet ministers. One analyst has recounted the students' anti-corruption demonstration organised in late 1988:

> the police restricted to campus an anti-corruption demonstration the students had planned for downtown. The students tried to march into town anyway, but were prevented by the police. The mood on both sides was very ugly. The students taunted those they called 'standard four thugs' and the police responded violently on a grand scale. The campus was sealed off while the riot police brutalised students . . .. Eventually, at the end of two days, the students responded to university appeals to stop the violence, and the police were withdrawn (Cheater, *op. cit.* 195).

Following this confrontation, the Willowgate car scandal was broken by the Chronicle newspaper severely embarrassing the Mugabe government. In a damage-limitation operation, the Justice Sandura Commission was appointed; as a result of its hearings and findings, five ministers implicated in the scandal resigned from government. The students had been vindicated.

Third, in a context of the dented legitimacy and hegemony of the ZANU-PF government, students held a demonstration on university premises in 1989 to commemorate the anti-corruption "demo" of 1988. State authorities reacted in a draconian fashion. The venue of the demonstration was sealed off, students teargassed in their rooms and running battles fought till the early hours of the morning (*ibid.*). The students lampooned the state for its provocation and added that "the institution of government had been rendered completely disreputable and hence the incumbents have completely lost legitimacy." (*ibid*). The president and secretary-general of the Student Representative Council (SRC) were detained; students vented their anger by stoning the university administration block and attempting to torch the vice-chancellor's vehicle. The entire SRC executive was also detained; so was the ZCTU secretary-general, Morgan Tsvangirai for expressing solidarity with the students. The university authorities closed the university for three weeks in October 1989. The university council then set up a sub-committee to enquire into the closure; the administration drafted modifications to the statutes, so that the 1982 Act could be amended; and police actions were publicly censured by the university.

Fourth, conflicts during the following two years (1990-92) would centre on the erosion of university autonomy and academic freedom and student grants in the context of unabated authoritarianism and structural adjustment. The University of Zimbabwe Amendment Act introduced a disciplinary system for staff and students that did not include legal safeguards to ensure that justice was done; conferred power to the Vice-Chancellor to sack any student, lecturer or worker without any obligation to provide reasonable justification; and made appointment of the Vice-Chancellor and certain key officials of the university a government prerogative. Students and staff were united in their denunciation of the authoritarianism encapsulated in the Amendment Act. Vice-chancellor Kamba castigated the legislation as constituting "academic and political intolerance, demise of legitimate debate and a threat to academic freedom and autonomy".

There is need to explain the factors which prevailed upon state authorities to draft this draconian, unsophisticated legislation. Political factors loom large in the states' concerted effort to bring the students "to heel". The first relates to state funding of the university which has increased substantially during the post-independence period. The state seeks to use its funding as some political capital to wield greater influence over the university and exercise some control over students. Its stance is a thinly disguised "he who pays the piper calls the tune" approach. This approach represents some continuity with that of the colonial regime's relations with the university. The colonial state sought to exploit its financial support for the university as a leverage to stifle debate on political issues amongst both staff and students. For example, a government circular demanded that students receiving grants, scholarships, bursaries and loans from the state should sign a pledge which virtually barred them from any political activities. Students defied this conditionality. When they heckled and booed two cabinet ministers attending a university function in 1966:

> the minister of education warned the government might withdraw grants from students. Government also notified individual students, lecturers and members of the University Council that unless strict disciplinary action was taken within two weeks, it would act (Gelfand, *op. cit.*).

The colonial government implemented its threat. Police raided the campus, arrested nine lecturers and nine students and served them with detention and restriction orders. The university was closed for several months.

The post-independence version of state leverage over the university included the withdrawal of grants from arrested members of the SRC following the 1988 demonstrations and those of 57 students including the entire SRC membership after the 1992 demonstrations. Whereas the grants withdrawn in 1988 were reinstated, those cancelled in 1992 were not. An appeal fund to raise fees for the penalised students was launched by students and staff at the university in mid-1992. Clearly, the state has punitively used the weapon of financial penalty to punish student activists. There have also been instances in which lectures have been briefly detained, and in one case, deported. The state was also been riled by the heckling of then government ministers (Joshua Nkomo and Fay Chung) at a meeting organised by students. The response of the state has been to reduce the grievances and activism of students to the problem of "student indiscipline". It was the intention of the University Amendment Act to address this problem once and for all. Of course, this has proved to be an inadequate and simplistic approach.

In concluding this section we should consider the significance of the 1991 and 1992 student demonstrations which were not only against Amendment Act but also against the abuse of human rights and the erosion of student grants in the context of ESAP. During the Commonwealth Heads of Government meeting in Harare in October 1991, students demonstrated against the undemocratic tendencies of the

Mugabe government and its abuse of human rights. The tight police cordon thrown around the university to contain the demonstration did not limit the extensive publicity given to the students' critique. In 1992, students reacted much more sharply against SAP which also undermines the value of their grants or "pay outs". A student magazine observed that:

ESAP has severely affected the student. Its meagre allowance has been heavily eroded by inflation. Few, if any, will manage to buy textbooks this year. For students staying off campus, they also have to bear the agony of everyone else. Yet despite these hardships, the student's life is even tougher this year . . . so ESAP tends to mean *Especially Students Are Prone to Suffering* (Focus, 1992).

The drastic erosion of student grants became the focal point for demands of a 45 per cent increase. In view of the inflation rate hovering around 40 per cent (in 1992) this was not a very substantial increase sought. The state could only concede a 25 per cent increase. In the ensuing confrontation, an ugly riot in downtown Harare provided a sufficient excuse to the state authorities to ban future student demonstrations in that part of the city. However, the austerity measures incorporated in ESAP will provide students with a broad, popular cause to attack government socio-economic policies.

The broad agenda of student's criticism of the Mugabe government included specific demands. Students called for the reduction in the size of the huge cabinet "during these hard times of drought and food shortages" (*The Herald*, 7 May 1992). They observed that the prices of all basic commodities had skyrocketed putting them beyond reach of most people; they demanded the improvement of people's standard which was currently "too low" (*ibid.*). The SRC recommended the resignation of the then Agriculture Minister, Witness Mangwende and the then Trade and Commerce Minister, Kumbirai Kangai for their "inept handling of the maize situation" (*ibid.*). The resignations of President Mugabe himself, certain senior cabinet ministers and the dissolution of ZANU-PF were also demanded. Thus issues on which there are sharp disputes between the state and students covered a broad range of social and political issues. The sensitivity of these issues to the incumbent government was clear. It hoped that student demands would not transform into popular demands by the fledgling opposition movement in the country. We should now turn to an overall assessment of the impact of social movements on political change.

Social Movements and Political Change

It should be enquired whether the social movements — the labour and student movements — assessed in this chapter possess the capacity to ameliorate their socio-economic conditions through political change. In other words, how significant has been the political impact of these movements? We have observed in our discussion that until the mid-1980s, there existed some unwritten pact or social contract between the state on one hand and both the labour and student movements on the other. Little if any confrontation occurred during this period between these social forces in a direct fashion. The state was viewed as playing a mediatory role in labour conflicts and a supportive role in the expansion of all levels of education, including university education. The contract was sealed by the boom, however short-lived, of the early 1980s.

However, we need to consider the organisational capacity of these movements as it has a bearing on their political weight. Until the mid-1980s, the labour movement was organisationally weak; the leadership of the ZCTU was inexperienced and self-seeking. Individual unions were undergoing restructuring and experienced an acute shortage of administrative skills and funding. External funding supported the bulk of the programmes both of the ZCTU and individual unions. The process of democratising the structures and procedures within unions went slowly. Thus the capacity of the labour movement to mobilise workers was extremely limited. There was no mobilisation of workers around issues outside the arena of the work-place: the voice of workers on explicitly political issues was not heard during the early post-independence years. Occasional statements by union leaders related to a bland endorsement of ZANU-PF's programmes. The situation changed radically in the late 1980s, as we observed from our discussion above.

As the social contradictions sharpened with the growing gap between the privileged and under-privileged classes, as the cancer of corruption ate deep and the squeeze of incomes leading to the collapse of living standards, the labour movement distanced itself from the state. Skills in administration and collective bargaining improved markedly. The workers' voice on broader national issues such as democracy, human rights, land reform and structural adjustment began to be heard. It constituted a critique of state policies and of the acquisitive and exploitative tendencies of the bourgeoisie. By 1993, the organisational capacity of the labour movement had improved substantially. Similar observations may be made about the student movement's transition from its introspective and quiescent phase in the early 1980s to its radical outspokenness in the late 1980s. The student population also trebled to about 10,000 during this period which put an enormous strain on services within the university. In 1991, two new universities had been established in Bulawayo and Mutare. A national student organisation to which different university and polytechnic student unions could affiliate was formed and called the Zimbabwe National Students' Union (ZINASU). ZINASU has made forceful statements regarding the handling of student demonstrations by state authorities; it has been scathing about police methods such as tear-gassing of students. During the May Day celebrations in 1991, 1992 and 1993 students participated in demonstrations organised by workers and gave solidarity speeches.

However, we should also consider briefly the ideological outlook of these two movements. Although their leadership espouse socialism, it is uncertain whether their broad membership subscribe to this ideology. There still remains a residual element of individualism characteristic of a petit-bourgeois outlook amongst students and workers. The focus and ambition of most workers and students still appear to be "individual self-improvement". There exists some ideological ambiguity. As avenues for most workers for self-advancement and accumulation become more restricted, the ambivalence over capitalism as an ideology may wane. The hardships associated with ESAP and the unabated rise in unemployment have dented the ideology of capitalism; the capitalist system is increasingly viewed as incapable of sustaining conditions of growth and putting basic commodities within the reach of most people. Nevertheless, the labour and student movements, in spite of their radical critique of capitalism, have not succeeded in constructing an alternative coherent and credible ideology. They have not gone much beyond paying lip-service to socialism; there exists a clear need for a counter-hegemonic ideology. The challenge of mobilising workers and students in a counter-hegemonic project relates to the construction of an alternative coherent ideology which incorporates the struggles and aspirations of not only these movements but those of other social classes.

Apart from these organisational and ideological dimensions, the labour and student movements need to consider strategic issues concerning their participation in the political process. Some of the strategic aspects relate to the organisation of protest demonstrations, class boycotts and industrial action. When these have occurred, the state authorities have unleashed their coercive paraphernalia in a relatively short space of time. To what extent could these movements pre-empt or obstruct this concerted state opposition? How can strikes be made more effective? Raising an issue of strategy and tactics it was pointed out that:

> we went for three weeks without lectures only to return without anything tangible. As a revolutionary act, there is nothing wrong with a boycott, in fact it represents a formidable psychological weapon against government intransigence in addressing student problems. But on its own, it is not enough, it needs to be supplemented by other modes of revolutionary struggle . . . (Focus, 1991).

To what extent such methods as hunger strikes could mobilise public opinion against the state is an open question.

The question of strategy and tactics also relates to strike action by workers in a context of extensive prohibition of strikes in many sectors, of high unemployment and state heavy-handedness which often includes the deployment of police and recruitment "shows" of strike-breakers. The dilemma often becomes the extent to which strike action is sustainable. Some groups of workers, such as bus-drivers, have resorted to less overt forms of striking such as go-slows but even these have soon attracted state coercion. Demonstrations on a nation-wide basis against specific government policies such as ESAP are similarly frustrated by politically-motivated police bans authorised at ministerial level. On the whole, true to its authoritarian instincts, the state tends to unleash its coercive apparatus when social movements challenge specific policies in a concerted manner. The challenge is for movements to extend their democratic space by mobilising public opinion decisively against state authoritarianism. This raises the issue of broader alliances between the labour and student movements and other social forces seeking change or redress.

This brings us to the question of social movements and participation in political alliances. In 1990 and 1991, labour and student movements played a critical role in Zambia in the formation of a broad political alliance under the auspices of the Movement for Multiparty Democracy (MMD). As Chanda shows in his chapter, MMD pressure on the incumbent Kaunda regime forced the latter to concede to demands for political pluralism and for general elections in October 1991. The MMD won a landslide victory. In South Africa, the Congress of South African

Trade Unions (COSATU) is a major player in the politics of the democratic movement; it is a major constituent force within the ANC and was represented in negotiations for a democratic settlement. In August 1992, a huge nation-wide strike organised by COSATU paralysed industrial sectors and sent a warning signal to de Klerk to abandon the sponsorship of political violence and to be less intransigent in the current negotiations with the ANC. In Malawi, strikes by workers and students in mid-1992 forced the Banda regime to bring the trade unionist and democratic campaigner, Chakufwa Chihana to open trial and subsequently make political concessions. The protests also dramatised increasing opposition to the dictatorial regime which was subsequently ousted in 1994.

Much more recently, relations between the state and the labour movement in Zimbabwe have entered a stalemate. In 1992 and 1993, both forces took uncompromising, diametrically positions on ESAP and this set the tone of the relations. Political and financial sponsorship of ESAP by the IFIs and most western governments have ensured that the programme could not be stalled for lack of funding. This sponsorship and a good agricultural season in 1992-93 ensured some growth estimated at 2% in 1993 from minus 8% contraction in 1992 and relief from the drought. The domestic slump has been ameliorated but not completely. In this context of emerging optimism, the labour movement finds itself even more marginalised. A sense of despondency and frustration within the movement was palpable by 1994 as it became quite clear that it could not block ESAP nor force its modification. At the same time, retrenchments which were destined to total more than 50 000 workers by 1995 had dented union membership levels as well as underlined the impotence of the labour movement in defending workers' jobs. Similarly, the comparatively low wage awards in 1992 and 1993 (in relation to inflation) continued to erode incomes, while the powerlessness of trade unions to stem that erosion was exposed.

Politically, the capacity of the labour movement to rally other social forces such as students, cooperative and consumer movements, and the peasantry against ESAP proved quite limited. The 'bread riots' and 'consumer boycotts' which broke out in many urban centres in 1993 soon petered out for lack of organisation and direction. The substantial number of strikes both 1992 and 1993 were organised and resolved independently of the national labour centre. The state through the ZANU-PF party apparatus was instrumental in defusing the bread riots and disorganising some community-based protests concerning wage conditions as at Dalny mine in February 1993 where fatal shootings occurred. As in the previous year, President Mugabe rejected an invitation to participate in the May Day rally of 1993. It could hardly have been more depressing year for the labour movement.

Finally, the state itself was not averse from fomenting divisions between some of the unions and the national labour centre. In certain cases, the personality factor loomed large in the fissions but the political pronouncements of the labour centre itself provided the context for them to distance themselves from the leadership. The state even saw potential allies in those handful of unions which attacked what they termed the ZCTU's political agenda.

In the latter period covered in our analysis (1993 and early 1994), there was also an emerging ambiguity in relations between the state and the student movement. The phase of direct confrontation was succeeded by one of dialogue, concessions to students (in the form of grants increased by 57%) and the courting of student support for land policy. Consequently, unlike in the previous six years, there was no anti-government demonstration throughout 1993. Rather the student leadership was co-opted into a ZANU-PF-sponsored demonstration on the land question. A discernible introspective mood seemed prevalent amongst students as some of their immediate material aspirations were met through enhanced grants (Interview with a University of Zimbabwe Student, December 1993). A more sophisticated strategy of the state towards students appeared to be paying off by the end of 1993. This was despite the moral victory of the student movement in forcing the university to reinstate three student leaders expelled in 1992 after the demonstrations on grants and the UZ Amendment Act in that year. Symbolic of the changed atmosphere at the end of 1993 was that the suspension of 2 000 striking non-academic staff which drew little solidarity from the student movement, some of whose members were engaged as strike-breakers in jobs of the suspended staff.

In the context of mounting unemployment, from which university graduates are no longer immune, the immediate concern of most students has become a good degree and job. In the context of ESAP, individualism has been abetted by the capitalist ideology from which students have not been immune. Although there was ritual participation by students in the May Day rallies, it was conspicuously absent in the 'bread demonstrations' and 'consumer boycotts' which ZANU-PF was able to co-op and deflect. The introspective outlook of students found expression in their pre-occupation with their parochial concerns such as the grants and flagging interest in national issues.

Conclusion

In summing-up this analysis of relations between the state and social movements, several issues stand out. First, the tendency of social movements to be dormant and amenable to co-optation by the state at certain conjunctures. Such a conjuncture was immediately after independence. That dormancy sometimes reflects the fluidity in the institutional base of a particular social movement but also ideological vacuity and lack of rallying local issue around which to mobilise. Second, at other conjunctures, social movements engage in spirited contests for both parochial concerns (improved working conditions and living allowances) and national issues (independence and democracy). This conjuncture occurred prior to independence but also in the late 1980s. However, we saw how dominant the nationalist movement became through organisational and ideological subordination of movements ranging from youth, students, to women and labour. In various ways, that legacy of domination has been replicated but with varying degrees of success by the post-colonial state in which the nationalist coalition wields considerable power. Clearly, the labour and student movements have not been demobilised nor co-opted by the state, but the same cannot be said of other movements such as cooperatives, youth and women which have specific state departments channelling and defining their interests. Even the more autonomous labour and student movements are not totally disinterested, it would appear, in negotiating some favourable pact or social contract with the state.

Two potential choices exist for both labour and student movements in Zimbabwe at this conjuncture. First, they could pursue a modest agenda centred on strengthening their organisational bases, sharpening their capacity in collective bargaining and thus wrestling more concessions from both private and public sector employers. At the same time, they would assert their autonomy *vis-a-vis* the state and its related institutions including the ruling ZANU-PF and the opposition movements. This would limit their political role and their intervention in national debates such as those on democracy, human rights and structural adjustment. In practice, it would be difficult to be detached completely from the political process: they may well earn the ire of the political actors and some of their activist membership.

Second, the labour and student movements could develop a grand agenda which would include provision to enter into tactical political alliances either with certain forces in the existing state or with opposition movements. The labour movement could develop a political wing and engage in the political process with the main objective of projecting the interests of labour. Whatever form those political alliances assume, there would be a strong reaction from existing political forces marginalised from the alliances. It could provoke fission within the labour movement itself. The current unravelling within the MMD in Zambia underlines the brittleness of tactical political alliances which incorporate labour. Furthermore, the current electoral structures in Zimbabwe are favourable to the incumbent regime, including the state subvention to ZANU-PF of Z$30 million per year.

Finally, the state has considerable resources at its disposal either to bait specific social movements or to invest in electoral success though such programmes as free seeds and inputs (for the biggest constituency) namely the peasantry. It could also be selective and tardy in the implementation of ESAP till it pulls off victory in the 1995 elections. The choices for social movements — for limited or expansive objectives — are very difficult ones, and terribly hard to reconcile.

Notes

1. Wood, 1987, p 50.
2. *Ibid.*
3. M. Von Freyhold (1987) "Labour Movements or Popular Struggles in Africa", *Review of African Political Economy* No. 39.
4. Cited in B. Wood 1987, *op. cit.*
5. L.M. Sachikonye (1986), "State, Capital and Union Since Independence" in I. Mandaza (ed), *Zimbabwe: The Political Economy of Transition*, Dakar, Codesria.
6. *The Herald*, 3 March 1983.
7. *The Herald*, October 1981
8. Prime Minister Mugabe as quoted in The Chronicle, 4 December 1981.
9. L.M. Sachikonye (1992), "From Equity to Structural Adjustment: State and Social Movements in Zimbabwe". Paper presented to a Conference organised by the Canadian Society of International Development (CASID), Prince Edward Island University, June 1992.
10. Botsch as quoted in *The Herald*, 2 December 1981.
11. Albert Mugabe as quoted in *The Herald,* 16 October 1981.
12. M. Burawoy (1985), *The Politics of Production*, London, Verso.
13. *Ibid.*

14. Maurice Nyagumbo as quoted in *The Herald*, 17 July 1984.
15. Jeffrey Mutandare as quoted in *The Herald*, 5 March 1981.
16. L.M. Sachikonye 1992, *op. cit.*

17. B. Chidzero, Interview, *Southern Africa Political and Economic Monthly (SAPEM)*, January 1992.
18. *Ibid.*
19. L.M. Sachikonye 1992, *op. cit.*
20. See, for example, I. Mandaza (1986) *Zimbabwe: The Political Economy of Transition,* Dakar, Codesria; and Lionel Cliffe and Colin Stoneman (1989) *Zimbabwe: Politics, Economies and Society, London* and New York: Pinter Publishers.
21. A. Mutambara (1991) "The One-Party State, Socialism and Democratic Struggles in Zimbabwe: A Student Perspective" in I. Mandaza and L.M. Sachikonye (eds.). *The One-Party State and Democracy*, Harare: SAPES.
22. K. Makamure (1991) "The Struggle for Democracy and Democratisation" in I. Mandaza and L.M. Sachikonye (eds.). *The One-Party State and Democracy*, Harare: SAPES.
23. M. Tsvangirai (1990) "Workers should not be Neutral" *Southern African Political and Economic Monthly (SAPEM)*, September 1990.
24. A. Musarurwa (1991) "The Labour Movement and the One-Party State Debate" in I. Mandaza and L.M. Sachikonye (eds.), *The One-Party State and Democracy*, Harare: SAPES.
25. Reserve Bank of Zimbabwe (1991) *Quarterly Economic and Statistical Review*, Harare.
26. *Ibid.*
27. Nicholas Mudzengerere as quoted in *The Herald*, 25 September, 1991.
28. L.M. Sachikonye and L.G. Dhlakama (1991), *Collective Bargaining in Zimbabwe: Procedures and Problems, Geneva:* ILO.
29. Morgan Tsvangirai (1992) "The Labour Relations Amendment Act 1992", Paper to the EMCOZ Conference on ESAP, Industrial Relations and Employment Creation, Harare: Friedrich-Naumann Stiftung.
30. *Ibid.*
31. *Ibid.*
32. *Ibid.*
33. Gibson Sibanda as quoted in *The Herald*, 2 May 1991.

34.	Gelfand, 1978; Sachikonye, 1991; Cheater, 1991.
35.	Gelfand, *op. cit.*
36.	Miliband, *op. cit.*
37.	Smith 1974 op. cit.
38.	Smith, op. cit.

References

Arrighi, G., Hopkins, T. K., and Wallerstein, I., *Anti-Systemic Movements,* London, Verso, 1989

Bhebe, N., *Benjamin Burombo: African Politics in Zimbabwe 1947-1958,* College Press Harare, 1989

Burawoy, M., *The Politics of Production*, London:, Verso, 1985.

Cheater, A., "The University of Zimbabwe: University, National University, State University or Perty University?" *African Affairs,* 1991.Vol. 90 No. 359.

Chigwedere, I., Trade |Unions in Zimbabwe, unpublished minutes, 1978.

Cliffe, L., and Stoneman, C., *Zimbabwe: Politics, Economics and Society* London and New York, Pinter Publishers, 1989.

Davidson, B., *The Black Man's Burden: Africa and the Curse of the Nation-State*, London, James Currey, 1992.

ESAURP (Eastern & Southern African Universities Research Programme), *University Capacity in Eastern and Southern African countries* London, James Currey, 1987.

Von Freyhold, M., "Labour Movements or Popular Struggles in Africa", *Review of African Political Economy* No. 39, 1987.

Gelfand, M., *A Non-Racial Island of Learning: A History of the University College of Rhodesia from Its Inception to 1966* Gweru, Mambo, 1978.

Focus (1991-1992) Various Issues Union, Harare, University of Zimbabwe Students, 1991/2.

Jacks, D., *Students Politics and Higher Education,* London, Lawrence and Wishart, 1975.

Makamure, K., *"The Struggle for Democracy and Democratisation"* in Mandaza, I. and Sachikonye, L. (eds.) *The One-Party State and Democracy,* Harare, SAPES, 1991.

Mandaza, I., *Zimbabwe: The Political Economy of Transition* Dakar, Codesria, 1986.

Miles, M. W., *The Radical Probe*, New York, Athaeneum, 1973

Miliband, R., *The State in Capitalist Society*, London, Quartet Books, 1969.

Musarurwa, A., "The Labour Movement and the One-Party State Debate" in I. Mandaza and L. Sachikonye (eds.) *The One-Party State and Democracy* Harare: SAPES, 1991.

A. Mutambara "The One-Party State, Socialism and Democratic Struggles in Zimbabwe" A Student Representative in I. Mandaza and L. Sachikonye (eds.) *The One-Party State and Democracy*, Harare, SAPES, 1991.

Nyagumbo, M., With the People Harare: Graham Publishing Co., 1980. Reserve Bank of Zimbabwe Quarterly Economic and Statistical Review, Harare, 1991.

Ranger, T., *Peasant Consciousness Guerilla War in Zimbabwe* London, James Currey, 1985.

Sachikonye, L. M. and Dhlakama, L. G., *Collective Bargaining in Zimbabwe: Procedures and Problems,* Geneva, ILO, 1991.

Sachikonye, L. M. (1991), "The Dilemma of the Zimbabwe Student Movement" *Southern Africa Political and Economic Monthly* (SAPEM) August 1991.

----- (1992), "From Equity to Structural Adjustment: State and Social Movements in Zimbabwe", Paper presented to a conference Organizeed by the Canadian Society of International Development (CASID), Prince Edward Island University, June 1992.

Smith, D. N., *Who Rules the Universities?,* New York and London, Monthly Review Press, 1974.

Tsvangirai, M., "Workers should not be neutral" *SAPEM*, September 1990

----- "The Labour Relations Amendment Act 1992", *Paper to the EMCOZ* Conference on ESAP, Industrial Relations and Employment Creation, Harare, Friedrich-Naumann Stifung, 1992.

Word, B., "Roots of Trade Union Weakness in Post-Independence Zimbabwe" *South African Labour Bulletin*, 1987, Vol. 12 No. 6-7.

ZCTU *ZCTU on the New Investment Code: Its Implication to National* Independence and to the Position and Conditions of Working People Harare, ZCTU, 1989.

Zimbabwe Government, *Labour and Economy*, Harare, Ministry of Labour and Social Welfare, 1987.

8

Agricultural Collective Co-operatives in Zimbabwe: A Vehicle for Rural Democratisation?

Louis Masuko

Introduction

The debate on democracy, civil society and the state is a major topical issue in contemporary Africa (Anyang' Nyong'o, 1987; Gitonga *et. al.* 1988; Mkandawire *et. al.* 1988; Shivji, 1990). It signals a recognition that behind every change or transformation, there lies a motive force, a force of change, namely social movements. Although independence in most states in Southern Africa was brought about as a result of liberation movements which were social movements in their own right, it was generally assumed that this was the end of the process of change as transitional states assumed the role responsibility for future national development. Little was it known that the quest for democracy expressed in civil action or resistance would put checks and balances or even haunt many a post-colonial state.

In Zimbabwe, independence was expected to signal change in all aspects of life and sectors of society, as gross imbalances existed across the board, particularly in the ownership of wealth-generating assets. The primary basis of these imbalances in the economy still remains the ownership structure of productive resources. These imbalances, along with the institutional structures which had been built to support them, made it difficult to undertake radical changes without causing destruction of economic activity, whose damage would take a long time to repair.

Of all the possible means of wealth distribution, collectivisation would not radically change the entrenched capitalist structures in the respective sectors of the economy with the possible exception of the agricultural sector. But even in this sector land was acquired on a "willing-buyer, willing seller basis", a Lancaster House conditionality. Thus collective co-operatisation is a concept which came with the advent of independence. Before 1980, emphasis in the co-operative sector had been on input supply and marketing, and every attempt was made to discourage or outlaw any nascent collective co-operative largely on political and ideological grounds (Mumbengegwi 1983). Political independence and the professed socialist ideology of the ruling (ZANU-PF) party provided the initial conditions for the development of collective forms of production and ownership. Economic empowerment of the dispossessed people, elimination of the exploitation of man by man and the achievement of collective or community control over socio-economic institutions by the majority of the people was on the agenda of the ruling ZANU-PF party. In line with its professed philosophy, the state provided seed money to agricultural co-operatives in the form of land from formerly commercial farms, establishment grants and work-plans.

The general premise of this chapter is that agriculture producer co-operatives in Zimbabwe provide institutions through which democratic participation by the rural population in production, consumption and decision making process can be realised. It is further argued that collectivisation entails social as well as economic re-organisation. However, the development of producer co-operatives requires social, economic and political initiatives from the state.

This chapter will attempt to examine and highlight the "missing link" in collective co-operative development in post-independence Zimbabwe. It then argues that the state, and not the co-operators, should bear the responsibility for the limitations of the co-operative movement. Finally, an assessment of the relationship between the co-operative movement and other institutions of civil society is undertaken.

Co-operatives Since 1980

Collective co-operatives in all sectors of society are a phenomena of the 1980s. In colonial Zimbabwe, proper co-operatives and industrial democracy were virtually non-existent (Chiwawa 1990). The first co-operatives were formed in the 1950s (Chitsike, 1986). After independence the ZANU-PF government encouraged producer co-operatives across all sectors as an important step to a new form of social and economic reorganisation that represents a community of free individuals, carrying on their work with the means of production in common in which social production is controlled by social foresight. This was not a completely new idea, but one which had been discouraged and proscribed by past regimes and which had for many years, constituted the production system practised and cherished by

ZANU-PF during the armed struggle, in military and refugee camps, "liberated and semi-liberated" zones.

Through collective co-operatives the ZANU-PF government aimed to achieve the following objectives:

i)   to enable the people of Zimbabwe to achieve economic power and through this power achieve control of socio-economic institutions;

ii)   to eliminate the exploitation of man by man;

iii)   to make the people of Zimbabwe self-reliant in skills, management, goods and services, and independently establish a sense of confidence and initiative; and

iv)   to provide an opportunity to develop community and collective ways of living that formed a sound base for socialism and national solidarity.

Collective Co-operative Movements' Size and Location

Given this impetus and encouragement, producer co-operatives were formed in almost every sector of the economy. A national survey by the Ministry of Co-operative and Community Development (1991) showed that there were a total of 1 892 co-operatives (across sectors) registered since 1980 and that 1 112 of them are functioning. In percentage terms, functional societies represents about 59 percent of the registered. Of the eight sectors in which co-operatives have been established, three sectors account for 1 664 registered co-operatives or 88 percent. The three sectors are wholesale and retail (970 registered and 637 functioning); agriculture forestry and fishing (386 registered and 195 functioning) and manufacturing (308 registered and 171 functioning).

Of interest is the locational distribution of the producer co-operatives. A closer look at the statistics shows an unquestionable rural bias in the location of co-operative activities. Unlike the more established enterprises whose activities are concentrated in the two big cities of Harare and Bulawayo (more than 75 percent of all industrial activities), 91.2 percent of co-operative activities are in the rural areas. Within the rural set-up, communal areas account for the bulky of the co-operative ventures (230), followed by rural service centres (136); business centres (114); small scale commercial farms (109); consolidated villages (49); large scale commercial farms (76); growth points (31) and district service centres (16). However of the 96 registered and functioning urban co-operatives more than 50 percent are found in areas designated as high-density residential areas and in the outlaying business areas as compared with the low density areas (18 percent) and central business areas (3 percent). Less than five co-operatives are located in industrially designated areas.

Manufacturing co-operatives, the majority of which are in the textile sector, are mostly located in the rural rather than urban areas. Nevertheless a bigger share of urban co-operatives are in manufacturing. The second major category in urban areas is wholesale and retail trade, which include hawking and vending, tuckshops and also registered wholesale and retail. Although co-operatives registered in the agricultural, forestry and fishing sector are largely rural some are also located in urban areas. These are small-scale farming operations conducted on allocated municipal land. Their location is predominantly in the high density residential areas and they are sources of low-cost food to low-income urban households. Real estate and finance co-operatives have an urban bias (more than 50 per cent are located in urban areas). These include savings and credit and housing co-operatives.

The shortage of accommodation has prompted the proliferation of housing co-operatives in both high density and low density residential areas. More are expected to be established in this sector as it is a relatively new dimension in co-operative development. The demand for a collective approach to housing is on the increase.

The Political Context of State Support for Co-operatives

The constraining factor on the expansion of the collectivisation programme was the limited resources available. Mumbengegwi (1988) argued that "political consideration aside the limited magnitude of state support to the co-operative sector can be construed as arising from resources constraints at a national level". However, over the period of four years (1981-1984) an amount of $5,72 million was budgeted for development purposes for 31 co-operatives which was around $184 000 per co-operative but only 15,8 percent had been disbursed by 1984.

A Zimbabwe Institute of Development Studies (ZIDS) study, (1991) *noted that the amount of resources so far allocated to Model A scheme has been phenomenal, and this seems to suggest that relatively more attention has been given to this scheme. This further implies that resources at a national level are available, but that 'assistance is given to co-operatives after consideration of foregone costs and benefits'.*

Second, the problem of concern is seen as fundamentally ideological and is squarely situated within the state itself (Moyo *et. al.* 1991, Mathema 1984, and Hanlon 1986). Mathema argued that for any government to achieve its goals and objectives it must be supported by civil servants who are dedicated professionals. Hanlon explicitly expanded on Mathema's point that co-operatives do face not only the problems encountered by most new business, but widespread discrimination by the private sector and some civil servants who see co-operatives as a challenge. An international dimension can be drawn from Moyo's (1988) observation that bilateral donors are unwilling to support co-operatives.

The success of producer co-operatives is a challenge not only to agri-business, but also to civil servants and politicians. Hedlund (1988) could not have missed the point that economically strong co-operative societies are regarded as a possible threat to the state. Successful co-operatives are both 'offensive' in the sense of seeking to change the established order and 'progressive' in the sense of seeking a better order for themselves. Co-operatives exist in the main to combat deprivation, and in so doing re-affirm the identity of those active in the movement (Gunder Frank, 1988).

Consequently the political significance of the movement has to be assessed. By reading between the lines one would argue that the political significance of this movement to the politician is negligible, and particularly so in the rural areas. Most members of parliament turn to the over-populated communal areas and the Model A resettlement scheme rather than to *Model B* co-operatives for their support. This could, however, be different in the urban situation where the co-operative movement is rapidly taking shape due to increasing poverty, unemployment, housing shortage, and to related problems.

After having grappled with the two arguments outlined above, an understanding the social base of the state and the correlation of power within it is arguably important. The state in Zimbabwe is manned mainly by a petty-bourgeois element whose main objective is to accumulate property and in particular land (Raftopolous, 1990). Its motto is to "transform" the inherited structures from within. Campbell *et. al.* (1985) captured the above in a more refined way:

> More specifically one might well expect cleavages between those who seek to use state institutions to prolong the forms of accumulation left by the colonial period as opposed to those strengthened by new sources of foreign credit and of expanded reproduction on which their interests depend. These cleavages and alliances are far from static. They are continually being redefined, depending on issues giving rise to policies which at times appear inconsistent and even contradictory.

State involvement in capital accumulation, in the absence of a local bourgeoisie, or local entrepreneurial class — whose emergence has been clearly frustrated, all in the name of nation-building-opened areas for a process of local capital formation under the umbrella of the state. Right-of-centre politics, took precedence, from the second half of the 1980s over the rhetoric of the early years into independence. The state in line with its capitalist development viewed co-operatives as a "stop-gap measure" so that its assistance in the form of infrastructure and financial support to co-operatives was quite limited (Chiwawa, 1990 *op. cit*).

The Collective Co-operative Movement and Civil Society

Civil society is a complicated organism. Lipton (1990) defined civil society as a complex of individuals, 'corporations', organisations and groups, in free competition to win minds as well as to buy support, but constrained to respect the right of rivals to do likewise. Important though is how these individuals, organisations, groups and so forth function and interrelate to each other particularly in an environment where there is competition for the scarce resources. This section focuses on the co-operatives in a capitalist environment, with the aim of bringing out the potential of these enterprises to democratically transform the rural economy and provide institutions through which the rural populace can get involved in decision-making processes both at the local and national level.

Producer Co-operatives and the Capitalist Context

Producer co-operatives in the agricultural sector can be categorised as "isolated islands" in a society which is predominantly capitalist. Two factors give them this attribute and these are: firstly, the physical location of co-operative farms is within local level territories dominated in most cases by large scale commercial farms. The latter have their own private administrative apparatus for the purpose of organising physical services and legal protection of private property, and political or interest group structures which exclude co-operatives (Moyo *et. al.* 1991).

Secondly, they represent a democratic form of ownership in a social and economic set-up arranged along principles of private ownership of the means of production and distribution. Private capital control more than 90 percent of all economic activities with around 50 percent of the above accounted for by transnational large scale commercial farmers.

About 40 percent of land was occupied by large-scale commercial farmers (LSCFs) at independence, and they have claim to 80 percent of the prime land in natural regions I and II. Small scale commercial farms (SSCF) and the state jointly account for less than 5 percent. Communal Areas (CAs) which occupy 41 percent of the total land mass are situated on over 60 percent of the low-quality land (Moyo 1990). This same ownership pattern has not changed much primarily because of the limited progress of the land reform programme.

The predominant capitalist relations of production have permeated all sectors of the rural economy. These social relations have shaped the spatial organisation of the rural economy in a way that produces, and reproduces, the dependence syndrome of the latter on the developed urban economy. If the access to active participation in the social and economic activities is an outcome of economic opportunities then the rural population has been denied this since the early colonial days. A chronic centre-periphery relationship has been created and strengthened.

Agricultural collective co-operatives were introduced starting from 1980 in the spatial arrangement compatible with the capitalist relations of production. The objective was to foster new social relations and a new spatial arrangement of the rural economy which creates economic opportunities for the rural population. What processes would the new actor generate?

The Zimbabwean experience has shown that there are only two main processes that are generated. On the one hand, co-operatives develop to levels where new social relations are cultivated and on this basis greater worker control over community resources is enhanced. On the other hand, co-operatives succumb to the logic of capital and remain in the ambit of the capitalist social relations of production.

Two scenarios can therefore be considered to explain the above. Firstly, it is a situation where the co-operatives have the following resources:

i)   land;
ii)   a few farm implements and draught animals (all individually owned) or none of these at all;
iii)   labour and;
iv)   freedom to organise.

For this scenario there is a complete retreat by the state. Observations from studies done in the 1980s indicate that the following features develop in most co-operative societies which fall in this scenario. These either

(a)   engage in subsistence farming (allocating plots to individuals) using old traditional methods in contrast to the scientific methods thus perpetuating and deepening the traditional habits, destroying in part the cohesiveness of the individual group of co-operators (between those who can use their own implements and those who do not own anything) in particular and the general movement at a national scale ;

(b)   they look for aid (as individual co-operatives) from private local companies and transnationals and NGOs (non-governmental organisations) opening up to capitalist exploitative mechanism mainly in the form of sub-contracting, provision of cheap labour; price transfer from co-operatives to capitalist firms via marketing arrangements or price setting by transnationals. The instructive example of this relationship is the well publicised relationship between Delta Corporation and Bethel Co-operative in Makoni District. The dependence syndrome is reinforced on the recipient's part; and

(c)   mostly trained co-operators defect from the co-operative looking for greener pastures in both the private sector and public sector. They steal the little the co-operative might have in the process, thereby negatively affecting the collective morale of the remaining co-operators.

The second scenario is that of co-operatives organised around the factors of land, labour, and endowed with appropriate means of production and freedom of organisation.

In this case the state provides the needed incentives to co-operate and to work. The observed outcome from this factor mix is outlined next.

(a)   The level of political and ideological consciousness of the members and the psychology of work (enhanced motivation and capacity to analyse and synthesise) develop progressively over time and through practical assimilation of the democratic ethos; division of labour, market management, etc.;

(b)   Problems, constraints or bottlenecks are encountered but are resolved consciously, by convocation of regular and frequent meetings for the consideration of the society's business and by the presentation of periodic reports and financial statements for questions, discussion and eventual adoption; and

(c)   Checks on balance mechanisms are developed to safeguard the society from being managed or manipulated in the interests of a minority of the members or of a single dominating individual or yet again of some external power, authority or institution (Watkins, 1985 *op. cit.*).

These are two different scenarios which are practically being experienced in Zimbabwe. Mumbengegwi (1988 *op. cit.*) alluded to the relationship between the two scenarios when he wrote that "those co-operatives which were not characterised by the internal disarticulation between material and technical conditions and the collective organisation of labour performed much better than those characterised by a low and thin material-technical base linked to a collective labour organisation". Democratic practice and the functioning of the organs which support it reproduce themselves in the second scenario. This approach has much in common with the "experimental organisational laboratory" methodology pioneered by a Brazilian sociologist, Dr. Clodomir de Morais.

Subsequently the potential for rural democratisation can therefore be explained by the following factors:

i) Co-operators are the owners of the society and are workers at the same time. The means through which the general will of the members is ascertained and expressed constitute the basis for a democratic system. Normally, this organ is the General Assembly which is the highest decision-making board of the cooperative. Each member has only one vote regardless of his or her position within the society.

Dissemination of information (market behaviour, production methods and techniques, political developments, dividend level and other social costs and benefits, etc) is facilitated by the above to the members. This enlightens them in the conduct of their own economic affairs and the needed changes in other structures such as the production structure. The typical peasant farmer or landless peasant knows little or nothing about the market for which his produce is ultimately destined. It is screened from his view by the host of middlemen to whom he directly sells but none of whom has any interest in enlightening him;

ii) By understanding the situation in which he/she operates the co-operator values his/her contribution and its impact on the changing of his position and that of others. He/she becomes a worker for himself/herself. This conscious approach is reproduced initially at each individual society and then at the regional or national level;

iii) The development of the co-operative movement entails the formation of a concatenation of activities cutting across sectors, and co-ordinated at different levels (enterprise, district, provincial and national levels). These include organised collective working of land, processing of agricultural produce, harvesting, construction of irrigation installations, roads, marketing and inputs supply etc. As Albert Thomas (1986) observed.

The structure of the cooperative economic system, based as it is on a very large number of small economic units which are like antennae through which it can sense the requirements and possibilities of everyday life, has a sort of sensory apparatus comparable to that of a living body. That apparatus does not simply transmit information step by step to the central organs which translate it into reasoned actions. It even, up to a certain point, permits automatic reactions, defensive or compensatory reflexes, which prevent maladjustment and avoid dangerous error; and

iv)   Much more important is the spill-over effect of this system to embrace the rural communities in which most of their activities are located. Economic opportunities are created, organised methods of production are disseminated to the rural population and access to cooperative markets is guaranteed. Information on new ideas of handling of stock or crops and cogent reasons for adopting them is given and the material or financial means of carrying them out is provided according to resource availability.

In turn, decision-making by the rural populace assumes a more organised posture. Community groups form their own enterprises, raising their organisational skills and consciousness in the process. Cooperation is fostered and through it the understanding and benefits from the practice of social division of labour are increased. This might sound more of utopia than real practice in Zimbabwean context, because of the gloomy picture painted of collective co-operatives. But already on a small-scale something along these lines is happening.

Ling (1985) observed the influence of co-operatives at the rural Vakuzenzele Co-operative in these terms:

the co-operators have run short training courses for local peasant farmers in irrigated market gardening and poultry rearing which have also made people aware of the benefits of the collective alternative to subsistence agriculture.

Experiments with this approach on communication in Zimbabwe, which is being conducted by the Southern Africa Development Trust (SADET) are still at an elementary stage. However, this process of cooperativisation of communities facilitates active involvement of the working people in solving society's economic and political problems, and simultaneously eliminate backwardness in education and culture (Maslennikov 1983). The strength of this method is in that it combines two critical elements of success: self-reliance in generating employment and income, and greater worker control over community resources (Lucena 1992).

The above presentation has been an attempt to present a theoretical context in which the performance of co-operatives has been assessed and simultaneously demonstrate that no conclusions can be drawn on co-operative policy changes before the relative contradiction between voluntariness, gradualness and state aid is understood and resolved. One cannot assess the process of change objectively if one of these three principles is not in place. These are basic principles whose balancing explains the level and direction of development of collective co-operatives over space of time. The following section briefly looks at the relationship between the co-operative movement and other institutions of civil society.

The co-operative movement is represented at the national level by its apex body which is the Organisation of Collective Co-operative in Zimbabwe (OCCZIM), established in 1983. At the tertiary level, the District Union (DU) brings together the individual co-operatives which fall within their respective jurisdiction and they co-ordinate their activities (agricultural activities, marketing of products), and disseminate information to co-operatives through meetings and/or visits to individual enterprises.

However, in Zimbabwe very few (about 3 out of a potential 52) district unions have been registered as the Registrar of Co-operatives felt that there was 'no hurry' to register them, regardless of the fact that unregistered DUs have no mandate to represent their affiliated co-operatives or to enter into contractual agreement with a third party on behalf of their members.

The 1990s are a challenging decade to the co-operative movement in Zimbabwe for the following reasons:

i)   The introduction of the Economic Structural Adjustment Programme (ESAP) and its emphasis on efficiency and market forces as opposed to social values;

ii)   Emphasis by the state on land redistribution manifested by the Land Acquisition Act (1992);

iii)   Intensified attack on co-operatives performance particularly the under-utilisation of land; and

iv)   The vulnerability of the co-operatives because of the land tenure system that does not protect them.

In the situation where the state has retreated, as is the situation currently and the institutions of civil society by their nature and purpose are constrained to respect the right of rivals to win minds as well as secure support, the inability of the movement to defend its position cannot be over-emphasised. In other words, the bargaining position of the co-operative movement (OCCZIM) can be considered to be very fragile reflecting in itself the under-developed resource base among collective co-operatives' members. However, the strong and weak institutions are in "free" competition for the scarce resources, in this case, land.

In Zimbabwe power is currently in the hands of a coalition of forces reflecting the interests of the emerging indigenous bourgeoisie (top civil servants and politicians in power included), agri-business and other social groups seeking to prevent the working people from taking power and to preserve private ownership of plants and factories and land (Sachikonye, 1991; Maslennikov 1983 *op. cit*). As co-operatives grow to a mass scale and the working people begin to play an active part in them; they pose a serious threat to industrial, agrarian and merchant capital and to the right-of-centre politicians. The antagonists are therefore ready to take extreme measures in order to prevent further social transformation in society.

The argument which has been advanced since 1980 clearly stipulates that land redistribution should not obstruct efficiency and productivity. The statistics indicate that LSCFs are way better off than agricultural co-operatives (in terms of efficiency and productivity) implying that in the event of acquiring land for Model A resettlement scheme, *ceteris paribus*, the latter would be the first to lose the land. While the representatives of different organisations, Commercial Farmers Union (CFU) for the LSCF; the Zimbabwe Farmers Union (ZFU) for the CAs and SSCF, can support their continued existence by efficiency, productivity and foreign exchange earnings for the former and by increase in food crops deliveries (which occurred in the 1980s) and pressure for land from the CAs, the future development of agricultural co-operatives would depend on state sponsorship and the political support the movement would be able to mobilise from non-commercialised and non-propertied civil institutions like students movement, the workers' movement, the church, etc. The fusion between industrial and agriculture capital makes it impossible for any support for the co-operative movement from organisations like Confederation of Zimbabwe Industries (CZI) who categorically supported LSCF during debate on the Land Acquisition Act. However, the outcome can be determined more by the role that the state will assume, firstly as the owner of the land on which co-operatives are situated, and secondly, as the provider of the material and technical resources for co-operative development.

Conclusion

The establishment of producer co-operatives in Zimbabwe after independence indicates change from past practices where only input supply and marketing co-operatives were encouraged. A policy document on co-operatives was drafted and made public in 1983 and from the number of producer co-operatives formed thereafter, it is evident that the policy document gave impetus to co-operative formation. Co-operatives in the agriculture sector (Model B) form an integral part of the resettlement package. Although this model occupies four percent of the total land acquired for resettlement it is the most controversial of all models implemented after independence. Ten years after the implementation of the Model B scheme, performance has been recorded as poor and the model a failure. Narrow economic indicators are used for evaluating their performance, deliberately overlooking the lack of much-needed technical material and institutional support for them to take off by the state. However, an assessment of the performance of the co-operatives therefore can only be done and objectively so, if it is done against the resource base of these organisations and not against the Agritex planned indicators or simple and subjective expectation of individuals.

The development of collective co-operatives and their assessment over time should be done within a context. It has been argued that this context is provided by the dialectical relationship between voluntariness, gradualness and state aid. If one of these principles is overlooked then internal disarticulation of co-operative societies cannot be ruled out. Obversely, the combination of the three allow for the development of an organic and democratic movement which allow for the full participation of its members and the rural community, in production and consumption and in decision-making process. However, developing in an environment which is predominantly capitalist means co-operatives have to interact with institutions which uphold capitalist values.

ESAP strengthens the grip of those who cherish these bourgeois values and the need for land redistribution has pressed the fragile co-operative movement against the wall. The 1990's therefore will, no doubt, be "a do or die" decade for most of the struggling agricultural co-operatives. But one would say that they are being sacrificed for a sin they did not commit and their only salvation rests with the political decision by the state to provide them with the needed technical, educational material resources and the support that they can mobilise from the non-propertied or non-commercialised institutions of civil society.

References

Anyang' Nyong'o P., *Popular Struggles for Democracy in Africa*. ZEB Books Ltd, London, 1987.

Bernstein, Henry, Campbell, K; *Contradictions of Accumulation in Africa*, Sage Publications, 1985.

Chitsike, L T., *Agricultural Co-operative Development in Zimbabwe*. Harare, May 1986.

Chiwawa, H., Co-operatives and Contract Mining in Zimbabwe Chrome Mining Industry. Harare, ZIDS Monograph No. 1, 1990.

Dahl, A. R., *A Preface to Democratic Theory*, University of Chicago Press, 1956.

Deshpande, S. H., *Some Problems of Co-operative Farming*, Haimabya Publishing House, Bombay, 1984.

de Lucena, H. P., Paper presented at ANC Basic Skills Workshop in Johannesburg, 1992.

Frank, G. A. and Fuentes, J., *Nine Thesis on Social Movements, Ifda dossier* Jan/Feb 1988.

Gitonga, A. K., et. al.; *Democratic Theory and Practice in Africa*. Heineman, Kenya 1988.

Hedlund, Hans (ed); *Co-operatives Revisited*. Bohuslanningens Boktryckeri AB, Uddevalla, Sweden, 1988.

Maslemikov, V., *The Co-operative Movement in Asia and Africa*. Progress Publishers 1983.

Moyo, S., *Agricultural Employment Expansion: Small Holder Land and Labour Capacity Growth*. Harare, ZIDS Monograph No. 2, 1990.

Moyo, S., Sunga, I., and Masuko, L., *Agricultural Collective Co-operativisation: A Case Study of the Socio-Economic Viability of the Makoni District Union OCCZIM Collective: Part II MDU Management and Overall Recommendations. Part I, The Socio-Economic Features of the Collectives*. Harare, ZIDS Consultancy Report No. 19 & 21, 1991.

Mkandawire, T., *et al.*; *Social Movements, Social Transformation and the Struggle for Democracy in Africa*. Working Paper 1, CODESRIA 1988.

Mumbengegwi, C., "Agricultural Producer Co-operatives and Agrarian Transformation in Zimbabwe: Policy, Strategy and Implementation". *Zimbabwe Journal of Economics* Vol.1 No.1, July 1984.

Mumbengegwi, C., "Some Aspects of Zimbabwe's Post Independence Agricultural Producer Co-operative: A Profile and Preliminary Assessment". Mimeo, Harare 1984.

Raftopoulos, B., *Beyond the House of Hunger: The Struggle for Democratic Development in Zimbabwe*. 1991.

Sachikonye, L. M., *State and Agri-Business in Zimbabwe: Structures and Procedures of Integration*, ZIDS Discussion Paper No. 13, 1991.

Shivji, G. I., *State and Constitutionalism in Africa*. SAPES Trust, Harare 1991.

Swain, Nigel, *Collective Farms which Work*? Cambridge University Press 1985.

Volkov, Alexander, *Confronting or Compromise? The Meaning of Worker Participation in the Management of Capitalistic Enterprises*. Progress Publishers, Moscow, 1989.

Wasserstrom, Robert, *Grassroots Development in Latin America and the Caribbean: Oral Histories of Social Change*. Praeger Publishers Division, New York, 1985.

Wright, David, H., *Co-operatives and Community: The Theory and Practice of Producer Co-operatives*. London 1979.

9

Conclusion

There have been epochal developments in Southern Africa since the drafts of chapters contained in this volume were presented to the SAPES Colloquium of March 1993. First, the democratic transition in South Africa took place relatively peacefully in April 1994 with the ANC obtaining almost two-thirds of the electoral vote. The broad popular base of the liberation movement represented by the ANC was generally confirmed by this convincing victory. The role which the mobilisation of mass organisations and movements by the ANC under the auspices, amongst others, of the United Democratic Front (UDF), the South African Community Organisations (SANCO) and the Confederation of South African Trade Unions (COSATU) was of crucial, if not decisive, importance. More than any other organisation in South Africa, the ANC demonstrated a significant capacity to weld together various social forces (ranging from youth to workers, from the peasantry to black middle classes) in the struggle to displace the apartheid regime. Like nationalist movements elsewhere in Africa in the 1950s and 1960s, the South African liberation movement represented the dominant social movement pressing for democratic change. The litmus-test for the consolidation of that democratic change in South Africa, as elsewhere in Africa after independence, will be whether the liberation movement will maintain a high level of mobilisation and representation characterised by decentralised authority and participation or disintegrate and develop authoritarian powers structures.

Second, there were processes of re-introducing multi-partyism in Zambia, Malawi and installing it in Mozambique. To the extent that these processes signified the demise of the one-party state system and recognition of voters' rights to choose between different parties and candidates, they were significant, indeed crucial preconditions, for the re-democratisation process in these three countries. However, the election outcomes in both Malawi and Mozambique demonstrate considerable ambiguities. Although the protest vote against the authoritarian Banda regime was convincing, the opposition movement itself was soon riven by feuds. That one of the major opposition parties, Alliance for Democracy (Aford) could nearly forge an alliance with the disgraced Malawi Congress Party (MCP) showed an unscrupulous pursuit of power; and the utilisation of the ethnic card also characterises the re-democratisation process in Malawi.

The considerable showing in the October 1994 elections by RENAMO, (it received 33% versus 44% Frelimo's of the parliamentary vote) demonstrated that there existed a significant base of political opposition to Frelimo, an opposition which had long been suppressed under the one-party system. The ethnic factor, as in Malawi, also is a major element in Mozambican electoral politics.

Finally, the democratisation process has proved to be more chequered in the two kingdoms of Swaziland and Lesotho. Pressure continues to mount on the Swazi monarchy to allow the installation of a multi-party system. Increasingly, the combined authoritarian and paternalistic tendencies of the Swazi oligarchy will be difficult to sustain and justify in a sub-region in which minimal democratic governance (as symbolised by multi-partyism) has attained broad acceptance. Indeed, the unsuccessful attempts by the monarchy in Lesotho to reverse the process of democratisation – by unconstitutionally unseating the elected government of Ntsu Mokhehle – belonged to this mould of politics of authoritarianism. Uncompromising opposition from both domestic and external sources rendered these unconstitutional manoeuvres unsustainable. Intervention by South Africa, Botswana and Zimbabwe was crucial for the reinstatement of the elected government in Lesotho and of King Moshoeshoe (who had been overthrown by the defunct military government).

These political developments relating to the restoration of the democratic process (despite its obvious ambiguities) provide some basis of optimism for the future of the sub-region. But they also relate directly to the conceptual issues discussed in the chapters in this volume. Here we will briefly recapitulate some of the major arguments and observations concerning democratisation and the role of the state in this process as well as its relationship with civil society, or more precisely, with social movements.

The process of building democracy – or democratisation – in the countries covered in this volume will inevitably be a long-term process. As it has been aptly put, democratisation is always and everywhere an unfinished process (Beetham, 1994). The minimal foundations, of installing and consolidating multi-partyism, are being laid but the more complex process of underpinning this process with material progress has hardly begun. Economic backwardness and austerity continue to pose a potential threat to the democratic arrangements currently being institutionalised. Establishing democratic electoral arrangements is one thing, sustaining them over time without reversal is quite another:

not all who make the transition will be able to sustain it *(Ibid.)*.

The material basis of the democratisation process will be a critical factor within the region.

Equally central to the sustainability of democratisation will be role of civil society, of which social movements, are a prominent part. It was demonstrated how such movements as those representing labour, women, students and community interests amongst others were active in the process of democratic change in South Africa, Zambia and Swaziland, and in the ideological contestation of the one-party state concept in Zimbabwe. Although not covered in this volume, similar social forces exerted powerful influence on the democratic change in Malawi.

Yet a generalisation which appears to retain considerable currency is that the civil societies in Southern African countries (with the possible exception of South Africa, and to some extent Zimbabwe) are still weak and sparsely organised. The predominantly agrarian base of most of the economies of these countries represents a constraint on the growth and strength of their civil societies. Hence the episodic character of the intervention of most social movements in the political process. Even allowing for their symbiosis with the state, the capacity of social movements is limited by the underdevelopment of civil society and vulnerability to co-optation by the state. As the concluding observations of most contributions to this volume suggested, euphoria about the capacity of social movements to speed up the democratisation process single-handedly would be misplaced. The movements will of necessity need to negotiate their role within specific political alliances and within the state, rather than detach themselves from these structures and processes. Their capacity and influence will be commensurate with the role and power they accrue in this institutional context.

However, the objectives of social movements do not centre exclusively on integration into the state or political process (as it relates to democratisation). As has been observed, social movements seek to go beyond "existing civil societies with their built-in inequality and unauthenticity" (Mushakoji, 1993). There will thus of necessity be often areas of tension between social movements and existing power structures.

The process of tension and collaboration is being played in such instances as the relationship between the new South African and Zambian governments and their national labour centres of COSATU and ZCTU respectively. Intensive negotiations continue over the terms of a social contract, against a background of austerity measures and industrial action. It is still uncertain whether the alliances between the ruling parties and national labour centres in these two countries will be sustained or whether there will occur a rupture as happened in Zimbabwe. Although student and other youth movements will continue to provide a radical voice on major political and economic issues, their effectiveness is likely to continue to be compromised unless they mobilise in concert with other social and political groupings. Cooperatives and entrepreneurial groups as well as groups emerging in the informal sector are becoming an important phenomenon, yet their dependence on state support is still vital for their sustainability.

Finally, the nature and role of the state itself is significant for the democratisation process. The legacy of the white-settler state in some of the countries in the sub-region — South Africa, Zimbabwe and Namibia— relates to continuity in state structures with built-in inequalities and constraints on redistribution of social and economic power. In the remainder of the countries, weak economic bases restrict options for alternative development strategies.

For "initiating the processes of democratisation and marketisation simultaneously is full of perils, not least because their time-scale are so different, and the early experience of economic dislocation and hardship that accompanies marketisation can readily undermine support for the democratic process (Beetham, *op. cit.*)

This is the broad context in which states in Southern Africa seek to pursue simultaneously, the objectives of democratisation and development. A proper balance must be struck between the two; the authoritarian model of development in East Asia (now much vaunted as a successful model) is not inspiring to states emerging from colonialism and apartheid. It is imperative that countries follow "a twin-track process of reforms, political and economic; while it cannot always be easy to guarantee success, it is structurally logical" (Aboyade, 1994). How much emphasis states will place on democratisation and development will not be a matter of voluntary choice. The emphasis and choice will be the outcome of contestation between various social forces and ideological perspectives. This is a contestation in which social movements have played, and will continue to play, a crucial role.

Select Bibliography

Aboyade, O., "Economic and Political Reform — Is a Combination Possible?", Synthesis Paper presented to a conference on *A Road to Development: Africa in the 21st Century* organised by the Scandinavian Institute of African Studies, Uppsala, October 1994.

Ake, C.,"Globalisation and Social Movements", Presentation to the Nordic Conference on *Social Movements in the Third World*, University of Lund, August 1993.

Amin, S., 'Social Movements at the Periphery' in P. Wignaraji (ed.). *New Social Movements in the South,* London and New Jersey, Zed, 1993.

Anyang'o Nyongo, P., *Popular Struggles for Democracy in Africa.* London: Zed, 1987.

Arrighi, G., Hopkins, A. and Wallerstein, 1., *Anti-Systemic Movements*, London: Verso, 1987.

Baile, S., and Breier, H., "A Turning-Point for Southern Africa", *OECD Observer*, No. 187, April/May, 1994.

Bangura, Y., "Authoritarian Rule and Democracy in Africa: A Theoretical Discourse" in P. Gibbon, Y. Bangura and A. Ofstad (eds.), *Authoritarianism, Democracy and Adjustment*, Uppsala, SIAS, 1992.

----- Gibbon, P. and Ofstad, A., (eds.), *Authoritarianism, Democracy and Adjustment*, Uppsala, SIAS, 1992.

Baylies, C., and Szeftel, M., "The Fall and Rise of Multi-Party Politics in Zambia", *Review of African Political Economy*, No. 54, 1992.

Beckman, B., "Empowerment or Repression: The World Bank and the Politics of African Adjustment' in P. Gibbon *et.al.* (eds.), *Authoritarianism, Democracy and Adjustment*, Uppsala, SIAS, 1992.

----- "The Liberation of Civil Society: Neo-Liberal Ideology and Political Theory in an African Context", *Review of African Political Economy*, 58, 1993.

Beetham, D., "Conditions for Democracy Consolidation", *Review of African Political Economy*, No. 60, 1994.

Bernstein, H., and Campbell, B., *Contradictions of Accumulation in Africa*, Beverly, Sage, 1985.

Bhebe, N., *Benjamin Burombo: African Politics in Zimbabwe 1947-1958*, Harare, College Press, 1989.

Bonner, P., *Kings, Commoners and Concessionaires*, Johannesburg, 1993.

Bratton, M., "Beyond the State: Civil Society and Associational Life in Africa", *World Politics*, Vol. 41, No. 3, 1989.

Buijtenhuijs, R., and Rijumierse. E., "Democratisation in Sub- Saharan Africa", African Studies Centre, Leiden, Research Report No. 51, 1993.

Burawoy, M., *The Politics of Production*, London: Verso, 1985.

Chazan, N., "Africa's Democratic Challenge: Strengthening Civil Society and State", *World Policy Journal*, Vol., 1992.

Cheater, A., "The University of Zimbabwe: University, National University, State University or Party University". *African Affairs*, Vol. 90, No. 39, 1991.

Chitala. D., and Lewanika, A., *The Hour has Come: Proceedings of the First Multi-Party Conference*, 1991.

Chitsike, L. T., *Agricultural Cooperative Development in Zimbabwe*, Harare, ZIMFEP, 1986.

Chiwawa, H., *Cooperatives and Contract Mining in Zimbabwe's Chrome-Mining Industry*, ZIDS Monograph, No. 1, 1990.

Cliffe, L. and Stoneman, C., *Zimbabwe: Politics, Economics and Society*, London and New York, Pinter Publishers, 1989.

Diuf, M., and Diop. M., Statutory Political Successions: Mechanisms of Power Transfer in Africa, Working Paper Dakar, Senegal, 1990.

Frank, A., "Revolution in Eastern Europe: Lessons for the Democratic Social Movements and Socialism?", *Third World Quarterly*, Vol. 12, No. 2, 1990.

----- and Fuentes, M., "Nine Theses on Social Movements", *Economic and Political Weekly*, 27 August 1989.

Fransmann, M., *The State and Development in Swaziland*, Ph.D Thesis, University of Sussex, 1978

----- "Labour, Capital and the State in Swaziland 1962-67", *South African Labour Bulletin*, Vol. 7, Nos. 6/7, 1982.

Frieling, I., *Population and Employment in Mozambique with a Case Study of two Maputo Suburbs*, Lusaka, ILO-SATEP, 1987.

Fukuyama, F., *The End of History and the Last Man*, London and New York, Penguin, 1992.

Garreton, M., "Social Movements and the Politics of Democratisation", Paper presented to the Nordic Conference on Social Movements in the Third World, University of Lund, August 1993.

Gelfand, M., *A Non-Racial Island of Learning: A History of the University College of Rhodesia from its Inception to 1966*, Gweru: Mambo, 1978.

Gibbon, P., "Structural Adjustment and Pressures Toward Multi-Partyism in Sub-Saharan Africa" in P. Gibbon *et. al., Authoritarianism, Democracy and Adjustment*, Uppsala, SIAS, 1992.

Gills, B. and Rocamora, J., "Low-Intensity Democracy". *Third World Quarterly*, Vol. 14, No. 3, 1992.

Gitonga, A. K., *et.al.*, *Democratic Theory and Practice in Africa*, Nairobi,: Heinemann, 1988.

Glaser, D., "Putting Democracy into Democratic Socialism" *Work in Progress*, 65, April, 1990.

Hall, R., *A History of Zambia*, Lusaka, Longman, Zambia,1969.

Hedlund, H., *Cooperatives Revisited*, Uddevaka, Bohuslanningens Boktrykeri.

Hermele, K., *Structural Adjustment and Political Alliances in Angola, Guinea-Bissau and Mozambique*, Uppsala: Akut, 1989.

Hoare, Q. and Smith, G. N., (eds.) *Selections from the Prison Notebooks of Antonia Gramsci*, London, Lawrence and Wishart.

Kaunda, K., *Zambia Shall be Free*. London, Heinemann, 1962.

Kasoum, F., *The Press in Zambia*, Lusaka, Multi-Media Publisher, 1986.

Keane, J., *Democracy and Civil Society*, London and New York, Verso, 1988.

----- *Civil Society and the State*, London and New York, Verso, 1988.

Leftwich, A., "Government, Democracy and Development in the Third World, *Third World Quarterly*, Vol. 14, No. 3, 1993.

Lehman, D., *Democracy and Development in Latin America*, Cambridge, Polity, 1990.

Lindberg, S., Friedmann, K. and Lundberg, S. *Social Movements and Strategies in the Third World*, Department of Sociology, University of Lund, 1992.

Macamo, E., *Internal Conflicts, Peace and Development in Africa, The Case of Mozambique*, Nairobi, AAS, 1992.

----- "Political Parties, Problems in Power and Opposition: The Case of Mozambique", Paper to the ESAURP Conference on *Political Parties in the Transition to Multi-Party Democracy in Eastern and Southern Africa*, Arusha, June 1993.

Majola, S., 'The Beginnings of People's Power: A Discussion of the Theory of State and Revolution in South Africa", *African Communist*, No. 106, 1986.

Makamure, K., "The Struggle for Democracy and Democratisation" in I. Mandaza and L. M. Sachikonye (eds.) *The One-Party State and Democracy: The Zimbabwe Debate*, Harare: SAPES Books, 1991.

Mamdani, M., Mkandawire, T. and Wamba-dia-Wamba, "Social Movements and Democracy in Africa" in P. Wignavaja (ed), *New Social Movements in the South*, London and New Jersey, Zed, 1988.

Mamdani, M., "State and Civil Society in Contemporary Africa: Reconceptualising the Birth of State Nationalism and the Defeat of Popular Movements", *Africa Development*, Vol. XV, No. 314, 1991.

----- "Beyond an Analysis of Peasant Movements as 'Tribal Pathologies'", *Paper to a Conference on Ethnicity, Identity and Nationalism in South Africa: Comparative Perspectives*, Rhodes University, South Africa, April, 1993.

Mandaza, I., (ed), *Zimbabwe: The Political Economy of Transition*, Dakar, CODESRIA, 1986.

----- and Sachikonye, L. M. (eds.), *The One-Party State and Democracy: The Zimbabwe Debate*, Harare, SAPES Books, 1991.

Maslenoikov, V., *The Cooperative Movement in Asia and Africa*, Moscow, Progress Publishers, 1983.

Masuko, L., et.al. *"Agricultural Collective Cooperation: A Case-Study of the Socio-Economic Viability of the Makoni District Union OCCZIM"*, 1991.

----- "The Socio-Economic Features of the Collectives" ZIDS Consultancy Report, No. 21, 1991.

Mayekiso, M., "Working Class Civil Society: Why We Need It, and How We Get It", *African Communist*, 2nd Quarter, 1992.

Miliband, R., *The State in Capitalist Society*, London, Quartet Books, 1969.

----- "Fukuyama and the Socialist Alternative", *New Left Review*, 193, 1992.

Mkandawire, T., "A Kind of Home Coming", *Southern African Political and Economic Monthly (SAPEM)*, July, 1994.

Molteno, R., *Politics in Zambia.*

Moyo, S., *Agricultural Employment Expansion: Smallholder Land and Labour Capacity Growth,* ZIDS Monograph 2, 1992.

Mumbengegwi, C., "Agricultural Producer Cooperatives and Agrarian Transformation in Zimbabwe: Policy, Strategy and Implementation", *Zimbabwe Journal of Economics,* Vol. 1, No. 1, 1984.

Mutambara, A., "The One-Party State, Socialism and Democratic Struggles in Zimbabwe: A Student Perspective" in I. Mandaza and L.M. Sachikonye (eds.) *The One-Party State and Democracy: The Zimbabwe Debate,* Harare, SAPES Books, 1991.

Mushakorji, K., "Foreward" to P. Wignaraj (ed.), *New Social Movements in the South,* London and New Jersey, Zed, 1993.

Narsoo, M., "Civil Society: A Contested Terrain" *Work in Progress,* No. 76 July/August, 1991.

Neocosmos, M., "Political Liberalisation in Lesotho and Swaziland: Recent Developments", Paper Presented to a Workshop on Experiences of Political Liberalisation in Sub-Saharan Africa, Copenhagen, June, 1993.

Nzimande, B. and Sikhosana, M., "Civics are part of the national democratic revolution", *Mayibuye,* June, 1991.

Pudemo, *Programme of Action, Mbabane, 1985.*

Qadir, S., Clapham, C. and Gills, B., "Sustainable Democracy: Formalism vs Substance" *Third World Quarterly,* Vol. 14, No. 3, 1993.

Raftopoulos, B., "Beyond the House of Hunger: Democratic Struggle in Zimbabwe" *Review of African Political Economy,* 54, 1992.

Russon, R., "Youth and Politics in Swaziland" *Economic Digest,* Vol. 3, No. 1, 1993.

Sachikonye, L. M., "The Dilemma of the Zimbabwe Student Movement" *Southern Africa Political and Economic Monthly, SAPEM,* August, 1991.

----- "From Equity to Structural Adjustment: State and Social Movements in Zimbabwe", Paper presented to a Conference organised by the Canadian Society for International Development (CASID), University of Prince Edward Island, June, 1992.

----- and Dhlakama, L. G., *Collective Bargaining in Zimbabwe*, Geneva, ILO, 1991.

Simelani, N. G., *Evolving Role of Trade Unions in Swaziland* Mimeo, 1991.

Smith, D., *Who Rules the Universities?* New York and London, Monthly Review Press, 1974.

Swain, N., *Collective Farms Which Work?* Cambridge: CUP, 1983.

Swilling, M., "Socialism, Democracy and Civil Society: The Case for Associational Socialism", *Work in Progress*, 76, July-August 1991.

Slovo, J., "Has Socialism Failed?" *African Communist*, No. 121, 1990.

Tengende, N., *Workers, Students and the Struggles for Democracy: State-Civil Society Relations in Zimbabwe*, Ph.D. Thesis, Roskilde University, 1994.

Tsvangirai, M., "Workers should not be Neutral", *Southern African Political and Economic Monthly*, September 1990.

----- "The Labour Relations Amendment Act 1992", Paper presented to the EMCOZ Conference on ESAP, Industrial Relations and Employment Creation, Harare, Friedrich-Naumann Foundation, 1992.

Vilas, C. M., *The Sandinista Revolution: National Liberation and Social Transformation in Central Africa*, New York, Monthly Review Press, 1986.

----- "Revolution and Democracy in Latin America", *Socialist Register*, 1989.

Wignaraji, P., (ed), *New Social Movements in the South*, London and New Jersey, Zed, 1993.

Wood, B., "Roots of Trade Unions Weakness in Post-Independence Zimbabwe", *South African Labour Bulletin*, Vol. 12, Nos. 6-7, 1987.

Wright, D., *Cooperatives and Community: The Theory and Practice of Producer Cooperatives*, London, 1979.

ZCTU, *ZCTU on the New Investment Code: Its Implications to National Independence and to the Position and Conditions of Working People*, Harare, ZCTU, 1989.

Zimbabwe Government, *Labour and Economy*, Harare, Ministry of Public Service, Labour and Social Welfare, 1987.

Newspapers and Magazines

The Economist
The Sunday Mail, Harare
Times of Zambia, Lusaka
The Herald, Harare

Index

Subject Index